THERE SHE GOES AGAIN

Gender, Power, and Knowledge
in Contemporary Film and
Television Franchises

AVIVA DOVE-VIEBAHN

RUTGERS UNIVERSITY PRESS
New Brunswick, Camden, and Newark, New Jersey
London and Oxford

Rutgers University Press is a department of Rutgers, The State University of New Jersey, one of the leading public research universities in the nation. By publishing worldwide, it furthers the University's mission of dedication to excellence in teaching, scholarship, research, and clinical care.

Library of Congress Cataloging-in-Publication Data

Names: Dove-Viebahn, Aviva Chantal Tamu, author.
Title: There she goes again : gender, power, and knowledge in contemporary
    film and television franchises / Aviva Dove-Viebahn.
Description: New Brunswick : Rutgers University Press, 2024. | Includes
    bibliographical references and index.
Identifiers: LCCN 2023017882 | ISBN 9781978836112 (paperback) |
    ISBN 9781978836129 (hardback) | ISBN 9781978836136 (epub) |
    ISBN 9781978836143 (pdf)
Subjects: LCSH: Women in motion pictures. | Women on television. |
    Women in mass media. | Franchises (Retail trade) | Feminism.
Classification: LCC PN1995.9.W6 D68 2024 | DDC 791.43/6522—dc23/eng/20230719
LC record available at https://lccn.loc.gov/2023017882

A British Cataloging-in-Publication record for this book is available from the British Library.

References to internet websites (URLs) were accurate at the time of writing. Neither the author nor Rutgers University Press is responsible for URLs that may have expired or changed since the manuscript was prepared.

♾ The paper used in this publication meets the requirements of the American National Standard for Information Sciences—Permanence of Paper for Printed Library Materials, ANSI Z39.48-1992.

rutgersuniversitypress.org

For Saoirse

CONTENTS

Introduction   1

1   Why Feminine Intuition?: The Gendering
of Knowledge and Power   8

2   Seriality and "Strong Female Characters": The Double
Bind of Women's Empowerment Narratives   25

3   From Girl Power to Intersectional Sisterhood:
Exceptionalism and the Imperatives of Belonging   57

4   Motherhood and Myth: Inside and Outside
the Family Circle   89

5   At the End of the World: Apocalyptic Bodies
and the Feminine Sublime   116

Conclusion   144

Acknowledgments   149
Notes   151
Bibliography   175
Index   189

CONTENTS

THERE SHE GOES AGAIN

INTRODUCTION

There is little question that women have seen significant gains in male-dominated arenas over the last several decades, from politics and STEM to business, industry, and beyond. The media landscape is no different: once heavily dominated by shows and films driven by white male leads, the popular film and television industries have increasingly created more and more leading roles for women. In a stark change from 2011, when a report showed only 11 percent of protagonists in the 100 highest-grossing films of the year were women, more recent numbers have trended upward.[1] According to an Annenberg Inclusion Initiative report, 43 percent of the top-grossing films in 2019 had a woman lead or colead, with the number dropping to 36 percent in 2020, but then returning to 41 percent in 2021.[2] Another recent report from the Center for the Study of Women in Television and Film indicates that, in the 2020–2021 television season, approximately half of all major characters on broadcast and streaming shows were women.[3] It may be worth offering the mild caveat that the definition of a "major character" is not the same as a protagonist; a prior report assessing "clearly identifiable" leading characters by gender indicated approximately a third of all programs had female protagonists, a third had male protagonists, and a third were ensemble shows.[4] It is precisely this upswing in women's representation as we near parity along solely gendered lines, as well as the relative popularity and familiarity of a certain brand of media feminism, that led me to ask a different sort of question. Rather than, "Why aren't more film and television protagonists women?" I began to wonder why, despite marked growth in roles for women, many of the characters I was seeing struggled in similar ways as their predecessors, even when well cloaked beneath explicit feminist messaging. The increased number of women in these leading roles does not necessarily mean the roles are particularly nuanced or that the fundamental representations of gendered difference have changed. This paradox mirrors recent attempts within the media industries broadly to improve diversity and inclusion via methods that may read to some as more lip service than meaningful or substantive progress along the lines of representation in terms of gender, race, or sexual orientation.[5] I found this tension vividly rendered in transmedia franchises, particularly those that historically focused on women, as these films and shows offer an opportunity to consider the same character or type of character over time.[6] Even in franchise installments overtly updated to complement shifts in viewers' sociopolitical perceptions of gender, long-standing markers of gendered exceptionalism remain.

Media analysis of U.S. television and film franchises, within their respective cultural contexts, informs the central thrust of this book. I limit my focus to shows and films with extended life spans via sequels, remakes, reboots, and revivals to highlight how women's roles continue to be reimagined but nevertheless inhabit the same logics time and again in similar yet differentiated embodiments. These issues are also timely, since real women (as opposed to fictional ones) face ongoing pressures to conform to contradictory roles. Debates regarding whether women are suited for positions of power or influence, and under what conditions, continue to be waged despite both perfunctory and sincere attempts at gender equality in sociopolitical arenas in North America and globally. Widespread institutionalized distrust of women's knowledge, abilities, and experiences, as well as a lack of space for women's voices or women's agency over their own bodies, endures; that distrust only deepens when women's intersectional identities marked by race, ethnicity, gender expression, sexuality, or class marginalize them further. Meanwhile, mainstream outlets and pundits continue to critique long-standing, patriarchal institutions dominating business, law enforcement, and politics by weighing stereotypically masculine virtues such as assertiveness and logic against stereotypically feminine ones like humility and empathy, as if gendered traits are or ever have been stable.

Much contemporary narrative media with so-called strong women protagonists portrays powerful women as explicitly violent, assertive, overly rational, or physically formidable, in part as a bid to combat accusations of excessive femininity. At the same time, emphasis on normatively feminine characteristics like altruism, love, collaboration, and diplomacy remain endemic to many representations of women. To unpack this conundrum—to claim ostensibly feminine traits as a standard for new ways of thinking about power or to discard notions of gendered traits altogether—my analysis converges on the concept of feminine intuition as a symptom of broader questions of gendered exceptionalism underscored by popular visual media. These representations of feminine intuition constitute largely unspoken, but repeated, performances of women's knowledge and power in contemporary serial narratives. As such, the concept illustrates a trend in the ambivalent (post)feminist representation of women protagonists as uniquely gifted in ways both gendered and seemingly ungendered, and yet inherently bound to expressions of their femininity. Constructions of gendered exceptionalism paradoxically highlight the singular and, perhaps, empowering possibilities for leading women (and viewers' expectations of them), while also undermining these characters' agency through insistent gendered messaging. I gesture toward a larger question regarding the function gendered exceptionalism can or should play in social and political action, as well as what forms of knowledge and power are presumed distinctly feminine.

In lived experience, gendered exceptionalism and other forms of identity politics can have far-reaching liberatory and progressive potential. Recent social movements speak to this potential: #MeToo, which started in 2006 but gained widespread traction in 2017; the 2017 Women's Marches and their subsequent incarnations; #TimesUp (2018); the activism around #BlackLivesMatter that began in 2013 and resurged to increased national attention in the summer of 2020 during the widespread protests after police killed Breonna Taylor and George Floyd; and recent campaigns to support and protect trans and gender nonconforming children and adults in light of harmful policies. And yet, the focus on exception and difference in North American news and fictional media highlights one of the ways all women, especially women of color, have been hemmed in and continue to be, often unintentionally, sidelined and tokenized. These practices of sidelining and tokenizing take many forms and do not always have their origins in misogyny. Scripted, fictional media, in fact, seems to rely on a series of familiar tropes that mark women characters as "special" or explicitly acknowledge tenets of (popular) feminism with the aim of presenting narratives of so-called empowerment.[7] Likewise, contemporary media frequently signposts its efforts toward greater diversity, equity, and inclusion, particularly in relation to gender, race, and sexuality. In both cases, emphasizing differences in this way has benefits but carries a level of risk.

An enduring leitmotif in popular culture—particularly in articulations of popular feminism across films and television programs—seems to be the differentiation of women's power and knowledge from agender abstractions of power and knowledge, or even as an explicit divergence from masculinized counterparts. Examples of this include assertions of "girl power" and attempts by media producers to affirm ideal womanhood as embodied by characters who are physically strong, confident, rational, *and* normatively feminine.[8] The same ideas filter through contemporary sociopolitical debate. To wit, discussions of global conflict resolution often center men as aggressors or protectors and women (and children) as either victims or interlocutors for peace in the face of masculine warmongering.[9] Female politicians who support wars may be decried as hawkish, while those who favor diplomacy are accused of being soft or without the conviction necessary to protect the free world.[10] The recent dissolution of *Roe v. Wade*'s federal abortion protections and the continuing battles over trans rights also signal the precarity of agency for those in sexed and gendered bodies that are differentiated and devalued, seemingly by rote and with little nuance. Establishing difference opens the door to hierarchical thinking, and yet eliding differences along the boundaries of gender, race, sexuality, and so forth, can erase the very real experiences of marginalization faced by those deemed outside the normative default(s). The problem, then, is not the emphasis on difference per se but on exceptionalism as it is specifically bound to conventional feminine gender expression as innate and immutable.

I center the idea of feminine intuition, explicated more thoroughly in the first chapter, to acknowledge how much of the power and knowledge bestowed on female characters is simultaneously gendered and passively acquired. As with the relationship between power and knowledge theorized by Michel Foucault, the structuring force of the power wielded by these characters is always in motion, ever shifting to accommodate how knowledge, intuitive and often unwitting, informs their actions.[11] This is not to say that these characters do not take an active role in their narratives, but rather that the source of their power often has little to do with something agential they have done to gain their special status. While this is sometimes the case with male heroes, for example, those who are created by the gods to fulfill some purpose or somewhat arbitrarily become invincible by birth/ upbringing/accident, they often eventually earn the title of hero via their hard work, intelligence, innovative spirit, or fortitude. Even in cases where heroines gain their knowledge or strength through training or study, the narratives sur-rounding their abilities frequently insist on their lack of agency in becoming powerful or bind that power to feminine traits that are presumptively nonagentic (desirability, gentleness, motherly instinct). The unconscious nature of many of these traits and abilities means that characters are not always able to access their respective forms of power at will and/or that they can easily be made vulnerable through the same avenues by which they engage their intuitive powers since these powers are not something they fully understand or control.

In the chapters to come, I further explore characters who access power through feminine forms of knowledge, employing the Lacanian concept of the subject-supposed-to-know (*sujet supposé savoir*) to examine the role of feminine intuition in these narratives. As delineated in chapter 1, I consider the performances of intu-itive mastery often required of women protagonists as related to both their gender and the repetition of these moments through the tenure of a transmedia franchise or series. Characters' abilities sometimes stem from specific forms of training or education but more often arise as if conjured from the depths of their psyches, a "natural" consequence of their feminine difference. Psychoanalysis has much to say about femininity—not all of it useful. While I do not lean too heavily on psy-choanalytic theory, it wends its way into popular culture, waiting to be unpacked, and can offer compelling insights into the relationship between representation and reality. As Jacqueline Rose explains in her introduction to a collection of Jacques Lacan's essays on feminine sexuality, "The question of what a woman is in this account always stalls on the crucial acknowledgment that there is absolutely no guarantee that she *is* at all. . . . For Lacan, masquerade is the very definition of 'femininity' precisely because it is constructed with reference to a male sign."[12] In many ways, referring to femininity's indefinability—analyzed at length by femi-nist philosophers and scholars such as Luce Irigaray and Judith Butler, among others—underscores a primary tenet of my argument.[13] As long as women pro-tagonists are an exception marked by feminine intuition or even empowered via symbolic gestures meant to signify how they are above-average *women*, we will continue to define the feminine as opposed to its masculine referent.

Much of the scholarship on visual representations of women and power has, understandably, focused on external manifestations of power vis-à-vis action heroines and superheroes.[14] Considerations of women's knowledge as unique, on the other hand, often take the angle of analyzing women detectives or, more broadly, women in the workforce or women's entanglements with traditionally male-dominated fields.[15] I simultaneously add nuance to and broaden these frameworks by considering characters who meet at least three criteria. First, they are the protagonists in their respective narratives and operate either alone or with a dedicated (female) partner or an inseparable group of other women (shows like *Charlie's Angels* and *Supergirl*, for example). I do not focus on ensemble shows with no distinct protagonist because the representations of each character may vary from episode to episode based on service to a larger story arc; this practice disrupts the serial assertion of mastery often thrust on exceptional female characters. Second, I primarily analyze characters whose power and/or knowledge is presented as an extraordinary ability of some kind. This does not require a supernatural catalyst, although it may; rather, the character in question has some acknowledged ability above and beyond those around her, whether it was gained through otherworldly intervention or exceptional talent. Rarely, as mentioned earlier, are transmedia heroines exceptional solely because of specialized training or hard work; even when they have received intense physical or mental instruction, the reason these characters are exceptional often stems from some aspect of their embodiment or via special instincts. Finally, I focus on characters who operate within repeated narrative frameworks via transmedia franchises, reboots, and sequels. While I highlight contemporary articulations of these characters to emphasize how representations of women's power and knowledge have been reformed in this era of heightened interest in gender parity across film and television, I ground my discussions in the historiography of each franchise, demonstrating how erstwhile gendered assumptions continue to rise to the fore, albeit sometimes in subtler ways. The primary reasons for this restriction are to avoid replicating the extensive, thoughtful scholarship published in feminist media studies in the past fifty years and to concentrate on articulations of feminine intuition and gendered knowledge and power in our contemporary era. By the turn of the millennium, mediamakers and viewers are familiar with mainstream conceptions of feminism, and most shows and films at least pay lip service to gender equality, which makes these articulations of gendered exceptionalism all the more complicated.

To set the stage for my analyses, chapter 1, "Why Feminine Intuition? The Gendering of Knowledge and Power," provides a selective overview of the ways debates around women's knowledge, power, and agency have a long history in literature, philosophy, mythology, and religion. Rather than a comprehensive review of the scholarship, which is legion and would prove impossible, I provide examples from a spectrum of writers and scholars to illustrate how femininity has long framed, and continues to influence, how a woman's gender is implicated in her ability to act on the world. This chapter, then, provides the playing field on which I arrange my interrogation of women's roles in the popular imaginary and in transmedia franchises throughout the remainder of the book.

I begin my media analysis in chapter 2, "Seriality and 'Strong Female Characters': The Double Bind of Women's Empowerment Narratives," which employs two decades-spanning transmedia franchises, *Charlie's Angels* (1976–1981, 2000, 2003, 2011, 2019) and *Wonder Woman* (primarily the 2017 and 2020 films, but with reference to the comics [1941–present] and the live-action television show [1975–1979]), to simultaneously interrogate the historical development of representations of feminine intuition and assess how they have changed in recent versions and remakes alongside shifts in popular articulations of feminism. Characters in both franchises are explicitly framed as "born not made" (that is, what makes these characters powerful is something intrinsic that supersedes any training they have had). *Charlie's Angels* allows me to focus on the process of rebooting—since each of its four iterations has created new characters using similar criteria—and the ways in which reboots of a familiar franchise attempt to inhabit aspects of a beloved but contentious original while addressing evolving ideologies. *Wonder Woman* similarly offers an opportunity to consider how representations within an eighty-year-old franchise have changed and the marked ways they have stayed the same, particularly in the case of Diana's enduring legacy as someone who fights for love.

My examination of comic-book-inspired superheroines carries over into chapter 3, "From Girl Power to Intersectional Sisterhood: Exceptionalism and the Imperatives of Belonging," in which I examine the television show *Supergirl* (CBS, 2015–2016; CW, 2016–2021) as a case study representing the media fervor for popular feminist narratives of young adult heroines who must make their way in the world. This chapter reflects on theoretical conceptions of the relationship between femininity, postfeminism, and neoliberal feminism in its analysis of *Supergirl*, the DC Comics Arrowverse franchise, and the CW network's erstwhile target audience of women aged eighteen through thirty-four. I also consider how the show's protagonist, Kara Danvers, and some of her companions consciously engage in several intersecting feminist ideologies, while the narrative of the show insists that coming-of-age means buying into femininized mores such as altruism, hope, and the power of sisterhood.

The second half of the book takes a darker turn, as I consider ways in which representations of powerful women intersect with narratives of social upheaval, political turmoil, war, violence, and the negotiation of masculinist apocalyptic futures. Chapter 4, "Motherhood and Myth: Inside and Outside the Family Circle," addresses the beliefs undergirding discourses of motherhood as a form of relational feminine identity that stands in as a political proxy. In congress with these ideas, I analyze the four-decades-spanning *Terminator* franchise (films: 1984, 1991, 2003, 2009, 2015, 2019; TV: 2008–2009), wherein a mother's defense of her child explicitly or implicitly serves as an allegory for her defense of democracy and freedom as essential feminine virtues. In this franchise, mothers and nurturing mother substitutes safeguard the social order via their particular intuitive relationship to the child or child surrogate.

Finally, chapter 5, "At the End of the World: Apocalyptic Bodies and the Feminine Sublime," advances the discussion of apocalypses from chapter 4 into an interrogation of biological determinism bound to the idea of woman-as-body in an imagined postapocalyptic future. The bulk of my argument in chapter 5 centers around the character of Alice from the *Resident Evil* films (2002, 2004, 2007, 2010, 2012, 2016), based on a popular survival horror video game franchise, as well as touching on the newest iteration of the franchise, Netflix's short-lived *Resident Evil* (2022) series. I draw on theories of beauty, the sublime, and the abject to parse how Alice's power and knowledge reside primarily in her representation as an iterative (given the films' fixation on cloning) and sublime subject whose body becomes the locus of the narrative. Alice represents both a destructive force and a possibility for humanity's salvation; she is situated as a primal feminine subject who operates on the boundary between life and death.

The chapters herein grapple with, in succession, innate feminine exceptionalism (*Wonder Woman* and *Charlie's Angels*), sisterhood and belonging (*Supergirl*), motherhood (*Terminator*), and the intersection of the woman's body with life and death (*Resident Evil*). This further allows me to tackle a progression of issues, from the ways in which these franchises take up the various iterations of feminist ideology over the last half century to how women's roles and ostensibly gendered traits continue to come to the fore. While this book focuses on narrative film and television and reflects on the ways feminine intuition, embodiment, and power resonate in progressive installments of each franchise, my conclusion returns to the considerations intimated earlier: how stereotypically feminine traits—love, empathy, altruism, diplomacy—are alternately lauded and repudiated as possibilities for effecting long-lasting social change. We may be less likely to hear the term *feminine intuition* in everyday conversation these days, but I argue it remains at the heart of many debates around women's roles, empowerment, and agency. The wheels set in motion by the earliest dismissals and admiration of women's knowledge as intuitive are similar to those driving ideologies behind political and social movements that insist women's voices, power, and knowledge take center stage. These constructions of gendered exceptionalism—feminine intuition qua women's empowerment—paradoxically highlight the productive potential of feminine power and knowledge as different from its masculine or agender counterparts, while also troubling women's agency through an insistence on accessing sociopolitical power via normative understandings of femininity.

1 · WHY FEMININE INTUITION?
The Gendering of Knowledge and Power

Our fantasy of a hero is that he's the good guy who is going to shut down the bad guy. That has got to change if we want to deal with the crisis that we're in. There is no bad guy. We are all to blame. New kinds of heroics need to be celebrated, like love, thoughtfulness, forgiveness, diplomacy, or we're not going to get there. No one is coming to save us.
> —Patty Jenkins quoted in Luscombe, "12 Questions with Patty Jenkins, Director of Wonder Woman"

Over the past 25 years, we have seen that when women and girls participate in democracy, the benefits ripple out across society. Women leaders are more likely to increase budgets for health care and education, and women's leadership contributes to greater cooperation, equality, and stability.
> —Hillary Clinton, "Power Shortage"

In her novella *The Murder of Roger Ackroyd* (1926), Agatha Christie illustrates how the concept of feminine intuition trickles into presumptive ideologies of women's knowledge. Christie's Belgian detective Hercule Poirot, a recurring character in her stories and known especially for his exceptional observational skills, offers this backhanded rebuke of women's abilities: "'*Les femmes*,' generalized Poirot. 'They are marvelous! They invent haphazard—and by miracle they are right. Not that it is that, really. Women observe subconsciously a thousand little details, without knowing that they are doing so. Their subconscious mind adds these little things together—and they call the result intuition. Me, I am very skilled in psychology. I know these things.'"[1] While by no means a central element of the case, in this moment Christie lampoons even her astute detective's masculinist assumptions about women's intelligence and its origins, notably characterizing his assertion as a generalization. Women are marvelous because of their innate talent for observation, in contrast to Poirot's years of psychological training; women intuit, but Poirot knows. We see a similar reference in Isaac Asimov's short story, "Feminine Intuition" (1969), in which scientists build a robot with an ostensibly female body and mind in order to gain certain astronomical knowledge they believe has been inaccessible to "male" robots. When the robot is destroyed, a female scientist is called in to reconstruct the robot's knowledge. She scoffs, "Feminine intuition? Is that what you wanted the robot for? You men. Faced with a woman reaching a correct conclusion and unable to accept the fact that she is your equal or superior in intelligence, you invent something called feminine intuition."[2] Despite the scientist's admonition, the premise and arc of Asimov's story do suggest that women's minds, whether mechanic or organic, offer a change in perspective necessary for the acquisition of certain kinds of knowledge. The attribution of this knowledge to intuition rather than study, exertion, training, or advanced preparation excises some of the agentic possibilities for the characters' application and control of their unique abilities, whatever those may be. These are only two, disparate examples of this phenomenon, and ones where feminine intuition is directly referenced. More often, the concept comes to bear on gendered framings of knowledge without being named.

Feminine intuition—whether expressed with admiration (feminine intuition as the special purview of women) or in the spirit of denigration (merely feminine intuition rather than intellectual knowledge or training)—has long functioned as a rhetorical signpost indicating knowledge both unexplainable and distinctly gendered. Anthropologist Margaret Mead defines *intuition* as a term "used to describe knowledge which seems to appear full-blown. It is knowledge which appears in a nonrational way, the steps leading to which are unrecognizable and difficult to articulate, either for the knower or for those who watch the knower. . . . It is used to describe those intuitive understandings which seem to come more easily and quickly to women by virtue of their sex."[3] Identifying here the ways women's knowledge is often defined as separate or different from rational knowledge and logic, Mead also emphasizes how the idea of feminine intuition frequently stands in for knowledge that even its bearer does not understand. While the term itself is rarely mentioned in contemporary parlance, the shows and films I examine in subsequent chapters shape their characters using backstories, experiences, challenges, and forms of power that are often distinctly gendered or grounded in gendered assumptions. I contend we see echoes of this belief about the purview of women's knowledge in the representation of women protagonists, particularly those in powerful roles, ones in which their abilities and strengths make them somehow uniquely suited for their (feminized) profession, destiny, or quest.

Although I am eager to examine the films and shows in question, this chapter provides a necessary if truncated foundation to frame the ways feminine intuition (named as such or implied) and attendant assumptions around "natural" feminine behaviors and abilities make frequent appearances in literature, sociology, psychology, and everyday life. One could easily become mired in a long overview chronicling the ways writers and artists have codified femininity and feminine virtues, from the Greeks to Shakespeare, from Buddhist scripture to the Catholic notion of sex complementarity (that masculine and feminine forces oppose and balance each other).[4] Many of these instances have been exhaustively chronicled and challenged by feminist scholars over at least the last century.[5] There is certainly no need to retread all of that well-worn territory. Instead, I take the liberty of highlighting here a few relevant aspects of the discourse around feminine forms of knowledge production—or, perhaps, knowledge *induction*—that directly relate to the idea of feminine intuition as a significant outlet of women's knowledge and power. This can only ever be a process of selection and distillation, the delineation of the contours of a space to be filled in subsequent chapters through my analyses. As such, I set the stage with an overview of a few relevant modern and contemporary articulations of feminine virtue, knowledge, and power.

WOMEN'S EDUCATION AND FEMININE KNOWLEDGE PRODUCTION

I start with the European Enlightenment not because of its inherent value as a bastion of philosophical insight but rather for its impressively essentialist arguments about women's roles that nevertheless filter into later feminist critiques. As stalwart contributors to the ongoing dialogue on social contracts, education, and the value and limits of knowledge, philosophers in this period reflect in part on the rights due to women and men by nature of their respective feminine and masculine virtues. Authors like Jean-Jacques Rousseau and Immanuel Kant clearly imagine themselves egalitarian—they are not in the least—when they bestow upon Woman certain powers and virtues that are hers alone. As Rousseau says in his treatise on education, *Émile*, "Woman is worth more as a woman, but less as a man; wherever she improves her rights she has the advantage, and wherever she attempts to usurp ours she remains inferior to us."[6] Literally proposing women keep to their place, Rousseau speciously suggests that husband and wife are both necessary to the function of society, if they each fulfill their roles properly: "One must be active and strong, the other passive and weak. One must needs have power and will, while it suffices that the other have little power of resistance."[7] This formulation echoes commonly understood, if often challenged, conventions around masculine and feminine binary oppositions and the ostensible balance of opposing forces in the occupation of gender roles. Kant offers a similar assertion in his aesthetic philosophy from the same period, arguing that women's understanding is that of beauty, whereas men's is deep and sublime.[8] A male-female couple, he later insists, should "constitute a single moral person, which is animated and governed by the understanding of the man and the taste of the wife."[9] For Kant, the emphasis on understanding and reason in the aesthetic determination of a person's values is notably a matter of intention. Women's tendency toward the beautiful is about the supposed passivity of feminine sentiment and ability to reason, an intuitive reaction to, rather than an intellectual and intentional interaction with, the world.

Pushing back against the edicts on feminine virtue, education, and sentiment offered by many male philosophers of the time, Mary Wollstonecraft's *Vindication of the Rights of Women* asserts the necessity of women's complete access to education while, in a perhaps calculated compromise, maintaining some of the conventions around gendered difference. To do so, she attributes what some consider masculine virtues to humanity as a whole, questioning why anyone would want to deny women these human qualities. Wollstonecraft asks, what is it that men are so afraid of when they fret over women being "masculine"? She continues, "If by this appellation men mean to inveigh against their ardour in hunting, shooting, and gaming, I shall most cordially join in the cry; but if it be against the imitation of manly virtues, or, more properly speaking, the attainment of those talents and virtues, the exercise of which ennobles the human character, and which raise females in the scale of animal being, when they are comprehensively termed mankind;— all those who view them with a philosophic eye must, I should think, wish with me, that they may everyday grow more and more masculine."[10] By invoking her readers' sense of reason, Wollstonecraft effectively utilizes the same dog whistle Kant and Rousseau, among others, rely on to assert the intellectual dominance of men: women's intelligence is intuitive and domestic, and men's is shaped by logic and intention. While allowing that physical strength and violent sporting activities are masculine, Wollstonecraft insists that intellectual pursuits, the acquisition of knowledge, and the cultivation of rational thought are human rather than gendered virtues.[11] She further argues that women deserve education if for no other reason than to be the best wives and mothers they can be—intellectual companions rather than merely beautiful objects, teachers of their children rather than just caregivers. Given Wollstonecraft's political and ideological leanings, this seems more likely a calculated emphasis on marriage and children rather than a firmly held personal belief that women should conform to these roles.[12] Still, in justifying her insistence that women can be men's intellectual equals, Wollstonecraft reaffirms gendered difference along physical and social lines, binding women to men as she frames her argument.

We see a similar insistence on women's roles vis-à-vis feminine and masculine imperatives in discussions around women's suffrage in the late eighteenth and early nineteenth centuries in the United States.[13] In *A Voice from the South*, sociologist and activist Anna Julia Cooper expressively asserts the ways the "feminine flavor" of women's peaceful and thoughtful natures has shifted the balance of the Western world, before moving on to discuss the egregious and, to her, bewildering differences in the way white and Black women are treated in American society.[14] She also emphasizes the complementary nature of men's and women's roles and abilities, in order to insist on the equitable treatment and education of women of all races:

> All I claim is that there is a feminine as well as a masculine side to truth; that these are related not as inferior and superior, not as better and worse, not as weaker and stronger, but as complements—complements in one necessary and symmetric whole. That as the man is more noble in reason, so the woman is more quick in sympathy. That as he is indefatigable in pursuit of abstract truth, so is she in caring

for the interests by the way—striving tenderly and lovingly that no one of the least of these "little ones" should perish.[15]

Both masculine and feminine traits should be encouraged and taught to children, Cooper admonishes, not to undo normative gender roles but to convey the significance of both women and men to the smooth functioning of a democracy, in which each has their place. Women are, after all, the moral center of the home, a position Cooper asserts is part of a woman's nature, "her contribution to the world." She continues, "Her kingdom is not over physical forces. Not by might, nor by power can she prevail. Her position must ever be inferior where strength of muscle creates leadership. If she follows the instincts of her nature, however, she must always stand for the conservation of those deeper moral forces which make for the happiness of homes and the righteousness of the country. In a reign of moral ideas she is easily queen."[16] As with Wollstonecraft, Cooper's assertions are certainly a product of her time; grounding a desire for women's equality in gendered difference and complementarity is one way of skirting accusations that women are trying to take the place of men or co-opt so-called masculine liberties and virtues. This is especially vital for someone writing in the late nineteenth century and attempting to establish a place for all women, but particularly Black women, in a rapidly modernizing but racially treacherous American cultural landscape.

Let us jump ahead a bit, to the mid-twentieth century, where we see what is commonly known as second-wave feminism beginning to take shape. Femininity as an enigma comes to the fore again and again in discussions of how to define women's roles, reinforcing the notion of feminine knowledge as something intuitive, ergo indecipherable, innate rather than learned (and, hence, unlearnable). French philosopher Simone de Beauvoir opens her volume *The Second Sex* by taking this supposition at face value: "We are told that femininity is in danger; we are exhorted to be women, remain women, become women. It would appear, then, that every female human being is not necessarily a woman; to be so considered she must share in that mysterious and threatened reality known as femininity."[17] As an existentialist, Beauvoir insists that no universal feminine exists; we make our meaning as we act in the world, despite social assumptions that define human virtues as masculine, positive, and neutral, with so-called feminine traits treated as Other, negative, or "in the wrong."[18] According to Beauvoir, "Woman can be defined by her consciousness of her femininity no more satisfactorily than by saying that she is a female, for she acquires this consciousness under circumstances dependent upon the society of which she is a member."[19] Her assertion aligns with that of psychoanalyst Joan Riviere, who, twenty years prior, described "womanliness" as a masquerade in an article that frequently informs gender performance theory.[20] Femininity/womanliness is "worn as a mask, both to hide the possession of masculinity and to avert the reprisals expected if she was found to possess it," Riviere posits. She further argues that "genuine womanliness and the masquerade . . . are the same thing," emphasizing the socially constructed nature of gendered difference.[21] While these scholars attempt to deconstruct notions of gender as a fixed binary, the semantics of social mores at the time (and still today, in many cases) insist on defining masculinity and femininity as known and understood quantities.

Digging into the real-world implications of gender norms, American feminist Betty Friedan latches more firmly onto (white) cultural definitions of femininity in order to critique 1950s gender politics:

> The feminine mystique says that the highest value and the only commitment for women is the fulfillment of their own femininity. It says that the great mistake of Western culture, through most of its history, has been the undervaluation of this femininity. It says this femininity is so mysterious and intuitive and close to the creation and origin of life that man-made science may never be able to understand it. But however special and different, it is in no way inferior to the nature of man; it may even in certain respects be superior. The mistake says the mystique, the root of women's troubles in the past is that women envied men, women tried to be like men, instead of accepting their own nature, which can find fulfillment only in sexual passivity, male domination, and nurturing maternal love.[22]

I quote this longer passage in full to emphasize Friedan's observations regarding the way privileging feminine ideals may be used against women with an insistence, as we see in the Enlightenment texts, that women are best at "womanly things" and should concentrate on excelling in those areas. Her book then dismantles these ideas of feminine exceptionalism, making a case against the "happy housewife heroine" and a case for an emphasis on women as individuals who can be intelligent, independent, and agentic without conforming to an enigmatic feminine standard. While significant attempts to deconstruct gendered relations of power and knowledge foment during this period, it is worth noting the caution that Bonnie Thornton Dill and others lay out in their critiques of the feminist movement. Dill clarifies, for example, that its "early emphasis upon the oppression of women within the institution of marriage and the family, and upon educational and professional discrimination, reflected the concerns of middle-class white women," rather than accounting for intersectional differences in need, desire, and experiences vis-à-vis gender equality.[23] Therefore, when Beauvoir questions the very idea of womanhood or Friedan considers the plight of housewives, they do not seem to take into account how a supposedly universal idea of femininity or womanhood was often automatically denied to women of color, queer women, and women living in poverty.

Unfortunately, while feminine exceptionalism is a worthwhile recipient of critique, emphasizing individual achievement only further dilutes the possibilities for collective social change and disproportionately benefits white women. This is an idea that bell hooks articulates throughout her oeuvre, arguing in her book *Ain't I a*

Woman: Black Women and Feminism (1981), "Although the contemporary feminist movement was initially motivated by the sincere desire of women to eliminate sexist oppression, it takes place within the framework of a larger, more powerful cultural system that encourages women and men to place the fulfillment of individual aspirations above their desire for collective change."[24] Individual fulfillment as a central aim interferes with both the collective action necessary for social justice movements to fully function and the need for women's emotional and political solidarity. Dill also asserts, "While Black women have fostered and encouraged sisterhood, we have not used it as the anvil to forge our political identities. This contrasts sharply with the experiences of many middle-class white women who have participated in the current women's movement."[25] Embedded in these critiques lies one of the central conundrums of gender politics, but also identity politics broadly writ: collective empowerment often requires an acceptance of a set of norms that define collective identity. However, normative definitions of "woman" too often rely on the experience of white, middle-class women *even when the aim is to dismantle those definitions*; this leads to an emphasis on individual empowerment as proxy for social change and an implicit or explicit denial of avenues toward revolution for those who did not fit the norms to begin with. Even in the contemporary feminist movement, journalist Koa Beck reminds us, "Coming to feminism with a centralizing of self was concurrent with the sharp mass uptick in 'women's empowerment,' a term that was searched to peak popularity on Google in 2014. Sanitizing 'empowerment' away from radical, deeply historical activism was pivotal for fourth-wave white feminism because it had to become transactional—something you could buy, obtain, and experience as a product rather than an amorphous feeling that rushed in from challenging power."[26] Here, Beck identifies one of several correlations between feminine forms of knowledge production and ideological constructions of women's power and/or empowerment. Whether embedded in activism, part of the sociopolitical sphere, or stemming from media representation, the idea that individual actualization, gendered knowledge, and the achievement of one's "potential" ultimately leads to empowerment is a central tenet of popular feminism.

NORMATIVE FEMININITY AND WOMEN'S EMPOWERMENT

I now turn briefly away from constructions of feminine intuition and knowledge to think more specifically about women's power. Empowerment narratives are not necessarily the same as narratives about women who are in positions of power or who have "powers," be they magical, supernatural, alien, divine, genetic, or due to preternatural human giftedness. And yet, there is a common elision in the stories I explore between portrayals of characters who are powerful and the idea of women's empowerment (or, in some cases, "girl power"). Influential media scholars Yvonne Tasker and Diane Negra define postfeminism as a movement that "commodifies feminism via the figure of woman as empowered consumer. Thus, postfeminist culture emphasizes educational and professional opportunities for women and girls; freedom of choice with respect to work, domesticity, and parenting; and physical and particularly sexual empowerment."[27] By this formulation, empowerment is a consumer narrative—one to be advertised, bought, and sold—but also a narrative about individual achievement and fortitude. Sarah Banet-Weiser similarly defines empowerment as embedded in popular feminism: "When girls and women are told to 'be' confident and empowered, it is framed as an individual choice: they just need to believe it, and then they will become it. This confidence will help them become better economic subjects, without interrogating the broad economic context that encourages women and girls to not be confident in the first place."[28] Both definitions of empowerment, in the contexts of popular feminism and postfeminism, underscore the centrality of girls and women following social cues that designate appropriate outlets for their agency and purpose, circumscribing their choices in order to fall closer in line with dominant ideas of women's roles. Contemporary philosopher Amy Allen's model of power attempts to negotiate feminist reflections on domination and submission by theorizing a "power-to," "power-over," and "power-with" model to categorize different enactments of power.[29] What all these definitions have in common is that, regardless of shifts in gender roles in the last century, certain forms of "empowerment" are still popularly understood as suitable for women and girls, while other forms of power (e.g., domination, or "power-over," in Allen's terms) are not.

An intersectional feminist approach informed by Patricia Hill Collins's "matrix of domination" can help parse out this distinction further. While Collins's writing focuses primarily on the lived experiences of Black women in the United States, rather than the fictional representation of women in literature, film, or television, her invocation of the ever-shifting and complex tendrils of situational oppression speaks cogently to the nuances of marginalization based on identity: "Her gender may be more prominent when she becomes a mother, her race when she searches for housing, her social class when she applies for credit, her sexual orientation when she is walking with her lover, and her citizenship status when she applies for a job. In all these contexts, her position in relation to and within intersecting oppression shifts."[30] Collins's critical insistence on the complexity of intersectional identities also illuminates a conundrum of diversity and inclusion initiatives as enacted in contemporary media, one that teeters between extremes of universality and individualism. We may also think of these ideas in Foucauldian terms. By considering an "analytics of power" rather than just a theory of power, Foucault expresses the need to take "relations of power" into account and interrogate both how to define "the specific domain formed by relations of power" and which tools are best to analyze that domain.[31] Fostering a sense of women's empowerment via media representation requires simplification and codification. Whatever the other complexities of the characters' lives, distillations of gender identity for the purposes of ostensible political efficacy often prevail.

Rather than ascribe these ideas merely to populist reimaginings of feminism, scholars grounded in critical femininity studies define normative femininity as related to Western patriarchal culture's obsession with feminine traits, behaviors, and ideals stereotypically ascribed to women.[32] On the other hand, there also exists in the literature a more inclusive version of femininity often, but not always, aligned with gender performance, femme studies, and critiques of toxic masculinity.[33] Popular feminism and postfeminism rely in large part on a broad understanding and acknowledgment of the primacy of normative femininity, the feminine as defined by cultural assumptions about women's roles and potential vis-à-vis men, and the traits ascribed most commonly to women. As such, normative femininity has its origins far back in the reaches of written history. As Mary Beard astutely asserts in her published lecture "Women and Power," women who acquire power, from ancient myth to the present, are frequently framed as stepping out of bounds (hence the phrase "breaking the glass ceiling"). In fact, she writes, "The unflinching logic of [ancient Greek] stories is that [women] must be disempowered, put back in their place. In fact, it is the unquestionable mess that women make of power in Greek myth that justifies their exclusion from it in real life, and justifies the rule of men."[34] Thus, the following example from ancient Greek drama serves as more than a tangential referent. It succinctly illustrates the enduring nature of the ways women's roles and behaviors—particularly in our classical heroic imaginary—are bound to forms of knowledge and power, but also the vulnerabilities gendered/feminine exceptionalism open through these very same avenues of seeming privilege, empowerment, or categories of distinction.

Written just shy of 2,500 years ago, Euripides's tragedy *The Trojan Women* chronicles the final hours before the wives, mothers, and daughters of the slaughtered Trojan soldiers are parceled off as slaves to the Greek victors of the Trojan War.[35] A unique play for the time in both its cast dominated by female characters and its sympathetic depiction of the losers of the conflict as they navigate the aftermath of defeat, *The Trojan Women* offers each of the women in the erstwhile royal family a stage on which to air her grief at her respective fall from power. The first two characters to share their stories, the former Queen Hecuba and her daughter-in-law Andromache, mourn the destruction of their city and their imminent degradation, including the death of Andromache's toddler son, the last male heir, who is torn from her arms and thrown from the burning walls of the city midway through the play. Moments before Greek soldiers take away her son, Andromache wonders how she, an honorable wife and mother, could be in such disfavor with the gods that she is destined to serve as concubine to the Greek Neoptolemus, whose father, Achilles, killed her husband, Hector. Andromache laments, "And yet the reputation I worked so hard to earn was the very means of my destruction."[36] Troy's other princesses fare no better. A third character, Hecuba's daughter, Cassandra, was cursed long before the events of the play by the god Apollo for refusing his sexual advances, afflicting her with the ability to see the future but never be believed. While she prophesizes her own death at the hands of her captor Agamemnon's jealous wife when their ship arrives in Mycenae, Cassandra still revels in the destruction her presence will cause to his family line.[37] Meanwhile, a fourth woman, Hecuba's youngest daughter, Polyxena, serves as a virgin sacrifice on Achilles's grave. The fifth, and only Greek, woman in the play, Helen, begs her husband, Menelaus, to spare her life despite her having set off the decade-long war resulting in untold loses on both sides by running away with the Trojan prince Paris. From Homer's earlier epic *The Odyssey*, we know Helen's entreaty is successful; she returns to rule Sparta at her husband's side.[38]

Even though Helen's beauty and sexual irresistibility save her life, Euripides's women are all at the mercy of Greek men, and they suffer in part because of the things that, in other circumstances, offer them some measure of feminized power. Neoptolemus chooses Andromache as his "prize" (sex slave) precisely because she was a loyal wife and good mother, horrifically emphasized by her breakdown when her son is killed. Odysseus selects Hecuba because she was once a wise and well-respected queen, formerly the most powerful woman among the now-slaves, and he sees himself as a wise and cunning man; she ultimately throws herself into the sea to escape her fate as the house slave of a man she hates. Polyxena is sacrificed because she was an honorable young virgin. Cassandra may speak freely of her desire for revenge only because the Greeks assume she is hysterical, and the larger ethos of the play allows it because she is destined to die. Normative femininity ascribes traits to women—fidelity, virginity, innocent youth or aged wisdom, beauty, vulnerability, irrationality, passivity—and reminds us that even traits that seem positive are no match for so-called masculine virtues or the wills of men.

Mythology and early religion offer many more such stories, morality tales showing us the ways normative femininity and normative masculinity inform the roles, abilities, and behaviors of heroes, heroines, gods, and goddesses. However, I offer the preceding example in particular because it concisely illustrates how feminine forms of power not only often serve as the foundation for a woman's inherent notability but also function as a catalyst for her actual or potential downfall. *The Trojan Women* also shows how trauma—especially femininized forms of trauma like rape or implied rape via bodily penetration, harm to children, and the threat of forced marriage—informs both women's power and its potential loss in popular narratives.[39] One of the central problems with the formula via which power and knowledge originate out of trauma, suffering, or implicit vulnerability is that the potential for an ostensibly strong woman's defeat is already built into the source of her power. And normative femininity, as an oppressive and obligatory construction, is itself a form of trauma. In all but one of the cases in this book, some form of pivotal trauma undergirds the power of the franchise's character(s). In the recent Wonder Woman films (2017 and 2020), Diana leaves her peaceful homeland to face war and hardship; then, Diana's trauma over the loss of her lover in the first film inspires a romantic divergence in its sequel that literally results in the waning of her superpowers and catalyzes the villains' rise to dominance. Supergirl suffered a cataclysmic loss of her home planet and family in her teen years that inspires her later altruistic heroism. Sarah Connor is hunted by machine assassins, faces the specter of nuclear annihilation, and is forced to bear a child for whom she constantly fears the worst. And Alice of the *Resident Evil* films experiences the primal trauma of being born into a world where her body becomes a locus of biomedical experimentation and retributive violence. Only the campy ethos of *Charlie's Angels* makes it an obvious exception; in this franchise, characters are underestimated and undervalued by the traditionally masculine police force (or other male-coded professions, in the later installments), but these microaggressions, insidious though they are, do not rise to the level of the devastating emotional and physical traumas endured by the other characters I discuss. As I will explore more fully in the coming chapters, many of these characters' traumas are intimately linked with expressions of normative femininity and/or with the ways they are represented as exceptional *gendered* subjects.

Contemporary film and television shows tend to put forward individual women protagonists as symbols of women's empowerment, an inclination even more likely when the character is part of a recognizable or well-known transmedia franchise, sequel, or reboot. Despite recent mainstream discussions and an at least surface-level, widespread understanding of concepts like intersectionality, popular media tends to rely on normative constructions of gender, even if the aim is to ultimately dismantle them. Assumptions and assertions surrounding standards of feminine knowledge and power reign supreme especially and ironically in cases where women protagonists are portrayed as empowered in part because of aspects of their character that correspond to their social construction as women. The historical, literary, and philosophical references just mentioned gesture at ways feminine knowledge has been theorized as well as how feminists have attempted to challenge and rearticulate women's relationship to power. Nevertheless, contemporary representations of women's power and knowledge often fall back on normative femininity, grounding women's abilities in a kind of intuitive wisdom that media sustains in part through repetition and the reassertion of familiar and recognizable tropes. This repetitive function further establishes feminine intuition as the sustaining force responsible for the specialized forms of power many fictional women possess.

SERIAL SUBJECTIVITY AND THE SUBJECT-SUPPOSED-TO KNOW

As franchises boasting an impressive series of reboots, remakes, sequels, and transmedia adaptations between them, the films and shows explored in this book serve as ideal models to begin a discussion of how women's representation frequently succumbs to the lure of gendered exceptionalism. One of the major factors informing assumptions of women's knowledge and power as intuitive and gendered is the repetition of these tropes, characters, and narratives. What better way to assess paradigms formed via repetitive representations than by looking to franchises spanning decades in which the characters have been excessively reimagined while maintaining some recognizable traits throughout their respective tenures? One way to articulate the relevance of concepts such as transference and repetition to the gendering of knowledge and power is to turn to psychoanalysis. There is a long history of using psychoanalysis to analyze screen media, grounded in part in the supposition that film and television, through their (fictionalized) representations, offer an insight into the unconscious desires, conventions, and ideologies of the cultures, eras, and individuals from which they originate.[40] Over half a century ago, Beauvoir and others, such as Gayle Rubin and Kate Millett, argued how seemingly de rigueur understandings of womanhood/femininity extend from repeatedly enacted narratives in ancient myths, modern literature, and social life.[41] Similarly, media representations of women rely on oft-repeated conventions and ideals that have become part of the tapestry of North American media production.

In her interpretation of Jacques Lacan, Juliet Mitchell writes, "Psychoanalysis should not subscribe to ideas about how men and women do or should live as sexually differentiated beings, but instead it should analyse how they come to be such beings in the first place."[42] It is in service of this understanding of psychoanalysis—in that it can bring to light the structural ideologies at work that undergird our sociocultural assumptions about gender and sexuality as well as the ways we have challenged them—that I conduct my analyses. Jacqueline Rose's assessment of "feminism's affinity with psychoanalysis" further supports these connections and their uses, as both scholars recognize "that there is a resistance to identity at the very heart of psychic life. Viewed in this way, psychoanalysis is no longer best understood as an account of how women are fitted into place. . . . Instead psychoanalysis becomes one of the few places in our culture where it is recognized as more than a fact of individual pathology that most women do not painlessly slip into their roles as women, if they do at all."[43] Along these lines, I do not subscribe wholesale to Lacanian psychoanalysis. Rather, I borrow the subject-supposed-to-know as a useful lens through which we can understand how repetition informs our identification with and trust in certain characters with whom we become intimately familiar through a serial franchise.

Lacan's theorization of the subject-supposed-to-know originates from psychoanalytic practice in a clinical setting. He describes it as part of a relationship of trust built through transference between analyst and analysand. Citing his reading of both René Descartes, whose "subject who is supposed to know [is] God," and Plato, who connects love and desire to the experience of transference as an assignment of trust, Lacan posits that an analysand will only cease to hold back information during analysis once they are able to envision the analyst as a subject who is supposed to know.[44] Lacan writes, "The subject comes into play on the basis of this fundamental support—the subject is supposed to know, simply by virtue of being a subject of desire. Now what actually happens? What happens is what is called in its most common appearance the transference effect. This effect is love. It is clear that, like all love, it can be mapped, as Freud shows, only in the field of narcissism. To love is, essentially, to wish to be loved."[45] The analysand begins to see in the analyst an authority with a certain degree of mastery and knowledge over the analysand's own life. The belief that the analyst *knows* the analysand and loves the analysand—cares for their well-being and understands them—allows the analysand to imbue the analyst with further imagined power. This, in turn, improves the process of analysis, which requires trust. The connection between the establishment of this link of trust and the designation of the analyst as the subject-supposed-to-know requires repetition—the repeated visits to the analyst's office, the repeated performances of presumed mastery.

In *Beyond the Pleasure Principle*, Sigmund Freud, on whom Lacan bases some of his theories, articulates repetition in a slightly different way. His use of the well-known example of the *fort-da* ("there-here") game leads to Freud's discussion of the relationship between pleasure and unpleasure and, thus, bears mentioning. A game purportedly played by Freud's grandson who repeats his mother's departure and return by continually throwing a reel on a string away from him and then pulling it back, *fort-da* sets up a possibility for the boy's pleasure in the unpleasure of his mother's loss.[46] In Freud's estimation, the boy envisions the reel as his mother and can therefore enact his agency over her when he sends it/her away from him, marking her absence and return not as an uncertain or random event but as one in which he is an active participant. By mimicking the departure again and again, his mother's absence becomes just one of many. The compulsion to repeat and the boy's imagined agency are both central to an underlying analysis of this account.

Freud's version is relatively straightforward: the boy learns he can send his reel-mother away and bring her back all with the pull of string, working through the loss by repeating the event. In his 1964 seminar, "The Unconscious and Repetition," however, Lacan maintains that the child's agency is of "secondary importance." Instead, he insists that the essential element of the *fort-da* narrative is a realization of a split in the subject of the child—the reel not only stands in for the mother but also is representative of "a small part of the subject that detaches itself from him while still remaining his," which Lacan designates the *objet petit a* or *objet a*.[47] It is ultimately the connection between the *objet a*, repetition, and the act of transference that brings us back to the subject-supposed-to-know. As he continues to discuss the game of *fort-da*, Lacan draws these elements together: "If the young subject [Freud's grandson] can practice this game of *fort-da*, it is precisely because he does not practice it at all, for no subject can grasp this radical articulation. He practices it with the help of a small bobbin, that is to say, with the *objet a*. The function of the exercise with this object refers to an alienation, and not to some supposed mastery, which is difficult to imagine being increased in an endless repetition, whereas the endless repetition that is in question reveals the radical vacillation of the subject."[48] According to Lacan, the repetition of *fort-da* only further alienates the player, marking a split in their subjectivity that has the potential to ever widen. Transference, during the act of analysis, allows the analysand to imbue the analyst with knowledge via these repeated engagements, presupposing a mastery onto the analyst that takes the form of the subject-supposed-to-know.

Both these frameworks are relevant to my objective. With Freud's *fort-da*, the boy tosses the reel, part of himself and a proxy for the loss and return of his mother, back and forth. His repetition garners pleasure by reenacting an unpleasurable experience of loss as he is able to visualize and control the experience of the return. The repetition is a symptom and response, a working through of a traumatic gap. For Lacan's subject-supposed-to-know, repetition establishes trust, a bond that *seems to* close the gap between analyst and analysand. It is not a working through of trauma per se but a construction of a connection between the analysand, who feels unease in their own split subjectivity, and the analyst who comes to embody—more and more with each passing session—a whole and masterful subject who understands the analysand better than they understand themselves. The analysand supposes the analyst knows them and imbues the analyst with power and knowledge they likely do not have but, paradoxically, gain in part through the assumption. These two readings of the function of repetition—as an enactment of agency over an experience of loss and as a projection of mastery onto an outside party—run parallel at first, but they eventually converge in the gap between lived experience and fictional representation.

As media viewers, we are shown protagonists who should appeal to our desires as both individuals and social creatures embedded in distinctive cultural contexts. Assumptions about what viewers want to see in women characters reveal some of the crucial issues at play in contemporary narratives of gendered exceptionalism and how we can or should articulate feminine knowledge and power while simultaneously eschewing gender binaries. In *Technologies of Gender*, Teresa de Lauretis asserts that "the construction of gender goes on today through the various technologies of gender (e.g., cinema) and institutional discourses (e.g., theory) with power to control the field of social meaning and thus produce, promote, and 'implant' representations of gender," while simultaneously offering the prospect of alternative, subversive constructions of gender and gender resistance through "micropolitics."[49] The repetition of the serial form—especially the protracted serial form we find in franchises and reboots—reinforces the first framing of gender's construction, as well as the seeming mastery of characters as they are articulated via feminine mores and gendered codes. And yet, in these narratives that sense of mastery is often a false one, moments away from being undercut, often precisely because of the ways it becomes tied to gender. If a female character's strength stems from her femininity/womanhood and is, therefore, intuitive, then her power and agency are also potentially unstable and under constant threat. Contemporary serial media frequently mask, more or less effectively, the gendered nature of a character's power, and yet it remains that many ostensibly empowered women characters' abilities or strengths actually extend from gendered aspects of their positioning within a given narrative.

The presumption of mastery is perhaps nowhere more prevalent in the popular imaginary than through the mien and exploits of the hero, broadly writ. When deliberately feminized as a heroine—or, more specifically, an action heroine, as one might define most of the characters I discuss—what emerges is a fraught assignation for powerful women. What makes someone a hero or heroine has its own field of study, with definitions that vary widely depending on where one looks; however, even a mundane, generalized definition proves revealing. The *Oxford English Dictionary* defines a hero as "a man (or occasionally a woman) of superhuman strength, courage, or ability, favoured by the gods; esp. one regarded as semi-divine and immortal." Alternatively, it defines a heroine in the same way, except that the phrase "a man (or occasionally a woman)" is substituted with "a woman." Here we can easily see the linguistic conundrum of gendered exceptionalism, wherein hero can function androgynously, but heroine cannot—wherein heroes are *occasionally* exceptional women. It is no wonder there exists a tendency to code heroines by traits that emphasize how their power stems from their femininity, lest they be confused with (presumed masculine) heroes. These coded traits then become fixed in the popular imagination via the repetition of these characters and further serve as comparative frameworks on which subsequent characters can be scaffolded—not to mention implying mastery that becomes bound to coded gender norms. Jeffrey A. Brown explains how differentiating male and female superheroes happens along gendered lines: "According to the dominant binary perceptions of gender, the idealized male characters have to be hypermasculine to fend off any hint of feminization while the tough and powerful female characters have to be depicted as hypersexual in order to fend off any accusations of being masculinized."[50] This contention, however, goes far beyond sexualization, with the feminized nature of action heroines' power embedded throughout many aspects of their characterization, as well as within the narratives in which they are found.[51]

The role of the action heroine has long required a complex negotiation of so-called feminine virtue and other overwrought tenets of femininity. This arises alongside generic conventions bound tightly to notions of machismo and/or masculine prowess and burdened further by the expectations implicit in celebrity culture, as well as what women viewers supposedly want to see. As such, many heroines find themselves simultaneously blessed and cursed under the auspices of femininity. According to Mark Gallagher, "The action film has historically been a 'male' genre, dealing with stories of male heroism, produced by male filmmakers for principally male audiences."[52] Yet action heroines have their own lush and varied history, from the serial queens of the early twentieth century to what Yvonne Tasker identifies as the "post-feminist character" of cinematic action heroines of the past few decades who are "physically strong, independent though often emotionally vulnerable, typically glamorous and even overtly sexy."[53] While the distended narrative structure of serial and episodic media allows for a greater depth of character development and nuancing of gendered norms, many characters remain framed by these and other tropes of the action heroine.

Contemporary action heroines possess the toughness, decisiveness, and wherewithal to be successful crime fighters, superheroes, and spies; they are also often imbued with special knowledge that I capture under the umbrella term *feminine intuition*. This specialized knowledge gives them insight and sometimes power that men in their roles do not possess; however, it also can make them vulnerable, often in the same way or for the same reason they are privileged in the first place—through sexuality, love, motherhood, empathy, and so on. We can see this even in a very early example from the "serial queens" of the silent film era, as Mark Cooper acknowledges in his essay "Pearl White and Grace Cunard: The Serial Queen's Volatile Present." Cooper interprets the form of silent serials like *The Perils of Pauline* as one that emphasizes danger as ever present: "Through repetition, this structure defined peril as persistent but punctual, omnipresent but extraordinary, inevitable yet unexpected. The dangerous moment ended only to be renewed."[54] This is certainly the case for Pauline, whose scheming guardian Koerner puts her life in danger any time (often through his encouragement) she veers away from the domestic safety of home. The adventures she so wishes to have—the premise of the series and the reason for her delayed marriage to her fiancé, Harry—lead her constantly into harm's way. Despite the fact that Pauline seems more than capable of handling herself—climbing down the anchor line of a renegade hot-air balloon, for example—she still requires rescue by a male figure before she is completely free from threat. Contemporary serial narratives configure female heroes in a similar manner; it is precisely their moments of empowerment that open the door to danger. The long-standing nature of these tropes speaks to an ongoing cultural need to emphasize the vulnerability qua femininity of women, even those who seem to defy gender conventions.

As we will see in subsequent chapters, the manner in which power and knowledge are defined, as well as how those definitions align with gendered expectations and norms, endures as a central stumbling block in narratives purporting to represent empowered or powerful women. It may be true that media should represent a diverse range of powerful characters, perhaps shifting away from conventionally masculine frameworks of power. However, to move away from masculine conventions explicitly toward feminine ones via heroines whose long and storied histories require a deep investment in tenets of normative femininity may open a space in which femininized forms of power can be easily dismissed as otherworldly or implausible—mastery promised and then found lacking. In her October 2020 piece in the *Atlantic*, quoted in this chapter's epigraph, Hillary Clinton reminds readers that she once coined the feminist rallying cry "Women's rights are human rights."[55] This assertion aligns women's needs and agency along the same lines as human needs and agency: women should be equal in all aspects of life, receiving equal opportunities, education, respect, and protection. And yet,

Clinton posits that women engage in politics and leadership differently than men, focusing their attention on issues like public health and the environment, as well as inspiring cooperative governance and greater social harmony. Similarly, director Patty Jenkins promotes the first *Wonder Woman* film by placing responsibility for the world's problems—and the onus of coming up with solutions—on a collective "us" while simultaneously urging a "new" heroics. It is no coincidence that Jenkins's emphasis on "love, thoughtfulness, forgiveness, diplomacy" signifies this new heroism as grounded in stereotypically feminized traits.[56] Hence, both Clinton and Jenkins insist on equality and actionable gendered difference at the same time, a paradox at the heart of the remaining analyses in this book.

2 · SERIALITY AND "STRONG FEMALE CHARACTERS"

The Double Bind of Women's Empowerment Narratives

> [Shonda Rhimes] said, for instance, that she hates it when people say she writes "smart, strong women." The alternative, she said, would be writing what? "Dumb, weak women?" Nobody, she pointed out, praises people who write smart, strong men. When you make smart, strong women in and of themselves noteworthy, you reinforce that they are exceptions to something, and it almost doesn't matter what.
>
> —Quoted in Holmes, "The Only One"

The 2019 film reboot of the iconic and controversial 1970s television series *Charlie's Angels* lays its cards on the table in the opening scene.[1] After an establishing shot of Rio de Janeiro's instantly recognizable Christ the Redeemer statue overlooking the city at dusk, the film's second shot, a close-up, reveals Angel Sabina (Kristen Stewart), candlelight augmenting her perfectly manicured nails and smoky eye shadow. She giggles, cooing at the camera and her off-screen date, "I think women can do anything." Her date, Johnny (Chris Pang), a wealthy Asian Australian embezzler, counters, "Think about women fixing cars, driving a taxi, installing drywall. . . . Look, trust me. A girl like you, you don't really want this." Sabina acts playfully incredulous, stroking a foot up Johnny's leg under the table as she breathily questions his logic and—with a bit of foreshadowing to which Johnny is oblivious—replies, "Well, at my job, it's actually considered a huge advantage to be a woman. Yeah, if you're beautiful, nothing else is really expected of you. And if you're not, you're pretty much rendered invisible. And in my line of work, invisibility, low expectations, they come in very handy." Sabina continues to play the part of an airheaded call girl, and Johnny continues to condescend as she starts to gain the physical upper hand by performing a comically seductive aerial routine on the curtains, eventually wrapping her thighs around Johnny's neck. By the time Johnny realizes he has been tied up and his date is choking him, it is too late. "Did you know," Sabina asks rhetorically, "it takes men an additional seven seconds to perceive a woman as a threat compared to a man? Isn't that wild?" At that moment, John Bosley (Patrick Stewart) and other Angels break into Johnny's apartment, quickly overwhelming his bodyguards and taking the erstwhile criminal into custody.

While this newest *Charlie's Angels* remake attempts to set itself apart from its forebears in myriad ways, the self-congratulatory, performative feminism of its opening scene feels familiar. After all, creator Aaron Spelling's 1970s original (ABC, 1976–1981) also aimed "to reconcile the 'feminist' with the 'feminine'—developing female characters who conformed to traditional notions of sexual attractiveness, but who could also be read as 'liberated' women."[2] Directed by Elizabeth Banks, who plays one of the Bosleys as well, the 2019 film eschews the nostalgia of its early aughts counterparts (*Charlie's Angels* [2000] and *Charlie's Angels: Full Throttle* [2003]) and ABC's failed 2011 television reboot and insists from its first moments on being different from the classic show, oft derided as "jiggle TV" due to its penchant for having one or more of the Angels run around braless.[3] To drive this point home, the film's opening scene transitions into a montage of girls and women succeeding at athletic, intellectual, and adventurous pursuits: dancing, going to school, scootering, swimming, skateboarding, performing scientific experiments, roping cattle, practicing archery, and white water rafting. Yet, despite distancing itself from the sexist critiques of the original, the 2019 *Angels* exposes a contemporary articulation of an age-old tension: How do you create media that showcases women's abilities without falling into a trap of gendered exceptionalism where women's power and knowledge must stem from their femininity? Without emphasizing femininity, how does one specifically empower women?

The most recent cinematic installment in the 80-plus-year history of Wonder Woman, *Wonder Woman 1984* (2020), runs into a similar problem, one made far more explicit in this sequel than in director Patty Jenkins's first foray with the character in 2017, discussed at length later in this chapter. By the time of the events in *WW84*, the former Amazon princess and demigoddess Diana (Gal Gadot) has spent 60 years living in the "world of men"—in other words, living among mortal humans rather than the 800 years she spent growing up on Themyscira, a mystical and secluded Amazon island. In her prior cinematic adventure, Diana bested the war god Ares and gained a lover and comrade in arms, American pilot Steve Trevor, only to lose him again when he sacrificed himself to help stop World War I. *WW84* finds Diana isolated from the humans around her, working a mundane job at the Smithsonian and performing hero work in secret; she seemingly has no friends and no prospective suitors. As such, the film hews so desperately to the notion that Diana's power and knowledge stem from her dedication to love that when a series of events brings Steve temporarily back from the dead, Diana seems all too willing to forget her heroic responsibilities in favor of a romantic dalliance, even going so far as to consider relinquishing her powers (strength, invulnerability) altogether and allow others to suffer if it means keeping Steve with her. *WW84*

FIGURE 2.1. Diana struggles with her fading powers. *Wonder Woman 1984*, directed by Patty Jenkins (2020).

ironically—yet not surprisingly, if we follow the threads of my argument—undermines Diana's ethos along precisely the lines that delineate her difference from comparative male superheroes. As I break down further in the latter half of this chapter, the exceptional nature of Diana's powers serves as a trap: her gendered representation becomes a vulnerability and a discredit to her heroism rather than a source of empowerment.

This book contends that contemporary representations of women are still informed by long-standing assumptions around what constitutes feminine power and knowledge despite an explicit push for gender equality. I underscore that discussion in this chapter by revisiting the historical underpinnings of so-called strong female characters and their representation in popular culture. The phrase "strong female characters" is primarily used in the popular press to address women's roles in contemporary film and television and vacillates from praise to pointed critique. In many cases, reviewers and critics have used the expression to condemn creators and promotors of mainstream female characters who reject ostensibly feminine weaknesses (emotionality, gentleness, nurturing behavior, altruism, obedience to authority, passivity, etc.) and replace them with toughness, strength (physical or emotional), rationality, or taciturn self-confidence—rather than creating a fully realized multidimensional female character.[4] In this chapter, I trouble the concept of the strong female character, noting ways in which assertions of feminine knowledge and power are bound to repetitive representations of mastery, which in turn are associated with feminine intuition, broadly writ.

As the paraphrased quote from Shonda Rhimes in this chapter's epigraph suggests, the idea of the strong female character presents a specious and knotty framework for exceptionalism. *Charlie's Angels* and *Wonder Woman* are apt vehicles for unpacking this term and related ideologies, since incarnations of characters in both franchises invoke and disavow, in turn, the tropes of the strong female character, at times emphasizing toughness and sometimes falling back on assertions of normative femininity. Their respective adaptations, both in film and on television, span decades; each subsequent edition or reboot incorporates the gen-dered ideologies of its cultural and temporal milieu. As such, these two franchises offer a distinct lens into the shifting landscape of women's representation through iterated versions that reinforce feminine conventions even when seemingly dis-avowing them. Although the Angels and Wonder Woman present different ver-sions of feminine power and knowledge, these iconic characters repeatedly serve as stand-ins for what writers, producers, directors, and actors believe will be finan-cially viable and culturally relevant. Viewers' responses to these characters, for better and for worse, further speak to how fictional women inhabit the popular imaginary and mark moments of both resonance and dissonance with the experi-ence of real feminine/feminized subjects.[5] As I discussed in the first chapter, a Lacanian understanding of the subject-supposed-to-know—via which repeated encounters with a subject who seems to have specialized knowledge and, hence, inspires a sense of love and trust, as well as an assumption of mastery—reinforces my argument in this chapter. In the case of media representation, the perspective of the other is embodied by the viewer, who may be encouraged to decode women protagonists in particular ways by the tropes employed frequently in the con-temporary films and programs that showcase them.[6] With women protagonists, this assumption of mastery extends specifically to intuitive forms of power and knowledge grounded directly or obliquely in the characters' gender.

We should avoid the temptation to measure *Wonder Woman* and *Charlie's Angels* against some abstract metric of feminist success. While reviews in the popular press often appraise each new adaptation according to how "well" or "accurately" its characters represent women's potential to achieve positions of power and/or showcase their superior intellects, I contend that assessing whether a series or film has laudable feminist values is an enticing lure, but a false one. Cer-tainly, 2019's *Angels* wants viewers to believe that its explicitly feminist messaging fully reconfigures the Angels for the contemporary moment. Similarly, 2017's *Won-der Woman* enthusiastically signposts its divergence from earlier and arguably more sexist versions of one of America's most iconic superheroines.[7] One could argue that *Wonder Woman* does this with a great deal more subtlety and (market/critical) success than either *Charlie's Angels* or *WW84*; however, in many ways that contention is secondary to the central tenet of my argument.

When we assess media representations of women according to whether or not they hew to feminist values, mercurial as those may be—common contenders include independence, choice, and empowerment, all of which are subject to the corruptive forces of neoliberalism, capitalism, racism, heteronormativity, and ableism—it becomes easy to forget that the inextricable element is always the woman. No matter how emboldening, inspiring, or discerning, any representation of a strong female character only further embeds her in notions of gender norms, gendered expectations, and gendered exceptionalism. What I intend to show, then, is not whether Wonder Woman or the Angels can serve as feminist icons, but rather how *both* franchises rely on the sometimes implicit, sometimes explicit concept of feminine intuition or feminized knowledge as the foundation of the characters' power. Wonder Woman's power stems from her Amazon heritage, training, and ability to prioritize love and truth; the Angels' skills and strengths come from their free use of feminine "wiles," turning supposed disadvantages into advantages. The question of whether either or both are "good" or "successful" representations is less compelling than the question of why creators—and perhaps viewers—so frequently insist heroines must be framed by the feminine origins of their power and knowledge, even in cases where they seem to reject them entirely.

"HE TOOK THEM AWAY FROM ALL THAT": CHARLIE'S ANGELS AND THE LEGACY OF THE ACTION HEROINE

Linda Mizejewski astutely designates Aaron Spelling's original *Charlie's Angels* as a "brilliant combination of feminism and antifeminism."[8] We need look no further than the opening title sequence to see this in action. Charlie's voice-over describes the show's fairy-tale setup: "Once upon a time, there were three little girls who went to the police academy, and they were each assigned very hazardous duties. I took them away from all that and now they work for me. My name is Charlie." In the first-season sequence, vignettes of Sabrina (Kate Jackson), Kelly (Jaclyn Smith), and Jill (Farrah Fawcett) punctuate this voice-over narration: first, they excel over and above the call of duty, besting the men in their police academy classes at sharpshooting, sparring, and fitness testing, only to find themselves assigned such "hazardous duties" as crossing guard, desk jockey, and meter maid. The implication is obvious: these superlative trainees were barred from real police work due to their gender, that is, until Charlie rescued them and helped them become private eyes. In exchange for their apparent empowerment working as PIs, the Angels constantly find themselves in danger. Thus, and in other ways, they embody specialized forms of power and knowledge, while remaining visibly and demonstrably vulnerable.

Why they are called Angels is never explicitly revealed (at least not to my knowledge), but the show was notorious for capitalizing on 1970s debates around women's lib in a very particular way, which ascribed the Angels only tenuous empowerment. While Sabrina, Kelly, and Jill (replaced by her sister Kris [Cheryl Ladd] after season 1) are unquestionably smart, courageous, and independent, they also rely heavily on their winsome good looks, seductiveness, and wide-ranging ability to get what they want from men. Sumiko Higashi's analysis during the show's original airing further elaborates on this tension: "The contradiction of three women rendered as sex objects but also functioning like men in a man's world at male behest is visible in the graphics and shots of the credit sequence. The Angels are successively shown in the graphics in aggressive postures thrusting out with rifle, gun, and hands in a martial arts position, but at the same time they are geometrically framed and encased. After each of the three graphics, there are five shots of each actress in conventional pin-up poses intercut with such male detective activities as driving cars in chase scenes and aiming guns."[9] Higashi emphasizes that, according to the ethos of the show, the Angels' beauty and sex appeal are feminine, whereas their activities are masculine. The show asserts that the intersection of these gendered traits is what make the Angels themselves exceptional. Reviews at the time of the show's premiere also emphasize that Jaclyn Smith and Farrah Fawcett were models, not actors; Kate Jackson, the only professional actor of the trio, also plays the least hypersexualized angel, Sabrina, treated within the context of the show as the brains and strategist of the group.[10] The primacy placed on physical appearance, via the casting of models, only reasserts the need for these Angels' femininity to remain front and center.

Some reviewers insisted on the show's broad appeal, and certainly its high ratings in the early years attest to a widespread interest in the *Charlie's Angels* phenomenon, whatever the cause.[11] Writing for the *Los Angeles Times*, Cecil Smith extols, "Women dig it as much as men. Which is a switch. There was a time when beautiful women were considered a liability on television, that no wife wanted to have some gorgeous electronic rival parading in front of her husband around her house at night."[12] This mindset encapsulates much of the thinking around *Charlie's Angels* and similar shows in the 1970s; female characters needed to be both titillating and nonthreatening to male viewers, while signposting women's empowerment to remain aligned with cultural concerns of the time. Even Jackson herself echoes this viewpoint; when "the talk turned to femininity and the need to redefine it," during a 1976 interview, she stated, "I am not for liberation but I am for women's independence on all levels."[13] The cognitive dissonance required to make a statement opposing liberation (by which she must have meant the "women's liberation movement") while championing independence is precisely the same required to create a show like *Charlie's Angels* in the first place. As Anna Gough-Yates articulates, the Angels "are successful precisely because they have found the perfect balance between women's liberation and traditional forms of femininity—though in attaining success the Angels effectively separate themselves from the world of 'ordinary women.'"[14] We can see this push-pull played out in almost every episode of the show: the Angels are both feminine—and, crucially, gain substantial advantages as investigators because of their femininity, whether due to their ability to infiltrate all-women spaces or because they are underestimated—and extraordinary, marked as different from the other women around them in significant ways.

In the pilot, the extended opening credits sequence includes an extra scene after Charlie "takes them away from all that" boring police work, showing Sabrina, Jill, and Kelly engaged in athletic pursuits designed to emphasize their upper-class, white femininity. Sabrina, fully decked out in riding gear, jumps a tall bay horse over a cross-country course before skillfully dismounting and handing the animal over to a waiting groom. Jill practices her tennis swing against a ball machine, fetchingly attired in white shorts and a fitted shirt. Kelly emerges dripping from a pool in a white bikini and matching swim cap. A phone call from Charlie interrupts each woman's graceful athleticism in turn; when they answer, Charlie tells them, "It's Charlie, Angel. Time to go to work," and they grin winsomely. Because this interruption of athletic leisure occurs for each Angel, we hear Charlie's summons in triplicate. In the episode's opening minutes, Jill coyly asks why they never get to see Charlie, and Sabrina teases her that she has already "fallen for" their boss. Charlie, for his part, begins the presentation of their case lamenting, over his iconic speaker, "This is a tough one, Angels. I doubt if I could do it myself. Needs the feminine touch." As such, the first three minutes of the pilot establish the Angels as athletic, wealthy enough for expensive leisure activities, charming, flirtatious, heterosexual, pretty, good at taking direction, obedient, witty, and happy in their roles of providing a "feminine touch" to private investigation. Gough-Yates describes them succinctly as "gun-toting glamour sleuth[s]."[15] The case itself—a matter of suspected murder and attempted inheritance fraud—hardly matters. Most episodes of the show proceed in a similar fashion, stressing the necessity of the Angels' femininity in order to solve these particular cases, while asserting the myriad ways they are above-average women.

In order to codify the Angels' extraordinary femininity as intuitive, bound both to the their expression of knowledge and power and to their ostensible mastery as subjects-supposed-to-know, the iconic and oft-referenced first-season episode "Angels in Chains" (1.4) bears a closer look. In this case, Kelly, Jill, and Sabrina investigate a client's missing sister, who was arrested on trumped-up charges, was thrown into a women's prison in small-town Texas, and has not been heard from since. The episode mimics 1970s exploitation prison films, complete with a strip-search scene, the Angels being forced to shower in front of lascivious guards, two lesbian-coded (and evil) prison matrons, attempted forced prostitution, and the Angels escaping chained together with handcuffs. Gough-Yates and others have commented on how the Angels in particular are set apart from the other women in positions of power in this episode—especially the statuesque female prison guard, Maxine (Mary Woronov), who has a strikingly deep voice, domineering approach, and aggressively sexualized demeanor.

The Angels are also set apart from the other women prisoners, who are terrified and obedient, afraid of being punished or even killed if they do not follow the prison rules. Sabrina and Jill, especially, deliberately antagonize the matrons, Sabrina in order to "sell their cover" and Jill to gain access to the infirmary. They talk back to the lecherous male guards, ask questions of the other prisoners even when given strict orders not to talk, show concern for their fellow inmates, and engage in a daring escape from the crooked sheriff and his deputy who shoot at them, give chase with bloodhounds on foot, and eventually crash after a high-speed car chase. This episode drives home the Angels' femininity as powerful and desirable, contrasting them with the masculinized matrons whose power is corrupt and distasteful. It also asserts their exceptional ability to wield that power, unlike the ordinary women prisoners who have fallen victim to the sheriff's and warden's machinations and do not possess the fortitude to save themselves. Most important, the Angels face mortal danger with almost a complete lack of concern, evincing an intuitive knowledge—shared by viewers—that they have ultimate narrative mastery. No matter what happens, the Angels are in complete control and will triumph.

Because they are women, the Angels can infiltrate a women's prison and are underestimated. Because they are women, the Angels can easily extract information from reluctant prisoners and productively entice or antagonize criminals of any gender they encounter. Because they are exceptional women, *Charlie's* Angels, they will always outwit the villains. Their abilities, moreover, are not due to special training but rather to an intuitive or instinctual embodiment of womanhood as it intersects with the masculinized profession of private investigation. If the Angels were not women, they would have no special abilities, as they are otherwise ordinary private eyes. If the Angels were not private investigators, they would be working in uninspiring police jobs because they are women. The Angels' keen ability to wield their femininity operates as both a blessing and a curse, as they labor under a framework of tenuous and conditional independence. As presumed keepers of special knowledge, they are hired for cases the police cannot handle, ones in which they rely on feminine intuition and wiles to great effect.

My aim in this chapter is to show how reiterations of these historical representations of feminine knowledge and power resonate in contemporary culture, so I will turn now to more recent portrayals of the Angels. After all, the assertion that a 1970s television show offers a skewed vision of women's empowerment is not news. In recent incarnations, we can see how attempts to update the Angels have nevertheless fallen back on conventional frameworks of gendered exceptionalism, perhaps in part because of the Angels' familiar ethos. The 2011 television remake bears discussion as a direct parallel to the 1970s show, although chronologically the 2000 and 2003 films were produced in the interim; I will return to them shortly. Developed and aired on ABC and canceled after only eight episodes, the 2011 *Charlie's Angels* was an unequivocal failure, unlike the six-season run of its precursor. Most of the show's reviews are negative.[16] For example, NPR's Linda Holmes describes the series as "an utterly unnecessary knockoff of a movie franchise that was an utterly unnecessary knockoff of a rudimentary '70s action show." She elaborates, "It's these dead, unloved, pre-chewed blobs that are spat out over and over again, truly serving no purpose other than filling time between commercials. Nobody thinks this show is fun, nobody thinks this show is interesting, nobody thinks this show is cool. Nobody thinks this show is anything. Nobody loves it, and you can tell."[17] Alessandra Stanley summarizes the new show in the *New York Times*, lamenting its refusal to veer from its predecessor: "ABC executives seem to consider [Aaron] Spelling a founding father of network drama, because they approach the original 'Charlie's Angels' like strict constructionists amending the Constitution. There are small adjustments: the crimes are more lurid; Bosley (Ramon Rodriguez) is now a hunk and a computer whiz; and the angels are ex-cons rather than former desk-bound police officers. But the cheesy

Spelling ethos remains untrammeled: sexy crime fighters dress like hookers to get the job done."[18] While ostensibly refreshing the show, the 2011 *Angels* maintains the overarching format of the original, even to the extent that the three Angels vary in ethnicity and complexion in superficial ways, with one Black Angel (Kate, played by Annie Ilonze) and two white Angels, a blonde (Abby, played by Rachael Taylor) and a brunette (Eve, played by Minka Kelly). Notably, the pilot begins with a Latinx Angel, Gloria (Nadine Velazquez), who is summarily killed off halfway through the episode and replaced by Eve, as if two Angels of color would be a step too far from the original formula, especially since Bosley is also Latinx. The racial makeup of the Angels' triad evinces a desire to pay lip service to a diversity mandate with little follow-through in terms of an intersectional feminist ideology that considers variations beyond hair and skin color.

In her review, Stanley also refers to the 2011 show as "neo-feminine," an apt term she defines in relation to the Angels embodying "martial arts Amazons who gracefully vanquish huge men without breaking a sweat or mussing their hair."[19] Stanley's identification of the "neo-feminine" may stem from Hilary Radner's contemporaneous conception of "neo-feminist" films, which she categorizes as post-1990 "girly films" evincing a strong correlation between mainstream ideologies of empowerment and highly feminized consumer culture.[20] In fact, a look at the 2011 *Charlie's Angels* remake of "Angels in Chains" highlights both the reboot's attempts to update its characters for the twenty-first century and the cracks in the facade of women's empowerment that emerge. In this version, the Angels go undercover as obnoxious American tourists in Cuba; they are framed for cocaine possession by the corrupt Cuban police, arrested, and thrown into prison—all in order to rescue a young woman named Tess on a client's behalf. Hearkening back to the 1970s episode, the Angels wear similar prison uniforms and are harassed by the tough Warden Galvez (Elizabeth Peña), who immediately slugs Kate upon the Angels' arrival at the prison in order to establish her authority. True to its contemporary crime drama aspirations, both the subject matter and the lighting are significantly darker: the captured Tess confesses to being raped by men under the guards' watch and explains how other women have been killed for refusing to comply.[21]

The Angels' planned jailbreak does not go smoothly; they are all recaptured, and Eve is tortured for information. Later, all three Angels and Tess are taken to the house of a wealthy American businessman where they will be forced into prostitution. When a furious Kate asks Galvez, "How could you do this to other women?" the warden replies, "Not to other women. To Americans. You've been doing it to us for decades." This striking political comment momentarily suggests the 2011 show's attempt to engage in an ideological critique, but this nod to the violence of American white supremacist heteropatriarchal capitalism is short-lived. Ultimately, the Angels and other trafficked women are extracted by Bosley and his CIA contact and former lover Sam (Erica Durance), who use a time-honored American political maneuver to facilitate the escape: Bosley encourages Warden Galvez to rebel against Cartwright's American capitalist chauvinism, only to double-cross her by recording the encounter and sending it to the police so that the warden will also ultimately face arrest. The show celebrates his scheme as a victory since the Angels and Tess escape, simultaneously undermining any criticism of the capitalist patriarchy inherent in the warden's earlier comments.

The episode dedicates a great deal of time to developing Bosley and Sam's sexual tension, which contrasts sharply with the Angels' relative lack of emotion or concern for their own safety as they coolly fight back against the baton-wielding warden, evade lascivious guards, withstand torture, seduce and dodge handsy johns, and rescue Tess. Their "neo-femininity," to borrow Stanley's term, emerges from their glamorous outfits, slim yet delicately muscled bodies, conventionally attractive features, and ostensible desire to help other women, whereas their seamless undercover work, no-nonsense attitudes, and eschewal of emotion fold them into the "strong female character" trope. During the party scene at Cartwright's mansion where the Angels are forced to change into cocktail dresses so they can entertain wealthy johns, Abby reminds viewers of these intersecting traits, both feminine and empowered according to the logics of the show, when she quips, "Never thought I'd be this pissed off in a room full of shoes." These contemporary Angels play the part of strong, independent private investigators, but if we scratch just below the surface, we are reminded how much they depend on Charlie and Bosley to bail them out, literally and figuratively. They may gain entrance into spaces closed to men, but their power and knowledge are ultimately just as limited as those of male investigators, perhaps more. Furthermore, attempts to update the Angels in terms of either sociopolitical positioning or gendered embodiments fall largely flat.

Unlike the dramatic turn of the 2011 television series, campiness and comedy dominate most iterations of the Angels franchise. The first film versions, *Charlie's Angels* (2000) and *Charlie's Angels: Full Throttle* (2003), ramp up the comic aspects of the show and play on understandings of popular feminism that foreground feminine conventions of knowledge and power. Starring Drew Barrymore, Lucy Liu, and Cameron Diaz as Angels Dylan, Alex, and Natalie, respectively, the films also hew to the rules of the franchises' opposing triads, illustrated not only by each character's ethnicity and hair color (Caucasian redhead, dark-haired Asian, Caucasian blonde) but also by its pastiche of the 1970s title sequence. Tweaking the script slightly, film Charlie intones, "Once upon a time, there were three very different girls who grew up to be three very different women," thus de-emphasizing the Angels' training at the "police academy" and placing prominence on the process of "growing up" from girls to women.

In the 2000 sequence, each Angel's theme music colors her youthful ambitions as symbolic of her adult personality and skills. Dorky young Natalie, wearing orthodontic headgear, performs stunts during her student driver training to the upbeat melody of Wham!'s "Wake Me Up before You Go-Go." High-achieving young Alex jumps her horse to the tune of Flying Lizard "Money (That's What I Want)." "The best things in life are free, but you can give them to the birds and bees. I want money," the singer chants, as Alex beams beside her many trophies. Dylan smokes in a high school bathroom, one arm in a cast, and flips off the security camera as Joan Jett's "I Love Rock and Roll" completes the thumbnail portrait of a tomboy rebel. The sequence then highlights them as adults: Natalie as a five-day champion on *Jeopardy*, Alex as an astronaut strolling confidently from her shuttle, and Dylan as a disobedient police cadet who punches her yelling superior before walking out. To assure viewers that these allegedly divergent women can still get along, Charlie adds, "But they have three things in common: they're brilliant, they're beautiful, and they work for me. My name is Charlie."

Putting aside for a moment the emphasis on beauty and brilliance in Charlie's cinematic voice-over, it is worth first examining the shift in tone in the 2003 title sequence, which has a similar style but focuses less on the Angels' strength and intelligence and offers a tongue-in-cheek emphasis on performative aspects of their personalities. Natalie morphs from a "girl" giggling in her high school mascot beaver costume to a woman handily birthing a calf, unperturbed as she navigates comic amounts of effluvia.[22] Dylan performs in a WWE-style wrestling match, then becomes a monster truck driver, screaming and hooting in both scenes as she glories in wanton destruction. Alex receives a perfect score at a gymnastics meet before winning a major chess tournament against a child opponent whom she intimidates by snapping her teeth at him. Here, *Full Throttle* offers further insight into the characters, portraying each Angel as disarmingly goofy or over-the-top—they are exceptional, but not to be taken seriously—while emphasizing key personality traits: Natalie's determination, Dylan's unconventionality, Alex's perfectionism. Unlike in the 2000 film, the flashback vignettes tell us very little about why these women make good Angels, homing in on their quirks instead.

What makes women good Angels, the films suggest, is their ability to be outrageously excellent at many tasks. This comic exceptionalism comes to bear frequently. The first film begins with Dylan on a commercial airliner, masquerading as a Black man for no discernible reason except to provide a cameo for rapper and actor LL Cool J while presenting the ultimate disguise: thin white woman becomes large Black man. Dylan/LL confronts a man in first class wearing a bomb, tackles him, and throws both him and herself out of the plane. Meanwhile, Alex waits in a helicopter hovering below; she dives out and plummets after them, dismantling the bomb in midair; then she and Dylan parachute effortlessly with their captive into a speedboat driven by Natalie. Alex removes her helmet, tossing her long, dark hair winningly as Natalie, resplendent in a gold bikini, grins. When the criminal screams at Dylan/LL, "You crazy bastard!" Dylan pulls off her disguise, retorting, "I think you mean crazy bitch." This seamless operation precedes the opening title sequence and succinctly frames the Angels as capable of death-defying acts of bravery in perfect synchronization without a hair out of place; it also reinforces the fact that they are women, with their bikinis, hair tossing, and insistence on the proper gendering of invectives used against them.

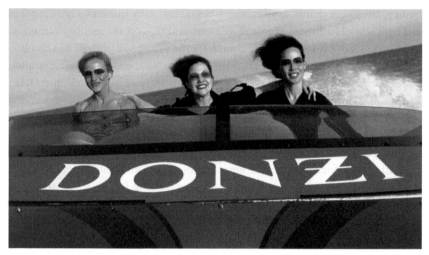

FIGURE 2.2. Angels Natalie, Dylan, and Alex (from left to right) skillfully complete their mission involving dismantling a bomb in midair while skydiving and landing on a moving speedboat. *Charlie's Angels,* directed by McG (2000).

The Angels display a similar—and similarly impossible—intellectual mastery. Midway through *Full Throttle,* the women masquerade as a crime scene investigation unit, Alex and Dylan in tight skirt suits and Natalie in an unflattering jumpsuit and mullet wig. In mere minutes, with minimal equipment and no laboratory analyses, they determine that the killer was a surfer with a limp, as well as other needlessly specific details; Dylan, for example, takes one look at the killer's footprints and declares, "He was wearing reissued 1989 Air Jordans, a limited promotional version that was sold only at the Foot Locker in Fontana in the summer of 2002." Demonstrations of their speed and accuracy, well above those of most experts in whichever field they are imitating, underscore the Angels as exceptional but also fantastical. When things do not go according to plan, they are able to adapt effortlessly, in most cases without any communication beyond meaningful eye contract or stating a need for "Plan B." Their precision and skill seem both orchestrated and instinctual, in that we might chalk up to intuition the Angels' ability to work together and to work so well at every task.

A further hallmark of the Angels franchise is the insistence on the triad as a bonded yet discrete group: there are three Angels and only three Angels, and they all work together. The insistence on the uniqueness of the individual Angels, their relationship to each other as members of a triad, and their combined and exceptional beauty and brilliance come explicitly to bear on one significant conflict in *Full Throttle.* Early in the film, Dylan worries that Natalie will leave the team because she and her boyfriend are moving in together. Alex inadvertently validates Dylan's concern by casually suggesting the three cannot all remain Angels forever.[23] In addition, the case blows Dylan's witness protection cover to her "bad boy" former boyfriend, Seamus O'Grady (Justin Theroux), a mobster imprisoned for eight years because of Dylan's testimony. As Seamus hunts her down, Dylan decides leaving Natalie and Alex is the only way to protect them. She runs away to Mexico, stopping for a drink in a dive bar, where she hallucinates a conversation with 1970s Angel Kelly (played faithfully by the original actress, Jaclyn Smith). Kelly instructs Dylan that her friends are in more peril without her and reminds her, "Angels are like diamonds. They can't be made. You have to find them." The idea that Angels cannot be taught but must be found, fully formed, highlights the mysticism of the Angels' abilities, including their uncanny and encyclopedic knowledge, their ability to perform any and all necessary martial feats and stunts, their unerring synchronization as a team both physically and intellectually, and their preternatural feminine charm.

Full Throttle's villain, a former Angel named Madison (Demi Moore), further underscores the dangers of individual Angels going rogue. In her first scene, Madison greets Natalie on the beach during a stakeout. Wearing a white bikini in counterpoint to Madison's black one, Natalie fawns over the former Angel as Alex and Dylan, from their positions of surveillance down the beach, observe the interaction through binoculars. Alex gushes over her headset, "She won the Nobel Prize in astrophysics for her research on flying mammals," with Dylan eagerly adding, "And predicted Carmine DeSoto's every move by using the *Cosmo* bedside astrologer." This initial scene frames Madison as an impressive feminine role model, emphasizing her intelligence—but comically; after all, astrophysicists do not generally study mammals—while praising her use of a horoscope from a women's magazine to catch a criminal. Later, when she is revealed as an evil mastermind, Madison explains how she wanted independence, demanding rhetorically, "Why be an Angel when I can play God?" In the film's climax, Madison holds Natalie in a headlock, gun to her temple, confident that she has the upper hand until Natalie reminds her, "I have something you'll never have . . . friends." On cue, Alex and Dylan arrive for the rescue, and, after a short fight, Madison dies in a ball of flames. When her villainy is revealed, the film portrays Madison as power hungry and arrogant: an intelligent, strong woman who went astray when she refused to work with her team and began to resent Charlie's control. The final fight scene and Madison's defeat are followed by Alex, Dylan, and Natalie assuring each other they will not become like Madison, instead continuing to work for Charlie and with each other.

Alongside these reassertions of the Angels as feminine subjects par excellence as well as best friends, the films continually insist on the Angels' heterosexuality— even while playing up Dylan as a rough-and-tumble tomboy, constantly showing the Angels draped over one another or otherwise physically touching, and having Madison flirt with Natalie early in *Full Throttle* before aggressively kissing her cheek during their final showdown. While flirtations and provocations between the Angels often seep into their undercover operations, these are demonstrably part of their "act," used to titillate and distract their (male) marks. For films that are largely a collection of stunts and action scenes, the *Charlie's Angels* installments of the early 2000s spend a significant amount of time documenting the love lives of the Angels. Near the beginning of the first film, Alex laments how her secret identity as an Angel impacts her relationships, declaring, "They come on all lovey-dovey until they find out I can shatter a cinderblock with my fists," succinctly asserting how romance is often deemed antithetical to "strong female characters" and suggesting the Angels can buck that trend. She has a boyfriend, an actor (Matt LeBlanc), who does eventually learn about her secret identity and finds it exciting, although he accidentally misrepresents her job to Alex's father, making him think his daughter is a sex worker. Shocked but remarkably tolerant in his confusion, Alex's father betrays how the Angels' missions serve to entertain, provide pleasure to, and satisfy viewers. Natalie also meets a man (Luke Wilson) as nerdy as she is during an undercover operation; the two date throughout both films, eventually moving in together. Overtly attracted to men, but never attached to any for the long term, Dylan has a series of strange boyfriends, several of whom turn out to be villains and betray her—prompting Alex and Natalie to joke in *Full Throttle* that if Dylan finds a man attractive, he must be the bad guy.

Dylan's inability to find a suitable romantic interest, combined with Alex's and Natalie's quotidian yet thriving relationships, ultimately serves as a foil for their action heroism—an avowal that these exceptional women, worrying about their boy-friends' motives or struggling to find a nice guy, are also "normal." Since the film Angels' embodiment of knowledge and power/ability is so comically improbable, their empowerment as women is ultimately unbelievable as well. They may be subjects-supposed-to-know, but they do not. Mariana Mogilevich elaborates along similar lines, noting, "The story is merely a vehicle for the substance-less display of the beauty of the three Angels, a surface display which is not, however, insubstantial. We might read the Angels as a postmodern mass ornament, like the capitalist mode of production that spawned it, an end in itself."[24] In her review in the feminist magazine *Off Our Backs*, Angie Manzano takes this line of critique further, asserting that, in contrast to overtly sexist films, "there's something much uglier, more insidious, and more demoralizing about a movie that packages misogyny and sells it as liberation."[25] She also argues that *Charlie's Angels* evinces a form of "free-market feminism," which "focuses on personal freedoms instead of women's rights, personal maneuvering instead of structural oppression, and per-sonal choices instead of collective action."[26] Both appraisals confront the Angels as performative stand-ins for the action heroine in the American popular imagi-nary: women who, like the 1970s and 2011 television Angels, use their femininity to their advantage and display martial expertise without sacrificing conventions of feminine beauty or heterosexual appeal. As Manzano's indictment of free-market feminism signifies, Charlie's brilliance-and-beauty model of gendered exception-alism fits neatly into sociocultural critiques of contemporary feminism as post-feminism, neoliberal feminism, and/or popular feminism. These ideologies, while distinct, share an emphasis on performative empowerment without the legislative, social, political, or cultural changes necessary to enact substantive progression in the fight for gender equality.[27]

It is all the more compelling, then, to return to the *Charlie's Angels* film from 2019 and find that it reads as savvy to the foibles of its predecessors within the franchise, explicitly asserting its feminism as unequivocal and engaged rather than merely performative. And yet even in this film—in which the Angels' feminism is meant to be read as intersectional, transnational, potentially queer, and interested in the community over the individual—the insistence on femininity as the font of the Angels' knowledge and power ultimately takes pride of place. Repeated bids to remake *Charlie's Angels* and the continued tensions in doing so evince both a desire to highlight the Angels as remarkable, powerful, and dynamic action heroines, as well as a lack of understanding that the very terms of their empowerment, grounded in normative femininity and feminine intuition, destabilize the concept from the start.

On the surface, the 2019 film diverges from its predecessors in myriad ways. Despite presenting itself as *Charlie's Angels* in its title and narrative context, the film otherwise refuses almost all nostalgic nods to the original, although there are a few references to the 2000 and 2003 films. Banks's 2019 film does not include any version of the opening title sequence or Charlie's voice-over narration proclaiming his stake in finding the Angels; we see no images of what the Angels were like before joining the Townsend Agency and hear very little about their pasts; the use of the iconic theme music is understated; and the iconography of the "Angel pose" (three women poised and ready to fight) is largely absent. Decentralized and international, the Townsend Agency now has branches across the globe, with dozens of Angels and many Bosleys to watch over them. The three Bosleys we get to know (played by Banks, Patrick Stewart, and Djimon Hounsou) are competent agents in their own right rather than mere bumbling middlemen. Whereas the Angels all appear to identify as women, the Bosleys are mixed gender. (Rebekah) Bosley (played by Banks) is a former Angel, the first Angel to be promoted to Bosley status.[28] Furthermore, the ending sequence reveals that Charlie, while still anonymous to "his" Angels, is now a woman using a voice scrambler.[29]

The Angels themselves are also not a bonded triad but a pair, Sabina (Kristen Stewart) and Jane (Ella Balinska), who have only worked together on one other mission—the one portrayed in the opening scene in Rio de Janeiro. They initially do not get along but are called to work together on a case protecting Elena (Naomi Scott), a whistleblowing programmer at a tech company. Elena joins Sabina, Jane, and (Rebekah) Bosley when she unwittingly finds herself embroiled in a complicated international criminal operation to weaponize her company's new device, Calisto, a source of sustainable energy that Elena designed.[30] As in earlier versions, each woman has her own distinct personality and accompanying skill sets. Sabina, a former American heiress who ran afoul of the law before joining up with the Agency, is somewhat awkward and unruly but imminently competent, especially at athletic pursuits, including hand-to-hand combat, horseback riding, and acrobatics. Jane, a former MI-6 British intelligence agent, is no-nonsense and cerebral, a meticulous martial artist who only shows emotional vulnerability when her mentor (Edgar) Bosley (played by Hounsou) dies and when Sabina is critically injured midway through the film. Elena, although not officially recruited as an Angel until the end of the film, is initially terrified of physical violence but is otherwise immediately capable of integrating with the team as a technical genius, throwing her intellectual weight behind surveillance, hacking, and data gathering.

Jane and Elena are both characters of color (as is Hounsou's Bosley, with a Beninese American actor playing a Black, French-speaking character). Balinska is mixed race (British, Polish, and Caribbean), and Scott, also an actress of mixed race (English and Indian), is ethnically ambiguous enough, by Hollywood's measure, that her most notable prior role was as Princess Jasmine in Disney's live-action *Aladdin* (2019). Since neither character's race or ethnicity is made explicit, or even discussed, in the film, it is unclear exactly how they should be identified. The film similarly avoids clear-cut discussions of sexuality. Jane flirts with an engineer from Elena's company, eventually beginning to date him by the end of the film, and (Rebekah) Bosley makes oblique references to her lack of a love life (implied heterosexual). Despite Banks's insistence in the popular press that Sabina's character is "definitely gay" (perhaps in part because actress Stewart identifies as bisexual), there is only one scene in the film that even hints at Sabina's interest in women, when she subtly checks out a female gymgoer.[31] We learn nothing about Elena's sexuality except that she has no current love interests, a significant change from the dating and sex-obsessed Alex/Natalie/Dylan triad of the earlier films. Irrespective of sexuality, race, or status, all the Angels-qua-women still love designer clothes, although the film does include a nod to the absurdity of earlier Angels' fighting outfits when Sabina hands Elena a pair of sneakers to trade in for her heels just before a stakeout turns into an action sequence.[32]

In other ways, the 2019 film attempts to set itself apart from the franchise while nevertheless relying on its premise. Unlike the earlier films and many episodes of the 1970s television show, the Angels are not shown in contrast to other women meant to serve as their foils, failed embodiments of feminine knowledge and power versus their successful ones. Instead, the Angels initially believe (Rebekah) Bosley has double-crossed them, following earlier tropes of another woman attempting to undermine them, only to discover the real villain is the first Bosley, John, who has tired of working under Charlie's thumb and, inspired by dreams of power and prestige, is trying to become a criminal mastermind in his own right. Both the betrayal orchestrated by (John) Bosley and Elena's interactions with men at her tech company emphasize how patriarchal assumptions of masculinist power are at fault for most of the Angels' troubles. In the latter instance, early scenes of Elena portray the daily microaggressions she faces, from a security guard using his position of authority to insist she should smile, to her immediate supervisor interrupting, patronizing, and silencing her when she tries to explain how she would like to fix a possibly fatal flaw in Calisto before the company begins mass production. Elena only escapes from her corporate nightmare into the protection of the Angels after an assassination attempt, a shoot-out in a café, a bullet-riddled car chase through the streets of Hamburg during which (Edgar) Bosley is killed, and a near drowning—all efforts to silence her for daring to speak out against capitalist patriarchal greed.

The world of the Angels introduces Elena to a strikingly different domain in which women's voices and ideas are valued and take precedence. In fact, most reviews of the film note, as I do in the opening of this chapter, the ways in which the 2019 film tries, perhaps too hard, to assert its feminism. Inkoo Kang's *Slate* review, tellingly entitled "The Dutiful Feminism of the New *Charlie's Angels* Made Me Miss the Sleazy Camp of the Old Ones," complains that "Banks' vision of women-empowerment heaven plays more like a checklist of topics from the feminist discourse of the past few years than a coherent movie, let alone a crowd-pleasing one."[33] In a similar vein, Peter Travers's *Rolling Stone* review conjoins praise and critique, proclaiming, "Good on Banks for obliterating the infamous 'male gaze' in favor of something less sexist and jiggle obsessed," but ultimately dubbing the film boring and clichéd.[34] On the other hand, Clarisse Loughrey, a reviewer for *The Independent*, argues that the film's feminism does not go far enough in "[trying] earnestly to bring these ladies into the 21st century. And it might have worked, if the film didn't so consistently pull its punches."[35] These and other negative to middling reviews hint at a central dilemma for action heroines who, always caught in a double bind, are either too feminine to be powerful or too feminist to be appealing.

The review in the feminist pop culture magazine *Bitch*, however, attempts to recuperate the film from these and other critiques; in a response titled "In 2019, 'Charlie's Angels' Isn't Just about Girl Power—It's a Critique of Male Leadership," Rachel Charlene Lewis posits that Banks's installment in the franchise is "less about impossibly perfect women saving the world and more about women joining forces to save the world. It's the direct opposite of the lens used by the men of the film, who are selfish, distrustful, and betray each other at every turn, and fail as a result. Instead, the angels truly are everywhere, and Banks has crafted a world where instead of bad men hiding behind every corner, strong women exist behind every corner, waiting and ready to support you when and if you need it."[36] Certainly, the climax of the film corroborates this interpretation. In it, (John) Bosley kidnaps Elena, taking her to a party thrown by the owner of her company, Alexander Brok (Sam Claflin), who has his own nefarious plans for Calisto and orchestrated the assassination attempts against Elena. Elena escapes using her intellect and coding savvy, and Jane and Sabina fight off other assailants working for either (John) Bosley or Brok. Eventually, (Rebekah) Bosley confronts (John) Bosley, and during their fight he seems to overpower her, throwing her to the ground for his henchmen to dispose of. "You're outmanned, Angel. You always have been,"

(John) Bosley taunts, clearly believing her incapable in her role as a Bosley and asserting a masculine prerogative of domination.

(Rebekah) Bosley, for her part, has called in the reserves. During a split-second, planned power outage, a dozen other Angels emerge, having disguised themselves as regular party guests, and easily defeat (John) Bosley's men with dermal tranquilizing pads disguised as mints. The men faint to the floor all around the two Bosleys; (Rebekah) Bosley reprimands (John) Bosley sternly, "You thought you made us. We made you." Here, (Rebekah) Bosley wrests ownership over the Angels' successes and abilities away from the male overseers and returns it, and allegedly the franchise itself, to the Angels. Although Sabina and Jane previously explained to Elena how the Townsend Agency employs many Angels, and other Angels make a brief appearance in the opening scene, the conventions of the franchise and the primacy of the Sabina/Jane/Elena triad gloss over the existence of other Angels for most of the film. In this final confrontation, Elena and, by extension, viewers witness the sizable network of Angels at the behest of the Townsend Agency who, when necessary, can all work together seamlessly. The blocking of this scene is particularly instructive: in one moment, (Rebekah) Bosley is surrounded by threatening men dressed in black suits; in the next, (John) Bosley stands alone, all other men unconscious, surrounded by a glittering bevy of Angels in cocktail dresses who have come to (Rebekah) Bosley's aid. The end credit sequence, in addition, shows Elena training and eventually becoming an Angel herself. The first comprehensive acknowledgment that Angels receive rigorous training, these closing vignettes include cameos from a host of celebrity women cast as Angel-instructors. Jaclyn Smith makes an appearance as Kelly, greeting Elena when she arrives. Other instructors include race car driver Danica Patrick, mixed martial arts fighter Ronda Rousey, and trans-rights activist and actress Laverne Cox. A few young up-and-comers perform roles as Elena's fellow recruits (actresses Hailee Steinfeld and Lili Reinhart, as well as Olympic snowboarder Chloe Kim, Olympic gymnast Aly Raisman, and superstar beauty blogger and entrepreneur Huda Kattan). (Rebekah) Bosley even implies that iconic Supreme Court justice Ruth Bader Ginsburg was once an Angel.

Seeming to recognize the drawbacks of the franchise as a vehicle for women's empowerment, 2019's *Charlie's Angels* addresses several salient sticking points from earlier iterations. It disperses the extraordinary nature of the Angels' talents among dozens of women rather than just three; emphasizes the need for training rather than preternatural giftedness; attempts to avoid gratuitous invocations of the Angels' sexual allure; and makes an effort at inclusivity in terms of race, ethnicity, and sexual orientation (somewhat), although much of this occurs in the credits. And yet, even Banks's film cannot resist the temptation to remind viewers that these Angels, no matter how tough, rational, intelligent, strong, and collaborative, also possess several seemingly de rigueur feminine traits: beauty, a love of designer fashion, and an intuitive desire to help people. As Sabina tells Johnny (and us) in the film's opening scene, there are "huge advantages" to being a woman, which

FIGURE 2.3. (Rebekah) Bosley (center) and her network of Angels defeat (John) Bosley's henchmen. *Charlie's Angels,* directed by Elizabeth Banks (2019).

include being underestimated due to normative understandings of feminine behavior and ability.

"TO STOP A WAR WITH LOVE": THE WONDER WOMAN PARADOX

The Angels embody the subject-supposed-to-know because they are in possession of a certain knowledge about femininity: it can support power, but only in its ideal form, which shifts from era to era as necessitated by the ever-changing media representations of women's empowerment. As with all articulations of the subject-supposed-to-know, including Lacan's, the subject does not actually possess the mastery they are presumed to have. Thus, for the Angels, the process of undermining the foundation of their knowledge—their feminine intuition, whatever form it takes—destabilizes their power. Since femininity is neither fixed nor anything more than a performative enactment of social mores, power based in representations of femininity presents a significant conundrum for real women who aspire to positions of leadership or wish to gain access to male-dominated fields. The character of Wonder Woman, long a complicated icon of women's empowerment, further exposes this stumbling block between representational feminine power and the lived experiences of women. While I acknowledge that Wonder Woman is unmistakably a fantasy figure—a superhero and, in many accounts, a demigod—I also argue that her symbolic feminist status, particularly in more recent incarnations, presents her as an ideal woman whose power is markedly grounded in her femininity.

As a feminist icon, Wonder Woman has fared far better, at least in recent years, than the Angels. And yet, a film, show, or franchise's ability to register as feminist or empowering to women and girls does not exempt it from relying heavily on notions of feminine intuition and knowledge as a baseline for its characters' powers and/or empowerment. Here, I emphasize again the imperative to sever presumed connections between feminism and a lack of overt femininity—or, significantly, anti-feminism and a championing of traditional femininity.[37] The divorce of these principles allows a clearer understanding of how feminist media may fall into the same traps as purportedly anti-feminist or misogynistic media. Because these dichotomies are specious, they ultimately throw the notion of women's empowerment into a double bind wherein female characters must identify as women, often using conventional metrics of femininity, but simultaneously not embody that femininity to the extent that they relinquish the unique positioning of their power. Whereas my analysis of *Charlie's Angels* interrogates ongoing efforts to both profit from and recuperate the Angels as icons of feminized liberation and empowerment, my discussion of Wonder Woman illustrates how even earnest attempts to assert femininity as powerful can fall back on similar tropes. I do not intend to attach a judgment value to these representations, in terms of *good* or *bad* portrayals of femininity or women. Instead, I assert that the impulse to embed the source of female protagonists' empowerment into the very substrate of their femininity by binding power to conventionally feminine forms of knowledge shapes how we evaluate real women, in positions of power and otherwise.

Wonder Woman's history spans over eighty years; she was created by psychologist William Moulton Marston in 1941, partly as a remedy for masculine superheroes' violence and brutishness and as an experiment to see if a female superhero would sell in the comics market. There has been ample scholarship on Wonder Woman, ranging widely in disciplinary perspective (women's studies, comic studies, film studies, sociology, psychology, and history, to name a few) and scope: from blog posts and magazine think pieces to scholarly articles, dissertations, and books.[38] She has also met with criticism and recuperation from many angles, sometimes lauded as a feminist symbol, sometimes eschewed as yet another pants-less female superhero wearing too-tight clothing and falling in love, literally, with the first man she meets.[39] In an appraisal conspicuously dovetailing with Mogilivech's assertion that the Angels embody a "postmodern mass ornament," Noah Berlatsky observes that Wonder Woman is "what most pop-culture icons are—a placeholder for nostalgia and recognizability, whose image provokes strong emotions in some people and moderate amusement in everybody else. She is an unassuming brick in the postmodern bricolage, famous for being famous— like Paris Hilton but significantly more charming, not least because she is less real."[40] As such, although Wonder Woman's mien fluctuates according to the cultural currents at large during each resurgence of her popularity, she still serves as an enduring, if mutable, symbol of women's political and social agency and its innumerable pitfalls. Therefore, I will be taking a far narrower view with her character, one that traces the legacy of a particular paradox of Wonder Woman's narrative and how that paradox comes to light in Patty Jenkins's 2017 and 2020 films.

Reflecting on her first Wonder Woman film, Jenkins asserts that she sees the eponymous hero as somewhat genderless—great not because she is a woman but because she is a classic superhero: "I believe in [superhero movies] as a metaphor for our own experiences . . . but I was missing the kind of superhero movie that got me interested in the first place, which really started with Superman, which was something incredibly beautiful, powerful, funny, grand, big game, lacking cynicism . . . that was my vision, not be more niche than that or more modern than that. . . . Wonder Woman is the grandest superhero that there is and so let's go back in time and make a great classic film."[41] Jenkins's insistence on Wonder Woman's universality as the "grandest superhero" intersects in compelling ways with reviews of the film, most of which nevertheless emphasize the character's gender. Some of these reviews present variations on a theme in which the summer blockbuster marks a new, important step for female-led action films, in part because Diana lacks conventional understandings of gender due to her upbringing on an all-woman island and her status as a demigod. Alyssa Rosenberg's *Washington Post* review asserts, "Diana . . . doesn't have any idea what women and men are—or aren't—supposed to do. Even when she does encounter other people's ideas about gender roles, she doesn't automatically accept them, and she never lets anyone stop her."[42] On the other hand, in a review titled "Dear Men: You Should Absolutely Feel Excluded from *Wonder Woman*," Jill Gutowitz writes, "When you watch *Wonder Woman* and you feel like an outsider, or you feel a pang of missing out, or you get a sudden urge to yell 'What about me?!'—hold on to that feeling. Cherish it. Recognize it. Because every woman, girl and non-cisgender male on Earth has lived a lifetime with that experience. That feeling is the slightest glimpse into what oppressive sexism feels like. Now you know what it's like to be a secondary character in our culture."[43] For *Vulture*, Angelica Jade Bastién writes, "Wonder Woman has still managed to reach icon status, which isn't accidental— it's indicative of the hunger for female-oriented stories, especially coming-of-age tales, that go against the usual depictions of female strength."[44] It is the intersection of and tension between these three positions—Wonder Woman as universal, as an exceptional woman demonstrating feminine-exclusive abilities, and/or as an icon of unconventional "female strength"—that shape the remainder of my argument in this chapter.

Two aspects of Wonder Woman's early years bear emphasis. The first is her positioning in the comics as a symbol of American democracy; after all, when the comics were published, America had just entered World War II, and a patriotic warrior woman defeating Nazis was good propaganda for the Allies and the war effort.[45] To wit, in the premiere issue (December 1941/January 1942), Athena, the goddess of wisdom and war, begs the Amazon Queen Hippolyta to return the stranded pilot Steve Trevor to American soil: "American liberty and freedom must be preserved!" Athena extols Hippolyta, "You must send with him your strongest and wisest amazon—the finest of your wonder women!—for America, the last citadel of democracy, and of equal rights for women, needs your help!"[46] Note here the insistence that America is a bastion not only of democracy but also of equal rights for women, a compelling invocation given how Wonder Woman is frequently set apart from average, human women. Second, Marston's purported impetus for creating the character has significant implications for her contemporary representations. In an article in *American Scholar*, Marston writes:

> It seemed to me, from a psychological angle, that the comics' worse offense was their blood-curdling masculinity. A male hero, at best, lacks the qualities of maternal love and tenderness which are as essential to a normal child as the breath of life. Suppose your child's ideal becomes a superman who uses his extraordinary power to help the weak. The most important ingredient in the human happiness recipe still is missing—love. . . . [N]ot even girls want to be girls so long as our feminine archetype lacks force, strength, power. Not wanting to be girls they don't want to be tender, submissive, peaceloving as good women are. Women's strong qualities have become despised because of their weak ones. The obvious remedy is to create a feminine character with all the strength of a Superman plus all the allure of a good and beautiful woman.[47]

Progressive for the early 1940s, Marston's insistence that Wonder Woman's appeal rests in her merging of feminine allure and masculine power may seem antiquated now at face value. His assertion that conventional feminine archetypes inspire derision, however, gels with much feminist scholarship about the continued denigration of femininity in terms of gender expression/identity.[48] Even when the superhero first graced the cover of the feminist advocacy magazine *Ms.* in 1972, Joanne Edgar offered a similar rationale for highlighting Wonder Woman in the inaugural issue: "Wonder Woman captured the Amazonian spirit of strength and self-sufficiency, but added the peacefulness and revulsion toward killing that have culturally distinguished women from men."[49] This formula, then, the merging of presumed masculine and feminine traits, is one that extends to contemporary representations of many female superheroes, who must possess key markers of femininity while also deriving power from those traits so they are not dismissed as weaknesses.[50]

While Wonder Woman's origin story has been revisited and modified several times throughout her tenure as a superhero in the form of comics, animated and live-action television, video games, merchandise, magazine covers, and several recent films, its essence remains more or less the same. An Amazon princess born either from the sexual union of Hippolyta and the god Zeus or else parthenogenically via Zeus's divine intervention, Diana grows up on the hidden island of Themyscira among a nation of ageless Amazon warriors. She trains alongside her fellow Amazons in the absence of men, until American pilot Steve Trevor's plane crashes on the island. Diana then either falls in love with Steve or feels beholden to help the war-torn world outside the safety of her island home—or both—and leaves with him. Among mere mortals, Diana possesses superior strength, speed, agility, and, in some versions, other divine powers; she also has gauntlets that allow her to deflect bullets and a magic lasso that compels anyone bound with it to tell the truth. In many versions, and in the popular imaginary, she is known as

Wonder Woman; in most versions, her alter ego secret identity is Diana Prince, an average human woman.

Ever since *Ms.* magazine's co–founding editor Gloria Steinem famously petitioned DC Comics to revamp Wonder Woman's image (after the character had gone from superhero to fashion maven and even, for a time, given up her immortality), the Amazon warrior has frequently functioned as a feminist icon.[51] As Michelle Finn asserts in her analysis of Marston's own ambivalent feminist leanings, "Although Marston aimed to elevate women, arguments that base women's right to power on a set of assumptions about 'the female character' ultimately reinforce the idea that women must adhere to the standards identified by the dominant culture as appropriately feminine."[52] Hence, reifying love and altruism as feminine virtues may seem desirable but also further strengthens the gendered divide. What the persistence of Wonder Woman as feminist icon offers, most notably, is a series of questions that also frame my analyses in this book. How do we argue for gender equality, while recognizing the unique strengths of women? Are presumed feminine emotions (such as love and empathy) effective tools for social change? Can violence serve constructive political ends if levied at a great injustice and tempered by so-called feminine altruism? It is in attempting to answer these questions that I consider feminine intuition as a set of skills characters like Wonder Woman possess, particularly in her weaponization of love, as represented in Jenkins's films.

What I name the Wonder Woman paradox comes to the fore in the opening theme of the campy, moderately successful 1970s television show (1975–1979), which aired on ABC for its first season a year before *Charlie's Angels*, and then spent its final two seasons on CBS.[53] Starring Lynda Carter, the series maintains the feel of the comic book in its caricatured, over-the-top depictions of everyone from Hippolyta (Cloris Leachman)—who, in the pilot, practically swoons when talking about men, notably absent from her island home—to the Nazi soldiers, whose anti-American plots are always thwarted by Wonder Woman, Steve, and their friends. The upbeat theme music, opening title sequence, and stylized comic book intertitles of stars and stripes remind viewers of Wonder Woman's graphic origins, and the lyrics of the show's theme manage to squeeze in women's rights, American patriotism, and the apparent charm of the Amazon princess as a "new" kind of superhero: "In your satin tights, / Fighting for your rights, / And the old red, white and blue! . . . / Now the world is ready for you, / And the wonders you can do. / Make a hawk a dove, / Stop a war with love, / Make a liar tell the truth!" The lyrics play on contradictions, referencing two compelling parallels. The first is the feminine/feminist pairing of satin tights and (women's) rights well suited for a mid-1970s television show and an emphasis on both Wonder Woman's sartorial femininity and her status as an icon of women's empowerment. The second is the figurative transformation from hawk to dove and its attendant ideology of stopping war with love, a central element of Wonder Woman's raison d'être as it extends from Marston's vision to her contemporary manifestations.

While I focus the remainder of my analysis on Jenkins's films, Diana Prince (as played by Gal Gadot) actually makes two prior appearances as a supporting character in *Batman v Superman: Dawn of Justice* (dir. Zack Snyder, 2016) and *Justice League* (dir. Joss Whedon and Zack Snyder, 2017). Diana has a minor role throughout most of the former film, with her reveal as Wonder Woman in the final battle scene set up as a surprise for both viewers and Bruce Wayne/Batman (Ben Affleck). In the second film, Wonder Woman has a more substantial role as a member of the Justice League, which also includes superheroes Batman, Cyborg (Ray Fisher), The Flash (Ezra Miller), Aquaman (Jason Momoa), and Superman (Henry Cavill). She is conspicuously the only woman in the group. While she is easily able to hold her own in battle, demonstrating superior strength and power to all but Superman and the villain Steppenwolf, she is also overtly feminized in the films, both visually and narratively. Diana often uses other characters' assumptions about her femininity to her advantage and "knowingly employ[s] an exaggerated form of femininity that serves the desires of men as a strategy to gain access to male privilege."[54] In *Batman v Superman*, Diana exploits Bruce's sexual interest in her to distract him as she steals the hacking device he planted in Lex Luthor's home. In *Justice League*, the men interact with her in conventionally gendered ways: she serves as a nurturing figure to younger heroes Victor/Cyborg and Barry/The Flash; Alfred teases Bruce about his attraction to her; and Aquaman, a demigod himself, remarks dreamily how gorgeous she is while under the accidental influence of her golden lasso.

Diana's astounding beauty is a consistent feature of her representation. In one of the earlier failed forays to bring Wonder Woman to the silver screen, Joss Whedon's unproduced screenplay introduces Diana by qualifying her beauty as divine: "To say she is beautiful is almost to miss the point. She is elemental, as natural and wild as the luminous flora surrounding [*sic*]. Her dark hair waterfalls to her shoulders in soft arcs and curls. Her body is curvaceous, but taut as a drawn bow. She wears burnished metal bracelets on both wrists, wide and intricately detailed. Her shift is of another era; we'd call it ancient Greek. She is barefoot."[55] While we may be tempted to write off this description, as the script was never produced and was widely criticized after it leaked online, echoes of it resonate with Wonder Woman's first appearance in superhero attire in *Batman v Superman*, when she leaps into the fray of battle to save Batman from a fatal blast.[56] As the fire and smoke clear, Wonder Woman stands behind her crossed gauntlets, still glowing with red heat. Composer Hans Zimmer's Wonder Woman theme swells triumphantly on the soundtrack, and a breeze causes Gadot's perfectly coifed long hair to artfully frame her face; she pants, in slow motion—once, twice—before taking an offensive position and fighting back. As such, in the *Justice League* films, Diana's beauty *is* elemental; she is a literal and figurative goddess, and in many ways her beauty seems to underscore and augment her strength. She is also exoticized in terms of both her appearance and her accent. An Israeli actress of relatively light complexion, Gadot's foreignness intersects in compelling ways with her whiteness in the films, underscoring Diana as both familiar and distinctive.[57] This especially comes to the fore via Diana's ambiguous Amazon/Greek accent, traded in for Gadot's Israeli accent.[58]

The emphasis on Wonder Woman/Diana's exotic or otherworldly beauty, and on her grace and fluidity in battle, characterizes her representation in every form of media, although it is striking that we are introduced to her as a young girl in 2017's *Wonder Woman*, which serves as an origin story. In Jenkins's films, Diana is also never referred to as "Wonder Woman," despite their titles. Instead, she functions as a humanizing and humane force, reaffirming how her love for humanity and her ability to recognize its failures and foibles trump whether or not humans "deserve" help or compassion. Jenkins shifts the action to World War I, rather than the original World War II setting, and delays the romance between Diana and Steve (Chris Pine) until late in the film. In making these changes, the 2017 film veers away from beauty and romance as immediate signifiers of Diana's feminine virtue and bypasses the question of Wonder Woman as a stand-in for American patriotism.[59] Most of the film takes place on Themyscira, in London, or on Belgian bases and battlefields. Steve is an American soldier, but there is little discussion of American democracy. Diana's armor no longer features stars or stripes, although it still consists of metallic blue, red, and gold. The narrative revolves around the return of Ares, Greek god of war and Diana's half brother; Diana leaves Themyscira, then, not to follow Steve but to assist in what he calls "the war to end all wars." Diana, naive from her upbringing in a sheltered paradise where battles were merely training exercises, does not understand the reality of death and suffering or why humans kill each other. She fixates instead on Ares (David Thewlis) as the sole catalyst for war and spends the entire film searching for him, only to discover that he is not at all whom she imagined him to be; he has been masquerading in plain sight as a seemingly kind British general. Ultimately, she battles and defeats Ares, but not before realizing mankind's incomprehensible lust for violence does not stem from Ares's divine corruption but is simply a symptom of humanity's flawed nature.

In setting Diana apart from mortal humans, Jenkins's film leans on two juxtaposed paradigms to highlight her gendered exceptionalism and, perhaps paradoxically, her universality. These two concepts first come together when Hippolyta (Connie Nielsen), lamenting her daughter's imminent departure from Themyscira, warns, "Be careful in the world of men, Diana. They do not deserve you." The deliberate usage of the terms *mankind* and *world of men*, rather than the gender-neutral *humankind* and *human world*, "[sets] the island of the Amazons apart from our world, perhaps not literally a 'world of men,' but certainly one suffering under patriarchal and otherwise oppressive impulses to dominate and destroy."[60] Moreover, the question of who deserves protection appears frequently. Late in the film, after falsely assuming the German General Ludendorff (Danny Huston) is Ares and killing him, Diana addresses Steve, distraught that the Germans are still fighting, even killing innocents, despite her intervention. "My mother was right. She said the world of men do not deserve you," Diana exclaims, about to give up on humanity. Impassioned, Steve responds, "It's not about deserve. . . . It's about what you believe." This emboldens Diana; in her final battle with Ares, hair again swirling around her face in elemental fervor and energy crackling on her gauntlets, she parrots Steve's line but with one crucial addition: "It's not about deserve. It's about what you believe. And I believe in love." It is these tensions between Diana's exceptional and, indeed, supernatural prowess and the femininized altruism she displays throughout the film—wanting to hug babies, saving villagers the soldiers have left for dead, and feeling sympathy for the Germans, whom she imagines have been corrupted by Ares's influence rather than being inherently evil—that function as symbolic of a series of prescient questions in contemporary sociopolitical debate.

Briefly disillusioned by humanity's capacity for destruction, Diana eventually comes to realize that the complexity of humanity is not its downfall but its strength. Even here, however, the film evinces a separation between mankind as a stand-in for humanity and the Amazons (all women, isolated, ageless), who are great warriors but supposedly uninterested in war. We can see this contradiction reflected starkly in early scenes showing us young Diana (Lilly Aspell). A unique creation formed by her mother and Zeus to eventually defeat Ares, Diana the girl desperately desires Amazon training. She and the film revel in the concomitant beauty and militancy of the other Amazons and their supernatural martial abilities in its opening scene of training on Themyscira. Cast from an impressive range of martial arts experts and athletes rather than solely professional actors, the Amazons stand out from previous incarnations—they are muscular and not uniformly slim, and they hurl themselves from galloping horses, fling javelins, spar with swords, and deftly shoot arrows.[61] Young Diana watches them eagerly. Later, she begs Hippolyta to let her train and peers covetously at an ancient sword she thinks is the "god killer," not realizing that she (as a demigod herself) is the one who actually has the power to kill gods. Despite all this, the film ends with present-day Diana's voice-over telling us that "only love can truly save the world," a remarkable assertion for a demigod whose martial skills and supernatural powers rival even those of the god of war and who, as a child, desired nothing more than to fight.

Once she ventures off her island, Diana is often the only woman in a ragtag group of men—in stark contrast to her Amazon upbringing where she was constantly surrounded by other women. Together, Diana; Steve; Charlie, a Scottish former sniper (Ewen Bremner); Chief, a Native American arms dealer (Eugene Brave Rock); and Sameer, a Moroccan spy (Saïd Taghmaoui) cross the Belgian front to seek out General Ludendorff, who aims to disrupt the coming armistice and whom Diana falsely believes is Ares in disguise. Once Diana leaves Themyscira, the only other significant female characters in the film are Etta (Lucy Davis), Steve's plucky secretary, and one of the film's villains, Dr. Maru (Elena Anaya), a maniacal scientist working on inventing a chemical weapon that can penetrate gas masks and kill instantly. Hence, Diana is an exception to the rule in the "world

FIGURE 2.4. Diana crosses No Man's Land while deflecting bullets and missiles. *Wonder Woman,* directed by Patty Jenkins (2017).

of men," a woman so extraordinary that she not only can fight alongside men but also can easily best them and accomplish the battle campaigns of an entire army with minimal effort.

In a climactic scene from the film, Diana reveals herself for the first time as Wonder Woman (unnamed as such, but in costume and in full glory as a super-hero) when she defiantly strides across No Man's Land. She shows no fear as the German army's rain of bullets ricochets off her gauntlets and she staunchly deflects larger shells with her shield; the Allied soldiers charge behind her across the barren battlefield, capturing the German trench and eventually reclaiming the Belgian village of Veld. This battle is preceded by a cascade of events in which Steve and the others have told Diana she cannot intervene: their mission is too important to compromise by wasting time helping injured soldiers, exhausted ani-mals, and desperate mothers with babies. Diana grows increasingly exasperated by these denials of her empathy, proclaiming, "We cannot leave without helping them. These people are dying." When Steve counters that they have no time and need to move on, she retorts, furious, "How can you say that? What is the matter with you?" Frustrated himself with Diana's refusal to understand the conventions of war, Steve declares, "This is No Man's Land, Diana. That means no man can cross it, all right? . . . This is not something you can cross. It's not possible. . . . We can't save everyone in this war. This is not what we came here to do." Determined, Diana turns away from Steve, frees her hair from its ties to don the battle headband she inherited from her aunt and teacher, Antiope (Robin Wright), and discards her long coat before climbing the ladder out of the trench and onto the battlefield. "No," Diana concedes partially to Steve's enjoinder, "but it's what I'm going to do." Implied in Diana's response, although not explicitly stated, is that she is not a man— neither human nor male—so the terms of No Man's Land do not apply to her.[62]

In the scenes that follow, Diana displays impressive and superhuman martial skill, not only incapacitating German soldiers and repelling bullets with little effort but leaping great distances across rooftops in the sieged village and, at one point, hurling an enormous tank in the air with her bare hands. Steve and his comrades quickly take up arms to fight alongside Diana after seeing that she is more than capable of doing what Steve earlier warned the entire Allied battalion had not been able to accomplish in over a year. Intermittent slow motion dominates these action sequences, in which point of view shots reveal Diana's hyperhuman senses at work as she responds so quickly and accurately that, even surrounded by six soldiers in close quarters, she can navigate their simultaneous attacks without hesitation. The slippage of the film from slow motion to high-paced action and back again accentuates the degree of Diana's exceptional dexterity. Despite her skill, she rarely visibly kills her enemies, instead reserving her sword for defensive blows, deflecting bullets with her shield and gauntlets, and demonstrating an impressive prowess with her lasso. While she engages in extravagant acts of destruction during battle—slamming her entire body into a church tower containing a sniper, for example, causing the tower to crumble to dust—she spills no discernible blood.[63] Therefore, Diana's enactment of violence eschews ethical questions around its ostensibly masculine glorification. Since she does not visibly cause harm or draw blood, these actual battles have a similar tenor as her Amazon training exercises.[64] Diana's fighting style is also cooperative, in concert with her upbringing. She is by far the most accomplished fighter, and Steve and the others somehow intuitively understand how and when she needs their assistance.

Nevertheless, despite witnessing Diana's superhuman abilities on the battlefield, Steve and Charlie still refuse to believe in the existence of Ares, thinking Diana somewhat naive and deluded. Chief and Sameer, on the other hand, are willing to admit the possibility of Ares's existence based on Diana's performance and claims. Perhaps unwittingly, the film aligns the two characters of color—one North African and one Native American—with Diana, suggesting they all possess a deeper intuition and greater willingness to accept the existence of unexplained phenomena than the white men Steve and Charlie, who insist on rationality and logic to guide their beliefs. And yet, Diana's naivete about the human capacity for evil comes to light when the people of Veld, the village they just saved, are indiscriminately obliterated by Dr. Maru's chemical weapon the following day. In some ways, then, Steve's insistence that crossing No Man's Land to save the village would be a waste of time turns out to be true. Diana's efforts result in one night of freedom for the villagers before they are snuffed out. The experience horrifies but also emboldens Diana, sending her galloping off to kill Ares and, she believes, thereby end the war.

Empathy and love drive Diana to do what she feels is right—to seek out Ares and attempt to save "mankind" from itself. Even though she says as much during their final confrontation, in the end it remains somewhat ambiguous what love has to do with Ares's defeat. Berlatsky argues, "Love, from this perspective, is a better way to run the world not because it is the opposite of force but rather because it is the quintessence of force—because it is more coercive than coercion. Love turns people into superior, more erotically invested state cogs, who will socialize better, produce better, and if need be, fight better than their less submissive Just Warrior peers."[65] According to this assessment, Diana's love—for Steve, for humanity, for peace—spurs her violent overthrow of Ares, allowing her to harness lightning (like her father, Zeus) and overpower her half brother. While the film represents her love for humanity in general via her empathy, its final scenes highlight how her love for Steve teaches Diana to accept humanity's flaws. There is a moment in her battle with Ares when Diana appears to have lost hope; prostrate on the ground, she looks up into the night sky and watches Steve martyr himself in an airplane full of explosives and deadly gas. Enraged, she rises, attacking German soldiers with abandon as Ares glories in her sudden fury. He encourages Diana to kill Dr. Maru, now unarmed and at her mercy: "She is the perfect example of these humans and unworthy of your sympathy in every way. Destroy her, Diana, and know that she deserves it. They all do." However, his use of the word *deserve* triggers a flashback for Diana, as she remembers Steve's parting words and his declaration of love. Inspired once again, Diana spares Dr. Maru and tells Ares, "You're wrong about them. They're everything you say, but so much more." Catalyzed by the memory of Steve, Diana's powers take on their mature, omnipotent form; declaring her belief in love as the origin of her power, she easily defeats Ares, impaling him with a concentrated cylinder of lightning.

For much of the film, even until these final moments, Diana trusts her fighting abilities but has a limited understanding of the extent and possibilities of her powers. Her knowledge rests almost entirely on a structure of belief, partly grounded in Amazon legends she was told as a child and partly derived from her strong conviction that humans are inherently good, with any corruption due only to Ares's influence. Steve teaches her that the "world of men" is messy and complicated and that heroes cannot wait for someone to deserve their protection to be saved. Despite the emphasis on Diana's extraordinary powers and Amazon training, her knowledge of those powers stems primarily from intuition and belief. Moreover, she is only able to unleash her full range of powers through a recognition of her love for Steve and, therefore, via conventions of heterosexual femininity (romance as a driving force for change and action). While Jenkins's 2017 film purportedly creates Wonder Woman anew for contemporary audiences and in line with contemporary feminism(s), Diana nevertheless remains allied with Marston's vision from the 1940s of "super strength, altruism, and feminine love allure."[66]

The film's sequel, *Wonder Woman 1984*, draws even starker connections between Diana's heroic powers, her femininity, and her heterosexuality, as illustrated through her romance with Steve. The sequel also begins with a flashback from Diana's childhood, when the young princess ran a pentathlon (involving an impressive obstacle course, swimming, riding, and archery) against fellow, adult Amazons, only to come close to winning and then be yanked out of the race at the finish line by Antiope as punishment for taking an unsanctioned shortcut. Diana's adult voice-over frames this scene as a vivid memory of her childhood, "when the whole world felt like a promise, and the lessons that lay ahead, yet unseen. Looking back,

I wish I'd listened, wish I'd watched more closely and understood. But sometimes you can't see what you're learning until you come out the other side." One of the lessons young Diana learns from her profound disappointment at the end of the race is that her ability to outperform her fellow Amazons means nothing without honesty. Her aunt Antiope chides, "No true hero is born from lies." This opening scene serves as a seamless example of the core principles of Diana's ethos—truth and justice—but seems a more bewildering starting point for the actual story told in the film.

Loosely, the plot of *WW84* focuses on a magic stone that grants wishes but always extracts a price from the wisher, and a megalomaniacal, Trumpesque supervillain, Maxwell Lord (Pedro Pascal), who tries to use this power to his advantage by becoming a living embodiment of the stone. He grows stronger and stronger as people wish for false emblems of happiness; each wish extracts a consequence, and civilization starts to crumble—in some cases, literally. Diana begins the sequel more or less in isolation; she has a job at the Smithsonian and occasionally dons her Wonder Woman gear for superhero work while trying to remain anonymous and avoid publicity. She has no friends or other personal relationships and seems to still pine for Steve (who died more than sixty years prior in the first film). These circumstances set the stage for Diana's reckoning, somewhat echoing the difficult lessons she learned as a child in the film's opener, but also quite divergent from the well-known tenets of Wonder Woman as an icon.

The most instructive illustration of *WW84*'s articulation of feminine forms of power and knowledge comes in the form of Diana's relationship with Barbara Minerva (Kristen Wiig), an unassuming and awkward new coworker who eventually transforms into the supervillain Cheetah. At first, Diana and Barbara are fast friends, Barbara marveling that someone as gorgeous and charismatic as Diana will even be in the same room as her. The two converse easily, enjoy a dinner together, and share a camaraderie that both seem to lack in other areas of their lives; Diana even swoops in to rescue Barbara from a would-be assault, forcing her to explain away her superhuman strength.[67] With the arrival of the stone, both women make unintentional wishes that fundamentally shift their relationship to each other and to their sense of self. Diana wishes for the return of Steve, whose soul comes to inhabit another man's body—which I will address in a moment. Barbara wishes to be like Diana, specifying her desire to be "strong, sexy, cool, special." As Barbara's wish manifests in the coming days, she acquires Diana's charisma and allure, suddenly making friends and attracting suitors; later, she also develops the demigod's strength and speed. Barbara's eventual alliance with Maxwell Lord leads to her transformation into her feline supervillain form. But each wish exacts a price; Barbara pays for her power and prowess by losing the kindness and humanity Diana initially admired in her. She becomes a ruthless and aggressive adversary, at one point nearly beating to death the man who had previously accosted her in the park (when Diana saved Barbara during this first incident, she showed much more restraint). Barbara exemplifies "power's corruptive force" in the film but also "veers uncomfortably close to long-standing arguments that imply women are too emotional to wield power responsibly and will only end up abusing it."[68] Under the influence of her wish, Barbara transforms from a socially awkward scientist who has trouble walking in heels into "the stereotype of a woman who uses her femininity to seduce and beguile," before shifting even further into a reckless aggressor, "unable to control her rage and savagely protecting her power regardless of the consequences."[69] One of the ironies of *WW84* is that Barbara is unable to handle responsibly the strength Diana wields so effortlessly, just as she desperately clings to powers Diana is all but willing to give up for the promise of love.

Diana's wish for the return of the love of her life also requires a sacrifice, one that is revealed the longer she is in the presence of resurrected Steve: the dwindling of her strength and the waning of her invulnerability. However, a significant portion of the film's midpoint dallies around Diana and Steve's rekindled romance. Despite Diana's prior single-minded focus on uncovering the origins of the stone and tracking the movements of Maxwell Lord, Steve's arrival immediately draws her into a lengthy detour from her mission. Diana giddily marvels at Steve's presence; the couple make love (completing ignoring the consent issues around Steve occupying another man's body); there is a comedic interlude as Diana walks Steve through choosing a 1980s-appropriate wardrobe; and Diana even takes Steve on an inexplicable nighttime tour of Washington, DC. Mozart's "Voi Che Sapete"—a well-known aria from *The Marriage of Figaro* sung by a teenage boy marveling at the ecstatic, confusing, and all-consuming nature of young love—accompanies this particular diversion. A strange accompaniment to the reunion of an immortal warrior and her dead lover, "Voi Che Sapete" underscores Diana's willingness to step outside her heroic responsibilities and abandon herself to love newly (re) discovered. Steve is the one who must convince Diana to relinquish her wish and lose him again in order to regain her powers and save the world, leaving the superhero to fight in isolation once more. As I have written elsewhere, "In the comics, Wonder Woman frequently advises women not to allow themselves to be controlled by their relationships with men. In the films, she is routinely cut off from other women (first her fellow Amazons, later Barbara), a stranger in the world of men who can only feel at home with one man in particular."[70] In the first film, Diana has spent 800 years with the Amazons growing up and yet walks away without looking back. She then spends a few weeks with Steve, but his death causes her such emotional upheaval that she remains single and friendless for six decades.

Binding Diana's power to her recognition of heterosexual love as a stand-in for universal love/love for all of mankind strikes a particularly dissonant chord when we remember that she was raised on an all-woman island, that she gave up a peaceful life with her mother and sister Amazons in order to enter into the destructive world of men, and that she expresses greater rage and sadness over the death of a man she only recently met than over that of her aunt Antiope, who trained her for years and died on the beaches of Themyscira at the hands of the invading Germans. In order to undergird Diana's femininity in the films, she needs to find a love that matters within the world of men, thus framing her upbringing with the Amazons as absent of this type of love. More importantly, since childhood, Diana has been taught that the Amazons' "foreordinance" (her word) is to protect mankind from Ares, sublimating their own desires for altruistic ends. While Jenkins's Diana may not be overly objectified by the camera in line with a resistance against the male gaze one might expect from a socially conscious woman director, she nevertheless resides within the scope of the heteropatriarchal imaginary, in which a feminized subject must submit to the needs of men. *Wonder Woman* frames all of humanity as "mankind"—a rhetorical decision emphasizing the potential of women's power and knowledge as a panacea against masculinist warmongering and domination. *Wonder Woman 1984* belabors Diana's romance with Steve, pitting love against power and suggesting that women who are not like Diana cannot wield the same power as she does responsibly. As such, both of Jenkins's films ultimately reinforce the idea that women's power stems from feminized sources like love and that such power should only be wielded for the benefit of others. Women who use their power for good, like Diana, must therefore abdicate the self.

Perhaps more than any other heroine, Wonder Woman functions as an icon of women's empowerment, familiar regardless of an individual's personal beliefs or sociopolitical allegiances, and recognizable even for those who may not know much, if anything, about her history or media representations. In order to resonate as a symbol, aspects of Wonder Woman's iconography must remain fixed across multiple iterations—at the very least her origin as an Amazon, her ability as a warrior, and certain earmarks of her femininity that differentiate her from masculinized superheroes. In a similar manner, one cannot update or reenvision *Charlie's Angels* without maintaining aspects of their feminine knowledge and power, which originally distanced them from typically male investigators and contributed to their representation as extraordinary women. In all versions of each franchise, femininity becomes a central trait that requires clarification and emphasis. These characters' embodiment as subjects-supposed-to-know constitutes an impossible double bind wherein their power and knowledge become a form of presumed mastery yet are inextricable from their femininity. Moreover, marking their abilities as intuitive, instinctual, or divinely wrought (found, not made, as Kelly observes in *Full Throttle*) further accentuates the gendered exceptionalism at work. If these are strong female characters, the implication remains that they are outside of the norm.

3 · FROM GIRL POWER TO INTERSECTIONAL SISTERHOOD

Exceptionalism and the Imperatives of Belonging

> You're an arrogant dude-bro and I'm the personification of the American way!
> —Kara Danvers, *Supergirl*

> The gender-marked texts of women's popular culture cultivate fantasies of vague belonging as an alleviation of what is hard to manage in the lived real—social antagonisms, exploitation, compromised intimacies, the attrition of life. Utopianism is in the air, but one of the main utopias is normativity itself, here a felt condition of general belonging and an aspirational site of rest and recognition in and by a social world.
> —Lauren Berlant, *The Female Complaint*

Wonder Woman never made an appearance on the popular Arrowverse show *Supergirl* (CBS, 2015–2016; CW, 2016–2021).[1] Nevertheless, traces of her linger around its edges, not least of which via the casting of Lynda Carter as the president of the United States, Olivia Marsdin.[2] In this vein, a brief, one-off publicity video, designed to promote the 2017 *Wonder Woman* film during *Supergirl*'s second season finale, uses Wonder Woman's boots as a sign of the symbiotic relationship between these two superheroines.[3] In the promotional spot, *Supergirl*'s protagonist, Kara Danvers (née Kara Zor-El, a Kryptonian refugee and Superman's cousin), wears her own iconic outfit—dark blue top with its signature sigil, red cape and skirt, and red patent knee-high boots—as she struts through a bar. The chorus of "These Boots Are Made for Walkin'" plays in the background, reinforcing the sartorial centrality and metaphoric value of Supergirl/Wonder Woman's footwear in this forty-five-second promo.

Three prominent women from the show's second season, each with her own relevance to Kara/Supergirl, watch the young woman saunter by. Alex Danvers

(Chyler Leigh) nods to her adoptive sister proudly as Kara passes. President Marsdin watches her with a calculating eye. Then, Queen Rhea (played by Teri Hatcher), a formidable enemy from Krypton's rival planet who dominates the latter half of *Supergirl's* second season, materializes in her own pair of sparkly, rhinestone-encrusted stiletto boots. Rhea eyes Kara, impressed, and tells her, "Nice boots." In the next shot, Kara sits at the bar, wearing the nondescript clothes of her human alter ego, a dark skirt and gray sweater, which contrast sharply with her new footwear, now swapped out for Wonder Woman's iconic gold and red metallic boots. "You like?" Kara quips. "I borrowed them from a friend." The boots flash briefly with a supernatural inner light, and Kara clinks her wrists together in an imitation of Wonder Woman's gauntlets. From across the room, President Marsdin gives Kara a wink, and Kara coyly eyes the camera, pulling down her glasses to remind us of her split/secret identity, as the promo transitions to a shot of Wonder Woman/Diana's boots and a seconds-long teaser from Jenkins's film.

A rich tapestry of intersecting threads, this brief promotional spot accomplishes several things at once. It makes explicit the connection between Wonder Woman and Supergirl as characters belonging to the same comic franchise in the service of cross-promotion for the former's film and the latter's television show. In doing so, the promo marks an affinity between two superheroines as part and parcel of the same ideological background and implies a metareferential friendship between the characters (Diana never actually appears on *Supergirl* or in any of the Arrowverse shows) who can, literally in this case, walk in each other's shoes.[4] There is little doubt that a significant element of the connection established here is because both characters are women. In fact, another compelling aspect of the promo is the way it suggests a generational lineage between women in the franchise via casting: from Lynda Carter (known for her iconic role in the first live-action televised *Wonder Woman* [ABC, 1976–1979]) to Teri Hatcher (known for her role as Lois Lane in *Lois & Clark: The Adventures of Superman* [(ABC, 1993–1997]) to relative newcomer Melissa Benoist as Kara/Supergirl. The intricacies of these cast-specific and metareferential relationships come to bear on *Supergirl's* second season finale, which is concurrently promoted alongside *Wonder Woman* in this spot and prominently features these three women.

In the two-part season 2 finale, Kara finds herself at an impasse when Queen Rhea invades Earth intent on enslaving its people and establishing a new home for the Daxamites, inhabitants of Krypton's rival planet who were displaced when Krypton's destruction also resulted in severe damage to Daxam. In an added complication, Kara's boyfriend Mon-El (Chris Wood) is Rhea's son and, hence, a Daxamite prince who hid his parentage from Kara when he first arrived on Earth as a refugee at the beginning of the season. In the finale, Rhea kidnaps Mon-El as well as Kara's best friend, Lena Luthor (Katie McGrath), intent on installing them as rulers of New Daxam (i.e., Earth) once her warships have completed their invasion. Rhea exhibits an unrestrained lust for power, even assassinating her own husband when he hesitates to enact her plans. Her position as both invader and alien sovereign naturally puts her at odds with President Marsdin and another de facto ruler in Kara's circle, Queen of All Media Cat Grant (Calista Flockhart), a formidable CEO of a media conglomerate and Kara's former boss.

In the penultimate episode of the season, "Resist" (2.21), the Daxamites have already begun their invasion, driving Supergirl and forces from the Department of Extranormal Operations (DEO)—for which Kara's sister and several of her close friends work—into hiding. Desperate to rescue Mon-El and Lena, Kara anxiously watches a hacked video feed of President Marsdin and Queen Rhea's negotiations. As these negotiations devolve into threats, Cat, aboard Air Force One with President Marsdin, steps into the frame of the feed. In a misguided attempt to establish some kind of gendered unity, Cat extols the two women to talk peace instead of war, employing her typical tone of snarky arrogance: "Oh my god. Enough. All right, *ladies*. Ladies. If I wanted to listen to this adolescent macho posturing I would have stayed in DC. Is this really who you want to be? Testosterone-driven windbags boasting about your big guns? Surely we don't need to *measure anything*—we're women. We're tough, we're wise, and we're way above this pettiness, so let's just roll up our sleeves and talk peace." Kara, watching the exchange from a makeshift command center set up in an alien bar, cringes in horror. Immediately recognizing Cat's appeal to Rhea's femininity as the wholly wrong tactic, Kara transforms into Supergirl and rockets into the sky in anticipation of imminent violence. When Rhea unceremoniously shoots down Air Force One from her spaceship, President Marsdin, a disguised alien herself, is able to fly to safety, but Supergirl arrives only just in time to snatch Cat out of a freefall from the wreckage as the destroyed plane plummets to the ground.

The final episode of the season, "Nevertheless, She Persisted" (2.22), concludes this storyline by allowing Kara to become "the champion of Earth" and confront Rhea directly.[5] But, first, she must subdue her cousin Kal-El/Superman, who has been poisoned by Rhea with mind-controlling silver Kryptonite and believes Kara to be his mortal enemy. Kara proves that she is ultimately the stronger of the two Kryptonians, assuaging her longtime anxiety that she could never measure up to the strength and speed of her cousin. Kara challenges Rhea to a ritualized trial by combat, but the other woman cheats and attempts to invade National City while Supergirl is distracted. Calling in a last resort, Kara employs an anti-alien technology designed by Superman's archrival Lex Luthor (Jon Cryer) but adapted to work against Daxamites by his sister, Lena, and their mother, Lillian. The device saturates Earth's atmosphere with lead, poisonous to the Daxamites, and drives away the invading army—but Mon-El must also leave, tainting Kara's victory with a great personal loss.[6] In the conclusion to an episode that alternates spectacular CGI fight choreography with moments of quiet grief, Kara receives her own pep talk from Cat, who tells her that she is on a "hero's journey" and reminds her, "The thing that makes women strong is that we have the guts to be vulnerable. We have the ability to feel the depths of our emotion and we know that we will walk through it to the other side." More receptive to this gendered argument than Rhea,

FIGURE 3.1. Alex Danvers (left) consoles her sister Kara/Supergirl after their actions to save Earth from the Daxamites result in Kara's boyfriend Mon-El being exiled. *Supergirl* (2015–2021), episode 2.22: "Nevertheless, She Persisted," CW, aired 22 May 2017.

Kara ends the season a hero who has had to sacrifice her personal happiness for the sake of others, proving she was right to worry, as she had previously lamented to her cousin, that it is not "possible to have everything you want."

Rhea's violent response to Cat's appeal, especially as compared with Kara's mentor-mentee relationship with Cat and her related adoption of much of Cat's guidance in season 1, could be interpreted as merely a generational or cultural difference. Rhea is an alien queen around Cat's age and does not take kindly to admonitions from her enemies; Kara is an alien millennial adopted by the Danvers who spent her late teens and young adulthood trying to adapt to human ways. However, I contend that the contrast between Rhea's and Kara's responses to Cat's exaltations of women's empowerment and feminist unity signals something far more endemic about the show's representation of femininity and, more specifically, feminine power and knowledge. Rhea refuses to recognize herself as a woman under Cat's definition; indeed, she is *not* a human woman, nor does she ascribe to American notions of femininity (and why should she?)—not to mention justice, honor, or fairness. Kara, on the other hand, having come of age in the body of a white, human-passing woman in contemporary America has absorbed the gendered messaging of the culture and hews closely to the ideologies of women's empowerment she has been taught.

We can see *Supergirl*'s insistence on positioning itself as a feminist show in its characterization, dialogue, plotlines, and mise-en-scène but also extended even into a few of its episode titles, as the season 2 finale episodes exemplify.[7] "Resist" and "Nevertheless, She Persisted" are both post-Trump feminist rallying cries, whereas an episode like season 1's "Stronger Together" (1.2) reflects the same messaging as Hillary Clinton's election campaign slogan. Notably, this episode was written and aired before Clinton began using the slogan, with the phrase "stronger together" offered as a Kryptonian family motto (*el mayarah* in the original language) that Kara and her family and friends, particularly Alex and Lena, use frequently throughout the series.[8] Certainly, "*el mayarah*/stronger together" takes on a different meaning in the wake Clinton's campaign, but the fact that the show selected this phrase as Kara's family motto prior to Clinton's use of it evinces an ethos of cooperative strength and justice that dovetails with a certain brand of contemporary feminism. These references, before and after the election of Donald Trump, make literal the show's overarching adherence to progressivist politics, explicit social justice messaging, and acknowledgment of the complexities of coming-of-age as a powerful girl/woman in America. Kara Danvers also embodies a kind of ideal mélange of rudimentary feminist virtues, although divided between two identities: by season 2, she has established herself as a strong, fast, courageous, and nearly invincible international hero, *and* she is a principled, gregarious journalist, respected for her craft and integrity. And yet, despite her otherworldly acumen, she frequently faces challenges in both her personal (Kara) and her professional (Supergirl) lives.

In this chapter, I focus on *Supergirl* as an example of an adult coming-of-age saga in which superpowers become a stand-in for adolescent growth and identity formation. The show operates within a rich metareferential network, not least of which because of its relationship to the DC Comics versions of Supergirl and the rest of the televised Arrowverse but also due to its wider "brand" recognition that requires little to no prior knowledge of the character. Beyond the Arrowverse show, Supergirl has appeared in many other guises, from countless comics, the 1984 film, myriad *Justice League*–themed video games, and animated children's shows like *DC Super Hero Girls* (Cartoon Network, 2015–2018, 2019–2021), where she incidentally is also friends with Wonder Woman. A new film released in Summer 2023, *The Flash*, features Supergirl for the first time in the modern DC Extended Universe (DCEU), and another film is tentatively in the works based on the *Supergirl: Woman of Tomorrow* comic books. Although the most recent DCEU Supergirl is also named Kara Zor-El (played by Sasha Calle), she differs starkly from the Arrowverse's Kara, with dark short hair and an alternate universe origin story where she has been the subject of government experiments.[9]

Regardless of her provenance, Supergirl is immediately recognizable as a recurring franchise figure, like Wonder Woman, although her icon status filters through her cousin, Superman. In the Arrowverse's *Supergirl*, Kara establishing herself as different from—and, in some cases, stronger/better/faster than—her cousin occupies much of season 1 and crops up regularly in later seasons. Kara as a super*girl* remains an important sticking point for the character especially over the first two seasons. In later seasons, while they do not as obviously refer to progress from girlhood, Kara still finds herself at odds with others who seem to have life "figured out." As part of her family—both the metafamily of the Arrowverse/ DC Comics and her connection to Superman—Supergirl is a quintessential subject-supposed-to-know who is initially revealed to be in over her head as she tries to figure out what it means to be a superhero. While Supergirl eventually becomes a beloved idol of National City and proves herself publicly, in private, she experiences recurring crises of faith and competency that belie her seeming mastery. Throughout the series, Supergirl must contend with frequent invocations of Superman lore that mark her as part of an iterative tradition of superheroes who are well respected and established. Like Superman, Supergirl is highly vulnerable to the mineral Kryptonite, a constant danger. Furthermore, the introduction of Lena Luthor in season 2 as a powerful businesswoman and tech genius who becomes Kara's best friend invokes a continual anxiety that Kara and Lena's relationship could follow the friends-to-archnemeses arc of Clark/Superman and Lex. In order to foment both the unease about their relationship and the allusions to Superman, *Supergirl* also includes Lex as a villain in his own right for the latter three seasons. To fully come into her power, Kara not only must master her own abilities and vanquish her own and her cousin's enemies but also must prove that she can do so by honing traits often marked feminine: cooperation, altruism, hope, compassion, and a refusal to kill unless absolutely necessary.

In addition to these diegetic references, *Supergirl* takes great pains to introduce social justice issues endemic to its airing, such as anti-immigration policies, the dangers of transphobia, and the far-reaching trauma of racial injustice; these issues serve as foils to Kara's struggles in ways typical of the CW network's overarching ethos and its young adult–centered programming. The ensemble cast of the show is markedly diverse, including multiple Black, Latinx, and LGBTQ characters, among those from other marginalized groups, and yet recurring, long-form plot arcs (beyond "special" stand-alone episodes) circulate around Kara's relationships, primarily with other white women. The current televisual landscape echoes this dichotomy and serves as a compelling microcosm of the broad sociopolitical effects of renewed public interest in social justice and equality—as well as the inconsistent ways those interests are implemented in policy and action. While unequivocally feminist in tone, even if viewers and critics might argue as to its "brand" of feminism, *Supergirl* falls into traps that we can see echoed in *Wonder Woman* and *Charlie's Angels*. As Marcie Panutsos Rovan astutely observes in "What to Do with Supergirl? Fairy Tale Tropes, Female Power and Conflicted Feminist Discourse," Kara

> must be powerful and strong and able to hold her own with any man. She should not be too powerful or "masculine." She must reject "femininity" and show that she is no different from a male hero. She must retain her femininity and the powers and leadership abilities that many see as uniquely feminine. She must not rely on others for help, as this is a sign of weakness. She must be willing to work collaboratively with others—and especially other women—as this is a sign of feminine strength. She must seek nonviolent approaches to conflict resolution. She must be willing and able to kick ass just like a man.[10]

As with the split in her identity, that between Kara and Supergirl, these additional burdens of representation around masculine and feminine dichotomies of behavior and the ways a character might be understood in reference to a broader discussion of action heroines palpably underscore Kara's characterization in *Supergirl*.[11]

Even if we hew closely to the 2015–2021 series, *Supergirl* is still not only a television show but also one at the whims of a media franchise (the Arrowverse) and a network (the CW, for seasons 2 through 6) with sometimes competing aims. Unlike screen versions of Wonder Woman and Charlie's Angels, the characteristics of whom remain fairly static due to their representation in films and episodic/procedural shows, *Supergirl*'s contemporary televised representation comes to us as part of an hour-long drama. As such, the format and medium of the show demand growth and change from the character, while subjecting her to ever-shifting storylines not all of which are equally thoughtful and some of which completely contradict each other. Serialized television also places greater demands on an ensemble cast and, hence, other characters sometimes carry the burden of operating as metaphoric lightning rods for Kara's anxieties or the aims of the show. Rather than worry about the ideological inconsistencies or messy illogics of a television show with a six-season run, my analysis of *Supergirl* focuses on broader trends while highlighting a few specific examples that illustrate them. Prior to that analysis, I discuss the CW as a network, particularly its emphasis on a youth demographic and related development of progressive programming and promotion of diversity and inclusion initiatives within its shows. Then, I consider the shift from the concept of "girl power" in the early 1990s to the intersectional feminism of the present moment. I segue from this discussion into my analysis of the show, focusing primarily on how it employs two interrelated themes: the power of sisterhood and belonging (literal and figurative) and the feminine imperative of specialized knowledge and embodiment of that knowledge (feminine intuition). These themes come to bear on how invocations of sisterhood link Kara first to her friends, especially other women, and eventually to all of humanity.[12] They also reflect the tremendous anxiety Kara constantly experiences over the split between Kara/Supergirl and the related divide between humans and aliens.[13]

DARE TO DEFY: THE CW AND NARROWCASTING DIVERSITY

Midway through season 2 of *Supergirl*, shortly before Kara and Mon-El begin dating, Kara half jokingly tells him that the reason they are so different is that "You're an arrogant dude-bro and I'm the personification of the American way!"[14] Despite the blossoming of the pair's romance in the following episode, the show takes great pains to emphasize Mon-El's freewheeling individualism—indeed, performed as a kind of white frat-boy charm—in opposition to Kara's "American" altruistic heroism.[15] This study in contrasts epitomizes *Supergirl* as a show that vacillates wildly between explicit critiques of patriarchal arrogance and frequent retreats to familiar romantic and neoliberal tropes surrounding relationships and success. In this section, I examine the way the CW as a network not only encourages but also reinforces these seeming contradictions between its explicit acknowledgment of social justice via the language of intersectional feminism and its somewhat reductive reliance on the stereotypical fodder of the women's and youth programming that shaped the network in its first decade-plus. Founded in a merger between the WB and UPN, the CW is a network that "acts like a cable channel."[16] In other words, it is available free over the air, like the major networks ABC, CBS, NBC, and FOX, and has commercial advertising to partially support its programming, but it also caters to a smaller, niche market as cable channels do. Part of that niche market is a focus on a younger demographic (teens and young adults) and an audience that initially skewed toward women but eventually reached more of a gender balance.[17] As such, it weathered a reputation for shows that have variously been described as campy, cheesy, cringey, or soap-operatic—in other words, kitschy, guilty pleasure TV, much of which is focused on coming-of-age narratives both literal (with characters who are teenagers or twentysomethings) and figurative (with adult heroes learning how to use suddenly acquired powers).[18]

From 2012 to 2022, the network was the primary home for DC Comics' adapted television shows, known as the Arrowverse; at one point, 40 percent of its original programming was purely Arrowverse, a decision that increased its viewership significantly.[19] The CW's tagline "Dare to Defy" corresponded to its 2019 "We Defy" campaign, codifying the network's investment in increasing diversity and inclusion across its programming. One of the ways these campaigns have visibly manifested is through casting, with the intentional replacement of characters who were men or white women in prior versions with women of color.[20] Characters on many of these shows, including *Supergirl*, frequently discuss misogyny, homophobia, racial belonging, sexual harassment, and other progressive-leaning conversations that have made the rounds on social media in recent years. In brief promotional videos posted to Twitter in March 2019, the casts of many CW shows insist on the network's adherence to its "We Defy" campaign, contending, "We are open to all: all choices, all orientations, all lifestyles, all possibilities. When we defy assumptions, change happens. When we defy division, hope happens. When we defy judgment, love happens. We are open to all and defy anything that stands in our way."[21] The casts of many CW shows made similar promotional videos with almost identical messaging. *Supergirl*, as an earlier addition to the Arrowverse and predating the CW's "We Defy" campaign, began airing on the cusp of this shift toward explicit social justice messaging, as illustrated by the show's changing politics over its six seasons.

In the CW's early years, the smallest network took into account its size and stature comparative to the Big Four (ABC, NBC, CBS and Fox) and developed a "narrowcasting" branding strategy with a focus on eighteen- to thirty-four-year-old women, more niche programs, and merging the teen programming and more culturally diverse programming its parent companies (the WB and UPN) had been known for, respectively, prior to the merger.[22] In the CW's second year as a network, *Gossip Girl* (2007–2012) became one of its flagship shows; a teen drama steeped in consumerism, fashion, and plotlines about sex and dating, *Gossip Girl* proved popular and allowed the network to employ innovative advertising and social media strategies to augment its ratings.[23] After *Gossip Girl* had run its course, the CW began to branch out by incorporating more and more comic book–inspired shows into its lineup, first with *Arrow* (2012–2020) and then with *The Flash* (2014–2023), as well as other programs that broke away from the teen mold the CW had become known for. Within a few years, "the fifth network [had] managed to rebrand itself and to acquire a cultural legitimacy that was out of reach for its teen soaps. From DC superheroes to *Jane the Virgin*, the generic category of the 'CW show' has undergone major transformations."[24] Growing its teen and young adult base, the CW represented "a radical departure from any other broadcaster—focused on catering to the tech savvy, young-adult media consumer."[25] This focus on young adult viewers fundamentally shaped the CW's programming, and thus it becomes impossible to divorce *Supergirl* from its industrial contexts, particularly when interrogating how gendered exceptionalism influences the development of feminine knowledge and its associated power(s) in characters who are coming of age.

The CW was once thought to have hit a sweet spot between narrowcasting and wider appeal.[26] However, its 2022 acquisition by Nexstar Media Group and changes in programming suggest a potential collapse on the horizon.[27] CW's debt and its subsequent sale resulted in the cancellation of the majority of its Arrowverse shows, with the exception of *The Flash* and *Superman and Lois*, as well as the cancellation of most of its shows with women or people of color as leads. This change may mark the end of the CW's progressive youth platform and programming, but it is too soon to tell at the time of this writing.[28] Still, in 2016, the year *Supergirl* migrated from CBS to the CW in its second season, Maureen Ryan reported in *Variety* that the network had "carved out a distinctive niche by using hourlong shows that use music, telenovelas, superpowers and comedic flourishes to explore serious ideas about duty, the pressure to conform, ambition and frustrated expectations; these are all themes that have special relevance for women."[29] While, by that time, the CW was no longer deliberately narrowcasting toward women, its reputation as a network of special interest to women and teen girls remained.

GIRL POWER COMES OF AGE

Supergirl did well its first season at CBS, when the network was attempting to use the show to reach a younger, more female viewership, but its ultimate move to the CW fit easily within the latter network's culture for a number of reasons.[30] As Caryn Murphy elaborates, the CW "specializes in scripted programming that encourages long-term viewer engagement with story and character.... In the same way that CBS' success is tied to episodic, procedural dramas like *NCIS*, the CW is identified with series that encourage investment in a specific narrative universe or mythology."[31] The Arrowverse properties, steeped in decades of comic mythos, perfectly dovetail with these goals, and *Supergirl* provided an opportunity for CBS and then the CW to capitalize on an interest in girl power ideology popularized in the 1990s while redefining it. Debates, definitions, and deliberations of girl power are legion; instead of rehashing that well-worn territory, in this section, I highlight several aspects that translate explicitly into my discussion of *Supergirl*'s application of feminine intuition and the politics of sisterhood/belonging. Moreover, this progression from girl power ideology to intersectional sisterhood mimics the ways characters on this show come into their "womanhood" as they learn about and gain power.

Girl power as a cultural ethos was fomented in the 1990s and early 2000s as part of "third-wave" feminism or "postfeminism" and has been thoroughly elucidated by scholars since then. For example, Jennifer Baumgardner and Amy Richards's collection *Manifesta: Young Women, Feminism, and the Future*, originally published in 2000, reminds readers that the experiences of young feminists at the time were different from those of their foremothers who came of the age in the 1970s: "If feminism aims to create a world where our standard of measurement doesn't start with a white-male heterosexual nucleus, then believing that feminine things are weak means that we're believing our own bad press. Girlies say, through action and attitudes, that you don't have to make the feminine powerful by making it masculine or 'natural'; it is a feminist statement to proudly claim things that are feminine and the alternative can mean to deny what we are."[32] This encouragement to "proudly claim" femininity rests at the heart of girl power's original ethos, one received triumphantly by many young feminists at the time. And yet, the shifting uses of girl power and its concomitant philosophies makes unpacking its contours thorny work. Stéphanie Genz and Benjamin A. Brabon interrogate this conundrum, explaining how "Girl Power has been dismissed by a number of critics as an objectifying and commoditising trap that makes women buy into patriarchal stereotypes of female appearance and neo-liberal individualist principles. Yet girl culture also has the potential to uproot femininity and make it available for alternative readings/meanings."[33] While there is significant value in privileging and celebrating conventionally feminine behaviors and traits, a frequent critique of girl power remains its misuse as a popular, watered-down version of feminism, with little substance beyond making feminism marketable and asserting that girls and women should celebrate their femininity (read: embrace normative gender roles).

In one sociological study on girls who are told they can achieve anything without full acknowledgment of institutionalized gendered inequity, Shauna Pomerantz, Rebecca Raby, and Andrea Stefanik acutely articulate this "success" trap: "The original feminist intentions of this youthful movement, however, were stripped away once marketers began cashing in on female empowerment as an easily digested form of pseudo-feminist branding."[34] Karen Boyle offers a similar warning regarding girl power's focus on individual empowerment in her analysis of postfeminist media: "The critical focus on individual women allows the challenge of feminism to disappear as it is positioned as a lifestyle choice (being feminist) rather than a movement (doing feminism). If feminism is equated with women's agency, choice and subjectivity, then questions about gender, about structural inequalities, discrimination, oppression and violence are allowed to slip from view."[35] These assertions emphasize the danger of popular feminism if its primary focus rests on the power of femininity and sidesteps questions of systemic marginalization, institutional discrimination, and structural inequity along the lines of gender.

Angela McRobbie's theory of "double entanglement" applies here, in that she asserts how late 1990s and early 2000s media often reflected widespread knowledge and acknowledgment of feminist ideas while simultaneously, though sometimes subtly, condemning them.[36] Susan J. Douglas takes this argument a step further by linking the backlash against feminism to media and popular culture narratives in which femininity is linked to power, much as Sarah Banet-Weiser, writing almost a decade later, ties feminist empowerment narratives to endemic and virulent misogyny. As such, Douglas coins the term *enlightened sexism* in her 2010 book, asserting it as "a response, deliberate or not, to the perceived threat of a new gender regime. It insists that women have made plenty of progress because of feminism—indeed, full equality has allegedly been achieved—so now it's okay, even amusing, to resurrect sexist stereotypes of girls and women."[37] Enlightened sexism, encapsulated by films like the 2000 and 2003 remakes of *Charlie's Angels*, serves a different rhetorical purpose than girl power–influenced narratives of feminine empowerment. While the former utilizes a tongue-in-cheek articulation of feminism in order to "make okay" sexist humor and/or the sexualization of girls and women, the latter sets up a questionable dichotomy whereby empowerment should stem from feminized/feminine acts, choices, and roles so that girls and women will not be seen as disavowing their womanhood.

Since, as Banet-Weiser explains, feminism sometimes has been framed as a threat to conventional masculinity and to "conventional performances of heteronormative femininity, particularly in the ways that femininity functions to reassure men of their dominant position," popular empowerment narratives mitigate that threat by asserting femininity as a (preferred) mode of power acquisition.[38] These links between feminine "being" and characters' main modes of identity formation echo Sara Ahmed's invocation of Judith Butler's notion of "girling," by which gender definition, especially from without, becomes a process reinforced by repetition. "Sex is given as an assignment; homework. No wonder mere description (it's a girl; it's a boy!) provides the basis of a task (being boy! being girl!) as well as a command (You will be boy! You will be girl!)," writes Ahmed in her book *Living a Feminist Life*, illustrating how a concept like feminine intuition can remain unnamed at the same time it endures as an endemic property of character building for girl and women protagonists.[39]

It is worth noting here my emphasis on *popular* empowerment narratives. Especially in recent years, there are more and more stories being told in narrative and nonfiction media about nonbinary and trans characters, as well as other people who do not easily conform to masculine or feminine norms and have no desire to do so. These depictions are still few and far between and rarely take center stage in the narrative—with a few exceptions.[40] More to the point, my focus remains on narratives that have been serialized and revived over time. In these shows and films, despite sometimes extensive, culturally conscious updates, the emphasis on femininity as a font of power and knowledge remains. In fact, I would argue that *Supergirl* consciously avoids some of the traps of the girl power ideology so prevalent in the 1990s and early 2000s. As a show airing after girl power's heyday, the series makes significant efforts to clarify its feminist bona fides in ways that allude to, but ultimately dismiss, neoliberal girl power individualism, while favoring a contemporary model of intersectional feminism. *Supergirl* also explicitly addresses the political and social threats to womanhood during the Trump presidency, hashtag activism such as #MeToo, transphobia directed at trans women specifically, and microaggressions that constitute common forms of sexism, racism, and xenophobia in the twenty-first century. Nevertheless, *Supergirl* maintains the overarching impression that feminine sensibilities undergird its protagonist's power and knowledge, especially as she graduates from individualist girl power to a network of collective empowerment and comes into her identity as a woman.

SISTERHOOD IS EVERYTHING: KNOWLEDGE, NETWORKS, BELONGING

A discussion between Kara and Cat in the pilot episode of *Supergirl* includes the most obvious evidence of the show's indebtedness to girl power philosophy, while hinting at Kara's eventual dismissal of it. As CEO and founder of CatCo media, the company for which Kara works, Cat takes it upon herself to name the new caped crusader performing heroics around National City. She is shocked that Kara, her mild-mannered assistant/protégée whom Cat does not realize is also Supergirl, objects to the name on the grounds that it is "something less than what she is" and, therefore, "anti-feminist." Cat eloquently rebukes her, asking, "What do you think is so bad about 'girl'? I'm a girl. And your boss. And powerful and rich and hot and smart. So, if you perceive Supergirl as anything less than excellent, isn't the problem you?" This reversal, accusing Kara of denigrating the word *girl* as opposed to acknowledging that it denotes diminutive or childlike associations with femininity, marks Cat as firmly grounded in girl power ideology. Kathryn Miller and Joshua Plencer take this to mean that the show itself hews to this philosophy. In their essay expounding on *Supergirl's* grounding in neoliberal feminism, Miller and Plencer argue that it "routinely insists that the problem of gender oppression is actually a problem of (women's) perception, and that things otherwise recognizable as degrading, sexist, or misogynistic can be personally and socially resolved by simply seeing things differently."[41] In this scene between Cat and Kara, in particular, Cat tries to reframe Kara's perception of herself, which Miller and Plencer understand as evidence, among other moments in the first two seasons, that "*Supergirl* is a TV-series-length corporate sales pitch for neoliberal, white-supremacist heteropatriarchy cloaked in the language of feminism."[42] While I agree that *Supergirl* has a complicated relationship to its constructions of both feminism and femininity, I contend that its incorporation of femininity-as-power is more nuanced than mere neoliberal lip service. In fact, even though Kara receives advice from Cat and considers her a mentor, she ultimately rejects Cat's model of leadership even as she moves toward another feminized paradigm, that of collaboration and sisterhood.

Girl power ideology frames feminine knowledge production and empowerment as worthy of emulation and glorification, but this tendency persists in current popular discussions of the unique traits of girls and women. The origins of this messaging vary widely, from self-help books and op-eds to political commentary and advice about "getting ahead" in business and STEM. For example, the self-help genre offers suggestions about tapping into sources of feminine power.[43] These sources acknowledge that "'feminine' ways of knowing . . . are most often associated with intuition and other intangible forms of insight—which we tend to distrust, because they don't accord with established (masculine) systems of knowledge."[44] Texts like these remind readers that powerful women have existed throughout history and that feminine power is apolitical and accessible to all women willing to privilege feminine conventions. Chapter titles in one such volume suggest the "feminine revolution" can be achieved through a series of imperatives: "Be Emotional," "Cry Openly," "Be Mothering," "Own Your Intuition," "Surrender," "Be Agreeable," "Apologize," "Embrace the Supporting Role," and "Love Fully," to name some. While an example like this is overtly hyperfeminine, its model of acceptance and empowerment regarding stereotypically feminine behaviors is not far off from one side of a feminist culture war in which we have been engaged since, at least, the 1960s. It also openly contrasts the kind of advice offered by a book like Sheryl Sandberg's popular *Lean In: Women, Work and the Will to Lead* (2013), which loosely encourages women to adopt masculine tactics of negotiation and management to succeed in business contexts.[45]

Furthermore, encouraging women to embrace their femininity in a contemporary context is not limited to self-help manuals or conservative publications that wish to reify gender norms. A *New York Times* op-ed by Ruth Whippman extols women to "lean out" and asks men to do the same: "So perhaps instead of nagging women to scramble to meet the male standard, we should instead be training men and boys to aspire to women's cultural norms, and selling those norms to men as both default and desirable. To be more deferential. To reflect and listen and apologize where an apology is due (and if unsure, to err on the side of a superfluous sorry than an absent one). To aim for modesty and humility and cooperation rather than blowhard arrogance."[46] The adoption of conventionally feminine forms of power and knowledge and the request for buy-in from men is echoed in *Supergirl*. While Miller and Plencer compare *Supergirl* with the neoliberal politics of "lean in," this ideology is largely abandoned by midway through the second season, which may have something to do with the show's shift to the CW or simply a change in the zeitgeist. *Supergirl* acts as a real-time representational litmus for shifting social norms around articulations of feminine power. A more accurate contemporary comparison to *Supergirl*'s brand of feminist ideology would be its parallels to the #MeToo movement and #BlackLivesMatter, both of which are referenced in clear but coded ways on the show. The #MeToo movement's focus on what Michelle Rodino-Colocino refers to as "empowerment through empathy" and its "second mission: to become an agent for exposing systems of oppression and privilege of which sexual harassment and assault are cause and effect" further elucidate the way *Supergirl* employs the language of solidarity and belonging to frame its characters and their struggles.[47]

There is little question that *Supergirl* hews to the model of popular feminism Banet-Weiser identifies as a "return to earnestness, a return to a focus on gendered injuries, by centering on the cultural, economic, and political injuries women experience by living in sexist societies."[48] However, the series cannot coast along this narrow ideological territory for long. By the third season, and after Kara has discovered for herself that she is stronger and faster than her cousin, *Supergirl* turns away from gender politics as a central foundation of its conflicts. These early ideological signposts are easy to recognize in season 1's focus on Kara's empowerment as a hero and growth apart from her family legacy. Season 2 extends the clear-cut allegories of its predecessor as Kara grapples with the machinations of an evil, anti-alien organization run by Lillian Luthor alongside her burgeoning friendship with Lena and her romance with Mon-El, during which she tries and eventually succeeds in convincing him to stop being such as "arrogant dude-bro" and adopt her brand of altruistic heroism. By season 3, the stakes of the show shift to more complex understandings of personal identity and morality, such as protecting Lena from assassination and battling an all-powerful Kryptonian threat who awakens in the body of Lena's CFO Sam Arias (Odette Annable).

From season 4 onward, we see Kara's bifurcation tackled in literal and figurative ways: she contends with another anti-alien domestic terrorist group known as the Children of Liberty, and she faces threats from a clone, Red Daughter, indoctrinated by Lex to be anti-American and anti-Supergirl and who possesses all of Kara's powers. Kara spends much of season 4 tormented by the monumental secret she has kept from Lena, who has become antagonistic toward Supergirl but constantly worries about Kara's safety and frets over her friend's growing emotional distance. When the truth is finally revealed, Lena's spiraling protovillain arc has her at odds with Kara and the Superfriends.[49] This lasts for all of season 5 before the two women reconcile.[50] The admittedly convoluted final season of the show focuses on Kara's traumatic experiences in the Phantom Zone—a hellscape to which Lex exiles her for several episodes, where she is subjected to a loss of power, nightmares, and other terrors—and, once she is rescued, a series of battles against an interdimensional magic imp, Nxly. Given the many twists and turns of the series, I will not attempt to address all of these arcs, intending here only to give an overview of the ways the show grapples with Kara's identity. I will, however, touch on a number of these specific incidents in order to interrogate Kara's relationships with other women as they pertain to her identity and coming-of-age, as well as how *Supergirl*'s plots intersect with contemporary social justice issues.

In *The Female Complaint*, Lauren Berlant discusses women's culture as a form of "intimate public," such that participation in this form of gendered culture "seems to confirm the sense that even before there was a market addressed to them, there existed a world of strangers who would be emotionally literate in each other's experience of power, intimacy, desire, and discontent, with all that entails."[51] This idea that women's culture equates to an intimate public in which affinity is assumed by virtue of shared gendered markers, however imagined, echoes the invocation of sisterhood in *Supergirl*. Furthermore, the supposition that sisterhood—or even kinship—is enough to establish solidarity and loyalty is a continual wrench thrown into the affinities between women on the show. To provide fodder for these conflicts and betrayals, *Supergirl* offers sisterhood as the ultimate form of feminist power and knowledge on the show, invoking it steadfastly in myriad ways, both explicit and metaphoric. The two clearest manifestations of Kara's allegiance to the collaborative practice of feminist sisterhood are her relationships with Alex and Lena, alongside frequent invocations of the mantra *el mayarah*/stronger together. Other powerful characters, many of whom are women, challenge and buttress Kara, emphasizing the tenets of her collaborative, Kryptonian creed, so different from her cousin's erstwhile individualism.[52] Moreover, sisterhood in its various manifestations marks Kara as different from other heroes, a particularly feminine difference that also opens her to a specific set of vulnerabilities, including but not limited to her struggles with identity formation and belonging.

The fraught slippage between nature and nurture in the construction of sisterhood on the show best illustrates some of these tenets. Kara and Alex are adoptive sisters, living together since Kara was thirteen and Alex, a few years older. At the start of the series, they are both in their midtwenties and tightly bonded through their shared experiences dealing with—and keeping secret—Kara's alien powers. While occasional flashbacks and even whole flashback episodes expand on the ways Kara and Alex have had to negotiate their relationship as teens, there is little question of the strength of their bond.[53] Even in the first season, when Alex is forced to kill Kara's Aunt Astra (Laura Benanti), the identical twin sister of Kara's presumed-dead mother and a rogue Kryptonian who believes she can forestall climate change on Earth through mind control, Kara ultimately forgives Alex, understanding that she did everything in her power to save Astra first and was only acting defensively.[54] Years later, when Kara discovers her mother and a small group of Kyptonians survived the planet's destruction, she similarly makes the choice to return to Earth to help her adoptive family and friends rather than remain in Argo City with her biological kin.[55]

Ironically, Kara initially finds affinity with Lena because of a separation from family: Kara recognizes in Lena's struggle to distance herself from the other Luthors her own similar struggle to set herself apart from both Superman and the questionable actions of her Kryptonian parents. While Kara and Lena are not sisters in any sense, the logics of the show present Kara's friendship with Lena as a relationship of importance only secondary to hers with Alex.[56] As Lena tells Kara in the middle of season 2 when their friendship begins to intensify after Supergirl saves Lena's life, claiming to have been instructed to do so by Kara: "I've never had friends like you before. Come to think of it, I've never had family like you. . . . Supergirl might have saved me, but Kara Danvers, you are my hero." The frisson of Lena's divergent feelings toward Kara and Supergirl stems in large part from the fact that she sees Supergirl as an invincible hero lacking in humanity and feels kinship with Kara as a mere human, like her, who is trying to do good in the world.

Despite her nearly unlimited strength, speed, and power as Supergirl, Kara registers as less equipped to handle the vagaries of everyday life than both Alex and Lena. For the majority of the show, Alex is a skilled federal agent who does not have to question her intellectual or combat skills; Lena is a successful and wealthy businesswoman and scientific genius who answers to no one in her professional life. While all three women are around the same age, Kara begins the show as an assistant to Cat Grant and then a junior reporter at the magazine, constantly at the whim of her editors. In her day-to-day life, she is unassuming and easily flustered, only embodying the bravado of the hero in her Supergirl costume. Alex and Lena also serve as visual and temperamental foils in other ways: both women are brunettes, favoring severe, straight hairstyles in contrast to Kara's blonde updos (buns and intricate braids) and Supergirl's flowing shoulder-length waves. Kara's normal clothes are often simple dresses or neutral slacks, button-up shirts, and cardigans.[57] Alex, by contrast, frequently wears all black at work, favoring militaristic clothing that supports her position as a DEO agent; when she eventually adopts a superhero costume (at the end of season 5), it is similarly composed of black material with teal highlights. Lena, in line with her profession, wears all manner of pantsuits, pencil skirts, tailored dresses, and other expensive designer clothes articulating wealth and corporate feminine power. Certainly, Lena and Alex have their anxieties as characters—neither of them fully self-possessed despite their put-together demeanors. Alex struggles in season 2 with her sexuality, finally coming out as a lesbian, and later grapples with the apparent incompatibility of her desire to be a mother and her dangerous profession. In addition to her recurring family drama, Lena has deep-seated trust issues and a history of being betrayed by those closest to her, a narrative that her relationship with Kara feeds into in destructive ways. However, Alex's and Lena's anxieties are emotional and internal, unlike Kara's externalized and embodied negotiation of her secret identity and powers.

Through Kara's relationships with Alex, Lena, and others, *Supergirl* reifies the importance of sisterhood and belonging and its invocation of the collaborative work of the Superfriends. Two intersecting plotlines from the third season illustrate these tendencies. In the first, Lena is framed and accused of poisoning children with lead by corporate villain Morgan Edge (Adrian Pasdar). After Lena's name has been cleared through the intervention of Sam and Kara, the three women drink wine together while Lena thanks her friends for standing by her. Kara rejoins, "When you're family, you can say what you need to say, and the people that love you will love you," and Sam agrees. Lena, ever self-recriminating, laments, "I've never had anyone like that in my life." "Well," Kara says, matter-of-factly, "that's because you've never had a sister," to which Sam adds, "Two. Two sisters." This bond is then almost immediately tested in the season's second plotline as Sam begins to be subsumed, at first without her knowledge, by her alter ego, Reign, a Kryptonian Worldkiller sent to Earth to mete out justice through old-god-style wrath and destruction. It is no coincidence that both Kara and Sam are adopted Kryptonian aliens with secret identities, one good, one evil.[58] When Lena realizes that Sam and Reign are the same person—somehow still remaining completely unaware that Kara is Supergirl—she locks Sam in a secret laboratory to protect her from the hero and the DEO, whom she believes would kill Sam in order to stop Reign. When Supergirl discovers that Lena has been harboring Sam/Reign for weeks, the trust between the three erodes. Moreover, the Worldkillers, consisting of Reign and two other recently activated Kryptonians living within human hosts (Julia/Purity and Grace/Pestilence), also invoke the bond of sisterhood as their defining source of power, explicitly using the phrase *el mayarah* when they unite. Only Alex, Lena, and Kara working together—despite the precarity of the relationship between Lena and Supergirl—can ultimately stop the Worldkillers and allow Sam to return to her human life. There is little question that Sam's humanity is safeguarded in part because of the sisterly strength of her friends' love for her, but also because of her own love for her teen daughter, Ruby (Emma Tremblay), whom Reign rightfully sees as a liability and actively seeks to destroy. This invocation of motherhood alongside sisterhood as fundamental strengths and vulnerabilities among powerful women is something I explore further in the next chapter.

In *Supergirl*, sisterhood operates as an explicitly feminine model of strength and power, but also one of feminine knowledge production through networks and collaboration. This manifests in several ways. Only through the intersecting abilities and skills of each "sister," literal or figurative, can goals be achieved. Notably, disagreements about the most effective path forward are frequent but usually resolved by coming together as one mind. Discord foments in moments of fear or distrust of the group, as well as individualist arrogance; declaring independence from the need for others' help or support always ends poorly, as we see in Lena's

season 5 villain arc. The resolution to these deviations is the need for reconciliation, reunion, and an acknowledgment that, as Kara tells anti-alien villain Metallo
at the start of season 2, "You might work better alone, but we don't."[59] Here, we see
an explicit reminder that Supergirl's model of power is one in which she has
"power-with" others, to borrow Amy Allen's term, pushing back against masculinist assumptions of power-as-domination or control.[60]

The insistence on the power of sisterhood and the explicit frameworks of
knowledge it provides echo feminist arguments for the need for solidarity among
women. Moreover, the reframing of intuition, collaboration, courageous acts of
love, and other feminized forms of power in Supergirl offers unambiguous counters
to the hegemonic forms of power and strength championed by patriarchal institutions. In their article "Feminine Power: A New Articulation," Bernadette Barton
and Lisa Huebner remind us that "if a task (care-work), action (re-direction), personality trait (warm and affectionate), or skill (mediation)—is something women
and girls are disproportionately good at, patriarchy automatically constructs these
as insignificant and trivial. In short, the very fact that a woman does something,
much less does so better than a man, devalues the skill within patriarchy. Such a
formulation ensures that Westerners never perceive feminine ways of power as
compelling, effective, and something to emulate."[61] This framing presupposes certain behaviors and traits as gendered—an assumption often made throughout cultural representation and in social and political life—although whether they are
"naturally" so or socially constructed remains a frequent matter of debate. Either
way, the auspices of popular articulations of feminism in contemporary media and
the more narrow definitions of girl power take up the call offered here: in order to
confront the patriarchal hegemony, new forms of power and knowledge are
needed and, hence, feminine power and knowledge need to be privileged. The creators, writers, and executives who updated Supergirl to serve as a panacea against
patriarchy—and the CW as host network—understood a certain cache in making
feminine power political by framing their protagonists as bonded to and bound by
codes of unity and collective action.

On the one hand, political solidarity is necessary to enact change. As bell hooks
acknowledges in Feminism Is for Everybody (2000), "Feminist sisterhood is rooted
in shared commitment to struggle against patriarchal injustice, no matter the
form that injustice takes. Political solidarity between women always undermines
sexism and sets the stage for the overthrow of patriarchy."[62] On the other hand,
Bonnie Thornton Dill cautions that there are "limitations of the concept [of sister-
hood] for both theory and practice when applied to women who are neither white
nor middle class."[63] In fact, hooks herself asserts a similar warning in her essay
"Sisterhood: Political Solidarity between Women" (1986): "The vision of Sisterhood evoked by women's liberationists was based on the idea of common oppression. Needless to say, it was primarily bourgeois white women, both liberal and
radical in perspective, who professed belief in the notion of common oppression.

The idea of 'common oppression' was a false and corrupt platform disguising and mystifying the true nature of women's varied and complex social reality."[64] The complexity of these positions—sisterhood as powerful versus sisterhood as a specious form of limited belonging—further burdens narratives that insist on gendered exceptionalism, particularly ones in which women are in effect learning how to navigate lives transformed by the acquisition of extraordinary abilities.

THE FEMININE ORDER, MASTERY, AND THE VULNERABILITY OF KNOWING

In her discussion of intimate publics, Berlant notes how the "often sweetly motivated and solidaristic activity of the intimate public of femininity is a white universalist paternalism, sometimes dressed as maternalism," wherein white women "mobiliz[e] fantasies of what black and working-class interiority based on suffering must feel like in order to find a language for their own more privileged suffering at the hands of other women, men, and callous institutions."[65] Despite Kara's being constantly surrounded by friends and allies, and despite the fact that she inhabits a quintessentially ideal American body (attractive, fit, blonde), her sense of alienation—literal and figurative—operates as a central tenet of the show. Supergirl is a beloved hero (easily divested of this status when she falls out of public favor due to a mistake or miscalculation), and Kara Danvers is a respected reporter (subject to the whims of her bosses), but the tension of this split rises to the surface again and again, causing Kara to frequently doubt herself and her role as a hero and a person. A tactic not uncommon for coming-of-age narratives, Kara's precarious sense of self is not always visible to those around her, a dichotomy that only causes further problems.[66]

Supergirl highlights Kara's humanity as a choice, one that does not come naturally to her as an alien, and particularly to an alien who has superpowers. In doing so, the show allies Kara's Kryptonian nature with a kind of dangerous masculinist tendency toward brute force and a lust for power that she must guard against. In the beginning of season 3, Kara—mourning the loss of Mon-El—tries to push away her humanity, framing it as a weakness not dissimilar to the conventional definitions of stereotypically feminine emotionality. She tries to subsume herself into her Supergirl persona, telling Alex, that "being broken" and suffering from grief is "what humans do. And I'm better than that." She further insists, "Kara Danvers sucks right now! Supergirl is great. Supergirl saved the world! So, if I could choose to be her, why would I ever choose to be the sad girl whose boyfriend is gone? I don't like that girl."[67] Later in the season, she reconciles her feelings for Mon-El and is able to regain her sense of "heart," but the rift between Kara and Lena grows wider as the former grapples with this split in her identity.[68] All these tensions result in a clear assertion that Kara's femininity and her humanity are connected; her alien strengths (flight, invincibility, heat vision, etc.) are what make her a superhero, but they are also corruptible and open for misuse. It is through her human connections qua femininity that she is able access her true powers: the ability to act compassionately and instill hope in others.

Villains on the show, whether male or female, lack empathy and morality; they are the true alien threat Kara must face. The violence enacted by villains like Lillian, Rhea, Reign, Lex, and the anti-alien terrorist group Children of Liberty registers as masculinist because they inhabit power as something one uses to dominate and destroy. Supergirl's violence, by contrast, is mostly justified by the ethos of the show, even when it is cataclysmically destructive or results in unintentional loss of life, due to her overarching motto of compassion and justice for all. The distinguishing feature separating villains who are redeemable and those who are not seems to be their adherence to a moral code of compassion. Therefore, bloodthirsty, dishonorable villains like Rhea and Reign (but not Sam, who is an innocent hostage of her alter ego and requires rescuing) are irredeemable, whereas season 5's Lena and season 6's Nxly are redeemable due to their ultimate desire to do good (Lena) and occasional bouts of empathy (Nxly).[69] Therefore, when Kara begins to embody masculine tropes of leadership or heroics—including individualism, rage, or domination—her companions and the show's narrative mark these behaviors as problematic and requiring intervention. Lena accuses Supergirl in season 4 of having a "God complex" because the hero objects to Lena manufacturing synthetic Kryptonite, even if it is to help stop Reign (rather than hurt Supergirl).[70] But it is Lena in the following season who believes that she alone has the technology and intellect to save humanity from itself, telling her cyborg assistant, Hope: "Who needs friends when you can save the world?"[71] While her intentions are well-meaning, Lena's myopic devotion to her goal and her insistence that she is better off without friends after revelations of Kara's dishonesty play right into her brother's hand. Only when she tries to do things alone does she begins to take on the much-maligned "Luthor" traits exhibited by her mother and brother: self-righteous arrogance, manipulative backstabbing, and an insistence that the end justifies the means.

The seasons-long anxiety over Kara's identity and Lena's sense of betrayal exemplifies the dangers of thwarted truths and restricted knowledge, as well as the vulnerabilities inherent in relationships bound by a sense of belonging and deep, "sisterly" trust. Two related scenes in the show's fifth season help illustrate the vicissitudes of the Kara/Lena split, although the better part of three seasons addresses aspects of the conflict around Kara's identity and Lena's knowledge of it, or lack thereof. At the start of the fifth season, Kara tearfully confesses her secret to Lena just prior to receiving a Pulitzer Prize for her exposé on Lex's attempt at world domination.[72] Unbeknownst to Kara, Lena already knows because Lex taunted her with the secret just prior to his death (Lena shoots him, believing him dead, although a series of later events result in his return). Intending to "out" Kara at the ceremony, Lena has a momentary change of heart, instead deciding to milk Kara's guilt as long as possible by asking her to perform tasks requiring her special skill set as a superhero, including stealing Lex's journals from a federal facility and having Supergirl rescue her from situations in which Lena puts herself in danger unnecessarily. Six episodes later, Lena confesses that she knew about Kara's identity for weeks before the ceremony, has been manipulating her, and will never forgive her for her betrayals.[73]

These scenes offer compelling visual and symbolic fodder for an understanding of Kara's struggles with her identity and her morality, especially her public declarations as to the imperative of truth and justice and her private need for secrecy, which other antagonists also attempt to exploit.[74] It is no coincidence that Kara's tearful confession at the ceremony occurs while she is dressed as Kara and about to receive public acknowledgment of her human talent and integrity while Lena's later accusation occurs when the two women are alone, with Kara dressed as Supergirl, in the frosty confines of the Fortress of Solitude, an Arctic hideout containing alien weaponry and Kryptonian records. Both scenes are deeply emotional, the former governed by close-ups of the two women's faces, Kara's teary and urgent throughout her confession and Lena's stunned. As Kara explains how she first kept Lena in the dark to protect her, then later because she was a coward, worried the truth would ruin their friendship as Lena's acrimony with Supergirl surfaced, the shots tighten further on her face, blurring the opulent background where the ceremony is taking place. Kara and Lena stand close together, the lighting warm and hazy, but Lena walks away without responding, leaving Kara to frantically wipe the tears from her eyes. Despite this seeming dismissal, Lena publicly praises Kara moments later during the ceremony for her commitment to the truth even though "the truth isn't easy and certainly not for the faint of heart." In this moment, Kara's visible relief and the tearful smiles and eye contact between the women offer the possibility of reconciliation.

However, in the parallel confession scene several episodes later, Lena traps Kara using Kryptonite in the Fortress of Solitude and then lambasts her erstwhile friend with accusations of bad faith: "I confided in you that everyone in my past had betrayed me. And how much it hurt to have someone you love lie to you and betray you. I spelled it out to you over and over again, essentially begging you not to violate my trust. . . . And all the while there wasn't a single honest moment in our friendship." When Kara protests Lena's assessment, Lena screams at her, admitting that she killed Lex for Kara, to protect her and their friends, which only served to cement her heartbreak when she learned the truth. This scene contrasts sharply with Kara's confession, now dominated by dark, unnatural blue lighting, deep shadows, and the reflections of the ice walls that surround them. The camera focuses sharply on Kara and Lena in turn, employing canted angles, lens flares, and fog in primarily medium shots with the desolate isolation of the background looming behind each woman. These scenes emphasize both rhetorically and visually the depth of emotion between Kara and Lena and the dangers of reliance on the exact extrafamilial bonds of solidarity and belonging central to Kara's ethos.

FIGURE 3.2. Kara and Lena embrace just prior to Kara accepting her Pulitzer Prize for Journalism. Lena, heartbroken over Kara's lying about her secret identity, has nevertheless decided not to "out" Kara as Supergirl, for the moment. *Supergirl* (2015–2021), episode 5.1, "Event Horizon," CW, aired 6 October 2019.

Alex comforts her sister in the following episode, although her explanation evinces a slippage around the function of "family" and where exactly Lena belongs: "You were damned either way, Kara. Your choice to conceal your identity, it wasn't born out of a place of maliciousness. It was born out of love and compassion. And you were just trying to protect your family; you were trying to protect Lena from people who could use that information to hurt us."[75] Who, here, was Kara trying to protect? Alex and the other Superfriends, who all knew her identity far earlier? Or is Lena part of the family Alex references, part of the "us"? The lack of clarity in Alex's reassurance echoes the perplexing nature of Kara's secrecy to begin with, as there are no discernible reasons early in their friendship to explain why she would not tell the other woman her secret except for the fact that she is a Luthor (by contrast, Kara tells her friends James Olsen [Mehcad Brooks] and Winn Schott [Jeremy Jordan] almost immediately in season 1). Certainly owing in part to the *deus ex machina* of the television writer—the tension between Kara and Lena provides several seasons' worth of dramatic fodder, after all—*Supergirl* also attempts to address this conundrum of the delayed confession in its hundredth episode. Devoted entirely to Kara trying to right the wrongs of her omission, the episode features a wish-granting imp, Mxy, who offers her the chance to change the timeline by confessing to Lena earlier in their friendship.[76] Ultimately, Kara discovers that there was no "right" time to confess—her other attempts go horribly wrong, with alternate timelines resulting in catastrophes even more terrible than the rift in Lena and Kara's friendship: Kara's death, the simultaneous deaths of both Lena and Mon-El, the systematic assassination of every one of Kara's allies, and a truly evil Lena attempting world domination. From these alternate realities, Kara deduces that Alex was correct: her secret had to be kept from Lena's for everyone's protection. Kara devoting this life-changing wish, one that ultimately cannot be fulfilled, to attempting to repair her friendship with Lena, only further denotes how the show leans heavily on the importance of their bond as symbolic of a deeper struggle Kara faces with her identity as both alien and human, both hero and woman. While *Supergirl* emphasizes the significance of female friendships, sisterhood, and belonging, it simultaneously exploits these forms of unity as vulnerabilities. Moreover, Kara's collaborative ethos and reliance on networks of friends and family function symbolically as aspects of what makes her a *different* kind of hero for a progressive America, one governed by ostensibly feminine ethics of compassion and altruism.

"HOPE, HELP AND COMPASSION FOR ALL": FROM EXCEPTIONALISM TO EMPOWERING OTHERS

Leading up to Kara's Pulitzer Prize, much of season 4 focuses on Supergirl's attempts to protect her fellow aliens, who come under attack when President Marsdin is outed as an alien and forced to step down, and Kara's attempts to expose the anti-alien domestic terror group Children of Liberty via her investigative reporting. Tackling two sides of the same anti-alien movement through the strategic use of her two identities, Kara must negotiate her privilege as a humanoid alien with no identifiable difference from humans in a landscape in which aliens are trying to live openly and are often punished for their difference. A clear metaphor against anti-immigration policy, white supremacy, and race-based violence, Kara's encounters with the Children of Liberty offer a compelling concluding storyline to showcase how *Supergirl* aligns its heroine with an idealistic new progressivism and auspices of a reframed American Dream. This is then echoed in the final season, in which racial injustice is again used as a metaphor for injustice against aliens. As we shall see from these interrelated storylines, the show underscores contemporary values regarding feminist intersectionality and social justice but does so at the expense of Kara's agency, suggesting that coming-of-age for a hero like Supergirl means relinquishing key aspects of one's power and reframing one's identity to match.

Before tackling the Children of Liberty, we should take a moment to consider how Alex and Kara are tested in their resolve toward widespread (social) justice when other characters' intersectional experiences of oppression challenge their knowledge and its attendant values. Despite her own uncertainty, Alex's coming-out experience in season 2 is notably smooth, with all her friends and family immediately embracing her after her revelation. Kara even apologizes to Alex "for not creating an environment" where they could talk about Alex's feelings, with so much of their youth dominated by Kara's adjustment to human life. She further acknowledges that Alex's experience is unique, while reminding her sister of their affinity; after all, Kara is well aware of "how lonely [it] can make you feel" to hide a part of your identity.[77] In the following season, the show further nuances this discussion of sexual orientation with a storyline involving Alex's Latinx girlfriend, Maggie Sawyer (Floriana Lima), who is secure in her sexuality but estranged from the family that disowned her at fourteen. Maggie's father tries to reconcile with her but ultimately storms out of her bridal shower, seeing his daughter's lesbianism as an insult to his efforts to become a normative American citizen and telling Maggie that "the only thing they hate more than a Mexicano is a homosexual."[78] Maggie's family drama marks the show's clear attempt to signpost its commitment to progressive politics and acknowledgment of the complexities of intersectional experience—even referencing Trump's border wall in this episode despite the fact that Trump is not president within the fictional universe of *Supergirl*.

Much later, in season 6, Alex's then fiancée, Kelly Olsen (Azie Tesfai), a human psychologist and social worker who eventually adopts the mantle of the hero Guardian from her brother James, criticizes both Alex's and Kara's myopic attendance to large-scale superhero work when there are people suffering in poor communities in National City whose plight is being largely ignored. Kelly accuses the Superfriends of refusing to listen to the voices of the oppressed Black and brown people who "look like her" and who actually have valuable insight into what kind of intervention is needed in their neighborhood, currently under attack by an energy-zapping alien housed in the body of a scheming councilwoman.[79] "While you all have the luxury of focusing on tomorrow, they are barely surviving today," Kelly tells Kara in an emotional confrontation. Referring implicitly to the Black Lives Matter protests of the summer of 2020 and subsequent related activism, Kelly urges white allies like Kara and Alex to consider the needs of those they purport to help. Heavy-handed in a way unsurprising for a youth-centered show, the episode foregrounds Kelly's needs even in her personal life, as she admits to Alex how the trauma of racial injustice bears down on her. Toward the end of the episode, costuming and props underscore explicit attempts by the show to broaden how it includes those who are grappling with intersecting marginalized identities. At home awaiting Alex, Kelly attempts to unwind with her hair wrapped and in a robe over a prominently displayed "Say Her Name" black T-shirt with white lettering and an upraised fist. She discovers two new books on the coffee table, Ta-Nehisi Coates's *Between the World and Me* and Robin DiAngelo's *White Fragility*, corroborating Alex's earlier discussion with her Martian mentor, J'onn J'onzz (David Harewood), about how she wants to connect with Kelly despite their racial differences. When Alex returns to their apartment, Kelly admits to being "tired of fighting for something that we should all be innately fighting for," and she subsequently chooses to embrace a Pan-African aesthetic for her Guardian costume, now black and gold with built-in braids as part of its mask headdress. While this episode is the most prominent example of the show's negotiation of the Black Lives Matter movement and racial justice, earlier episodes tackle the experiences of other Black characters like James and J'onn in more tangential ways.[80]

Supergirl acknowledges human forms of identity-based oppression while simultaneously embracing the common science fiction and fantasy trope in which experiences of marginalization related to race, class, or sexuality are transposed onto supernatural or alien Others who must contend with their differences from humanity as a broad identity category. Notably, in many of these instances, humanity becomes synonymous with femininity, wherein characters' must adopt femininely coded forms of knowledge and power in order to reconcile conflicts in their identities or community belonging. We can see these aims at intersectional feminism and social justice–oriented progressivism illustrated in another notable character on the series. In season 4, Kara begins to mentor a young journalist, Nia Nal (Nicole Maines), whom she quickly learns is a mixed-species human-alien with a matrilineal set of powers that allow her to tap into dream energy. Nia, adopting the superhero moniker Dreamer, is openly transgender, and several storylines in the latter three seasons not only address the harassment Nia faces as an alien and a trans woman but also assert the legitimacy of her womanhood. Early in the character's development, family drama erupts when Nia's sister Maeve (Hannah James) discovers that Nia has inherited their mother's dream powers instead of her despite not being, in Maeve's words, "a real woman."[81] In counterpoint to Maeve's transphobia, *Supergirl* frames Nia as an unequivocal woman, both by emphasizing how her family's powers pass down to her as a daughter but also in smaller ways, such as the brief but prominent use of Lenny Kravitz's "American Woman" as the soundtrack for a major fight scene Nia undertakes as Dreamer.[82] Nia/Dreamer's introduction also coincides with the season-long arc featuring the anti-alien group Children of Liberty, making her character a direct referent for violence against trans women as well as a metaphor for the U.S. DREAM Act and its attendant backlash of hatred toward immigrants (Nia was born in the United States to an alien mother and a human father).[83] Indeed, she even faces deportation alongside other aliens in season 4.[84] While Kara and her friends immediately accept her and do not manifest even the slightest transphobia, Nia eventually must take Kara to task for the ways Supergirl's sense of justice lacks nuance, making little room for Nia's rage at the way the trans community has been and continues to be attacked.[85]

The first episode of the fourth season, "American Alien," sees the introduction of Nia's character alongside a dichotomous plotline that highlights Kara's privilege and sets up the dissolution of her attempts to delineate strictly between her two personas. Kara starts the episode by announcing, "For the first time in my life, I've got everything under control" and asserting hope for the improvement of alien acceptance into U.S. society because of President Marsdin's recently enacted Alien Amnesty Act, but J'onn cautions that many aliens do not share her optimism. Some aliens, those with less humanoid features, have been using image inducers to change their appearance to avoid harassment and attack, contradicting Kara's careless assessment that "the world is better than it's ever been," with "more diversity, more acceptance." Naturally, Kara eventually discovers that J'onn is correct and becomes overwhelmed with the level of hatred she witnesses toward aliens with more distinguishing features than her invisible powers. Even so, J'onn asserts that Kara's optimism "will help save us," since Supergirl is a "beacon of hope that sets an example, fighting for justice everywhere. The voice of unity and compassion that will inspire change." In the following episode, a prominent moment of symbolism seems to corroborate J'onn's assertion.[86] During a protest against the president, in which protesters call aliens "roaches" and counterprotesters chant, "peace for all," Supergirl swoops in to protect the crowd when a runaway news van crashes into a large flagpole, causing it to topple. She catches the pole before it can crush the surrounding protesters, cracking the pavement with the force of her landing and briefly halting the scuffle. In a brief wide shot in front of the White House, Supergirl stands, one hand holding the American flag, the other on her hip in a show of defiance, her perfectly coifed hair blowing in the breeze. The protesters gape at her in silent awe, momentarily distracted from their chanting and fighting. At the end of the episode, Supergirl addresses the nation in a live news broadcast, proudly proclaiming, "I'm an alien, and I love this planet that I am proud to call home. I want what we all want, to be a good American," further cementing the immigration metaphor that dominates season 4. The episodes in the first half of this season address a spectrum of responses to the relationship between aliens and humans, from the corrupt U.S. government's pro-human stance and Lena's experiments to see if she can find a way to give humans superpowers to a militant alien rights group known as the Elite who are set on defending aliens by any means necessary. Asserting herself as pro-justice, rather than pro-human or pro-alien, Supergirl fights back against both the Children of Liberty and the Elite, proclaiming herself a peace-loving American citizen first and foremost.

Part and parcel of Supergirl's ethos is her ability to inspire hope and enact change through compassion, as J'onn proclaims and as we see carried out in other episodes. For example, in several prominent incidents, Supergirl uses her powers of persuasive speech to convince billions of people to save themselves through the sheer force of her optimism and creation of a sense of empathy and belonging.[87] In these moments, Kara forms connections not based on the strength of her alien powers or her heroism but via her feminine/human markers of compassion and empathy. To wit, in the conclusion of the Children of Liberty storyline halfway through season 4, Kara is finally able to bring people together under the banner of American compassionate progressivism by agreeing to walk with the alien protesters dressed not as Supergirl but as Kara Zor-el—not quite forgoing her secret identity but swapping her Supergirl uniform for Kryptonian robes to mark her as a person rather than a hero. She does this at the urging of Brainy (Jesse Rath), one of the Superfriends, who invokes the motto *el mayarah* and tells Kara, "In times like this, change won't come from someone with a ring or a cape. It will only come when each one of us answers the call to stand up and be heard. *El mayarah*. Stronger together. Just because we're superheroes, doesn't mean we forget who we are."

FIGURE 3.3. Supergirl catches a flagpole about to crush demonstrators outside the White House, where a protest has broken out over the resignation of President Olivia Marsdin after the revelation that she is an alien. *Supergirl* (2015–2021), episode 4.2, "Fallout," CW, aired 21 October 2018.

When the anti-alien Ben Lockwood attempts to incite violence at the rally, spurred on by the presence of the Elite, average human and alien citizens unite to help each other escape the violence rather than take part in it. Supergirl and her friends also join the fray as helpers rather than fighters, and James takes photos for CatCo to show how humans and aliens can come together. Like other invocations of unity and collective empowerment on the show, the conclusion of the Children of Liberty storyline suggests the power of the press and the power of the people are more significant than the power of the superhero.[88]

In fighting the Children of Liberty, Supergirl must contend with several intersecting threats. While the Children of Liberty systematically target and attack aliens and those who support them, Lockwood, a radicalized nativist history professor (who goes by the alias Agent Liberty and leads the terrorist organization in secret), channels his twisted knowledge of America's past to influence public opinion via biased political news segments and, eventually, infiltrating the U.S. government. Right-wing media spins Lockwood's approach as "human rights activism," and the DEO takes a hard line against defending aliens from the Children of Liberty's attacks, with its new director Colonel Lauren Haley (April Parker Jones) insisting that the organization's role is to protect humans from aliens, not the other way around. Ultimately, Supergirl discovers that she cannot fight the Children of Liberty using her usual powers, as any forms of physical defense are willfully misinterpreted as alien aggression. While she bests the Children of Liberty with nonviolent protest, Lex capitalizes on the latent fear around alien powers in the second half of the season to manifest a plan to demonize Supergirl and make himself a hero. In doing so, he uses a brainwashed Kaznian Kara-clone, Ryzhaya Dch/Red Daughter to masquerade as Supergirl, causing the new anti-alien U.S. president to accuse Supergirl of terrorism and driving Kara and the Superfriends underground.[89] Here, again, we see *Supergirl* making explicit references to contemporary politics, as the actions of both Ben Lockwood (e.g., his anti-alien rhetoric and nativist cable news rants) and Lex Luthor (e.g., alien deportation and collusion with the Russian-speaking Kaznians) echo real-life events surrounding Donald Trump's presidency—up to and including Kara winning a Pulitzer Prize for her investigative reporting exposing Lex.[90] However, unlike in real U.S. political life, Lex eventually fails because Kara's moral compass is so unwavering that it remains embodied even in her radicalized clone. When Lex ultimately betrays Red Daughter to glorify himself, she recognizes that he never had the best interests of her country at heart; this, in addition to her unbidden affinity for Lena and Alex, whom she has been taught to hate but still finds herself drawn toward, catalyzes Red Daughter's ultimate sacrifice when she saves Kara to stop Lex. Again, sisterhood and belonging resonate as innate and immutable forces driving Red Daughter's sacrificial actions, even without access to Kara's experiences in order to undergird her feelings of affinity for these other women. Invoking Supergirl's ethos of protection, love, and belonging, she tells Kara with her dying breath, "Protect your people as I protected mine."[91]

There is little question that Supergirl is an unmatched powerhouse when it comes to her strength, endurance, and speed; the show emphasizes time and again how she is stronger than her cousin Superman, tougher than the sternest of super-powered criminals, and nearly as fast as The Flash.[92] Even when confronted with Overgirl, an evil, Nazi version of herself from an alternate universe, wearing dark lipstick and a black and red suit with a sigil that forms an ominous pair of SS-shaped bolts inside the familiar shield crest, Kara ultimately comes out on top. Overgirl accuses Supergirl of being a "perversion" for squandering her potential, "the most powerful being on the planet rendered weak by saccharine Americana."[93] The ironic twist of their encounter is that Overgirl has been overpowered by solar radiation and kidnaps Kara so she can steal the hero's healthy heart. Supported by her friends, both human and alien, powered and "normal," Kara escapes Overgirl's machinations, and the latter explodes like a dying star.[94] Despite all these overt acknowledgments of Kara's strength and superlative powers, the ways in which she falters often stem from situations in which her physical powers are useless or used against her; her emotional vulnerabilities, including her compassion, altruism, and insistence on maintaining her secret identity to protect those she loves, can have equally devastating consequences for Kara and those around her, as we have seen. Certainly, a show in which a superpowered alien blasts away her enemies in every episode with no variation and no challenges would make for exceptionally boring television, so it is no surprise that *Supergirl* developed a host of threats for its characters to face that offered unusual challenges to Supergirl's superpowers. However, the series finale points to ways that the show's ethos of collaborative power and belonging, alongside its social justice bona fides, also serve to de-power Supergirl, suggesting that one aspect of coming-of-age for powerful women is to learn that the prospect of coming into the self often requires the relinquishment of some agency and control.

Season 6 is a muddied final installment for *Supergirl*, as its plotlines are difficult to codify and not always coherent when taken together in an arc; part of this may have to do with the COVID-19 pandemic, which disrupted the film and television industry throughout 2020 and 2021. Nevertheless, if one could draw out a motif in the sixth season, it would seem to be how Kara continually fails at tasks where she previously excelled; her power ultimately redistributes itself among her friends and allies, and she experiences a traumatic loss of powers during six episodes spent in the Phantom Zone. For example, in a race to acquire the Courage Totem, a magical vessel Kara and the Superfriends are attempting to keep from the villain Nxly, Kara fails the totem's gauntlet despite the fact that courage is something Supergirl has in spades by any metric.[95] In the series finale, Kara laments to Lena, "I'm supposed to be the strongest person on Earth, but I think I'm actually the weakest," and confides that she realized she could not pass the gauntlet precisely because she has been hiding who she is for her entire life.[96] At many points, it is Kara's refusal of this specific kind of emotional vulnerability—admitting her identity as Supergirl—that makes her weak, which we see most starkly realized during Kara's rift with Lena but then echoed in her failure to pass this particular gauntlet.

The first half of the series finale includes an epic battle against Lex and Nxly but also employs many of Supergirl's earlier nemeses and the assistance of all the Superfriends, plus other allies like Mon-El. The second half is dominated by Alex's wedding, marking the division of *Supergirl* as part action-adventure, part coming-of-age drama, although Kara does not get to partake in the series' romance plots with the exception of her relationship with Mon-El in season 2. In the first half of the episode, color and tone alongside Supergirl's emotive and affective powers of speech illustrate this ostensible transfer of power from one hero to many. Lex and Nxly prove powerful enemies, slowly draining the global population of their life force. Having watched aliens and humans alike band together to try to fight back, Supergirl rallies the Superfriends, admitting to them her ultimate failure: "My whole life as Supergirl has been built on a premise that is deeply flawed. . . . I've been driven by this idea that people need to be rescued, that it was my job, my mission, to save them. I believed it was my calling to be Earth's hero. It's just so clear to me now. We don't need to be heroes. We need to be partners. And we need to actively empower every single person to be the hero of their own life." Mirroring meme wisdom to "be your own hero," Kara's speech is met by immediate agreement from the Superfriends, even as it fundamentally invalidates much of their and Supergirl's prior ethos. Aided by Lena's magic to make people emotionally responsive and Brainy's thirty-first-century communication technology, Supergirl creates a worldwide telepathic broadcast to the people of Earth, who have literally started to gray out, becoming desaturated of color and despondent as their life force drains. She extols the people to empower themselves. "Together we will shine," Supergirl proclaims with passion as people hear her message and begin to regain lifelike color tones again. "Together, we will be unstoppable. Together we will create a better world." Using words instead of brute force, Supergirl rallies the people of the world; as their power grows, that of Lex and Nxly diminishes, allowing the Superfriends and their many allies a final victory.

In the second half of the series finale, we see Kara's friends setting up foundations to help people, organizations that mesh with their superhero skills and recognize the real-life social justice issues different characters represent. Lena founds the Lena Luthor Foundation, the logo of which suggests its dedication to environmental sustainability; Alex and J'onn spearhead a newly revamped DEO championing alien-human cooperation and national defense; former CatCo editor Andrea Rojas (Julie Gonzalo) founds a Spanish-language journalism school in honor of fallen colleague William Dey (Staz Nair); and Dreamer opens the Center for LGBTQ Outreach. Kara, however, remains at a loss. She cannot even save a kitten caught in a tree because average citizens band together to do it themselves instead of calling for Supergirl's aid. "Everybody is so empowered," Kara tells Alex, "and I feel less powerful than ever." The lead-up to her sister's wedding and the event itself are dominated by Kara's dialogic working through of her problems in conversation with each of her friends in turn and catalyzed by an out-of-the-blue offer from Cat to become CatCo's new editor in chief. Contradicting James's assurance from the first season that the people of National City need a hero, Alex urges Kara to remember that she does not have to protect humanity on her own.[97] Cat, in turn, tells Kara that she has known her erstwhile assistant was Supergirl for quite some time; in response to Kara's insistence that "the two parts of me just don't really go together," Cat offers that Kara may feel "bifurcated" or "inauthentic," but that she has the power to change her life—a frequent mantra from Cat in the first season. At last, it is Lena who codifies these points, helping Kara realize that she has another option, that of relinquishing the division between her personas. In their conversation at Alex's wedding, Kara helplessly concedes that she does not know how to take Cat's job offer, admitting that hiding "behind these glasses . . . [has] gotten in the way of every job I've ever had, everything I've ever wanted to do, every relationship, every friendship." Worried, as always, about the danger of hurting others, Kara ultimately accepts Lena's exaltation that "you can't always be our savior" and breaks down in tears when Lena urges her friend to remember that they handle all conflicts together, again invoking the Kryptonian motto, el mayarah. The episode ends with a televised interview between Cat and Kara, in which Supergirl finally comes out, relinquishing her secret identity for good as the reporter and the superhero become one. Fleetwood Mac's "Landslide" dominates the soundtrack in these final moments, exalting the melancholy but necessary impacts of coming-of-age as Kara steps into a new identity as her whole self.[98]

While Kara Danvers coming out as Supergirl functions as a compelling ending for the series and wraps up seasons' worth of anxiety about Kara's identity, it also effectively undermines many of the struggles Kara overcame in the previous seasons. In the end, we are left with Supergirl's potential as she comes of age and embraces her identity, but none of the payout regarding what this new form of empowerment might look like. By reconciling her two identities, Kara also joins her alien otherness—sometimes rendered through masculinist terms—with her human normativity, often marked by her emotions and state of belonging. Throughout the series, *Supergirl* transforms the classic Superman motto, "Truth, Justice and the American Way" into "Hope, Help and Compassion for All," a mantra Kara offers frequently, particularly in the latter two seasons.[99] It is in this avowal of hope that we can most vividly see how the auspices of feminine intuition undergird the many trials and tribulations Kara must face, as well as the open-ended nature of the show's finale. While shifting linguistically away from the "American Way" of Superman's tenure, the symbolism of the show still conveys Supergirl as an American ideal, even if the America she purports to represent has been lost along with way. The democratization of power made explicit in the finale only reifies this concept, that Supergirl, like Barack Obama, has the "audacity [to] hope" for a better future in which heroes help rather than dominate.[100] These are certainly not unworthy goals; my contention, however, rests in the understanding that this relinquishment of power comes from a particularly intuitive and feminine place in which peace, altruism, collaboration, and compassion govern action. Moreover, throughout the show—and particularly in this finale—Kara's ostensible mastery over her powers, her self-worth, and even whether she is needed as a hero destabilize along the same fault lines as their conception. If Supergirl is a "personification of the American way," as she tells Mon-El, then it is precisely those bastions of idealistic citizenship and the abdication of self in favor of democracy that cause her the most distress.

In *Against Citizenship*, Amy Brandzel argues "that there is nothing redeemable about citizenship, nothing worth salvaging or sustaining in the name of 'community,' practice, or belonging. Citizenship is, inherently, a normativizing project— a project that regulates and disciplines the social body in order to produce model identities and hegemonic knowledge claims."[101] Despite its visible and explicit efforts toward diversity and inclusion in both casting and narrative, *Supergirl* hews to a kind of normative project of citizenship—eliding alien differences, literal and figurative, in favor of a model of intersectional sisterhood and community empowerment that, while arguably feminist, comes about in such a way that it undercuts the power of its eponymous heroine. By insisting on privileging feminine models of heroism as central to its character's coming-of-age—and forestalling viewers' ability to see what becomes of the character once she has reconciled her split identity and fully embraced "who she is"—*Supergirl* reifies normative conventions of feminine embodiment and links them to notions of proper citizenship. That said, as we will see in the second half of this book, even franchises that rely on the undoing of the social order, rather than its maintenance, still fall back on models in which women's power stems from feminine forms of intuited or embodied knowledge.

4 · MOTHERHOOD AND MYTH
Inside and Outside the Family Circle

"How wonderful to bring a man into the world!" they say; we have seen that they dream of engendering a "hero," and the hero is obviously of the male sex. A son will be a leader of men, a soldier, a creator; he will bend the world to his will and his mother will share his immortal fame.... Through him she will possess the world—but only on condition that she possess her son. Thence comes the paradox of her attitude.

—Simone de Beauvoir, *The Second Sex*

War and childbirth are recognized in classical thought as two moments when the fabric of the social order is rent. Unlike today when, against all the bloody evidence, armies and mothers—lynchpins of the social order; although at opposite poles of the human spectrum—are called upon to secure our futures and make a precarious, dangerous world feel safe.

—Jacqueline Rose, *Mothers: An Essay on Love and Cruelty*

While it was not the focus of the previous chapter, *Supergirl* plays out against a backdrop of significant trauma related to mothers and family: Kara Zor-El is forced to leave the dying Krypton as a young teen, only to be stranded in the Phantom Zone "replaying the destruction of [her] planet for nearly a decade," including the presumed death of her parents, before crash-landing on Earth and having to adapt to a new family and a life full of superpowers and secrecy.[1] Her adoptive sister, Alex, struggles to balance her desires for motherhood with her personal relationships and with the high-stress, dangerous nature of her job.[2] The mother of Kara's only major love interest on the series, Queen Rhea of Daxam, attempts to kill Supergirl and take over Earth. And, as a child, Lena Luthor watched her biological mother drown only to be adopted by the Luthors and find herself the frequent victim of their machinations and betrayals: an adversary of her alien-hating stepmother and a target of assassination attempts by her megalomaniacal brother. As such, there is no question that motherhood, family, and their attendant complexities of love and loss haunt *Supergirl*, but, in this coming-of-age narrative with a twentysomething protagonist, issues of the maternal are mostly on the periphery, primarily affecting characters in terms of their relationship to parental figures. Whereas *Supergirl* ends with a hopeful rendering of future promise—despite the trauma of the past, characters can move forward to embrace their identities and, thus, ostensibly inspire change and hope—the franchises I explore in the second half of this book take a much darker turn as they reflect the possibilities of the future. In both the *Terminator* and the *Resident Evil* franchises (I discuss the latter in chapter 5), characters grapple with terrible, apocalyptic landscapes of both the present and the future. They are filled with dread instead of promise and battle foes that are institutional and widespread, the horrors of the world writ large to accommodate our deepest nightmares.

The much-lauded forty-year-spanning *Terminator* franchise (films: 1984, 1991, 2003, 2009, 2015, 2019; TV: 2008–2009) brings us the recurring protagonist Sarah Connor. In the early films, Sarah evolves from mousy nobody to mother of the savior of all humankind, continually forced to defend her son, John, from cybernetic assassins who want to bring about a future apocalypse. This chapter focuses on the more recent installments from the franchise, including the television show *Terminator: The Sarah Connor Chronicles* (2008), which showcases Sarah's relationship with John and with her maternal responsibilities as a fighter, the reframing of Sarah's role in *Terminator: Genisys* (2015), and the revision and expansion of women's roles in the latest film, *Terminator: Dark Fate* (2019), in which John is removed from the narrative in favor of a young woman who shares a similar destiny.[3] I touch on the other films, primarily to set up Sarah's backstory and reference the rich theoretical ground on which I construct my own analysis, but also to acknowledge a broader argument around the role of women in war and how the auspices of motherhood and maternal intuition shape cultural understandings of these roles whether or not individual women are mothers.

When we consider how feminine forms of knowledge and power are welcomed and perpetuated by the cultural imaginary, motherhood presents treacherous terrain. Mothers are simultaneously venerated and dismissed, as well as subjected to the many idioms that involve special maternal ability: mama bear, tiger mom, mama's boy, mother hen, mothers having eyes in the backs of their heads, and so on. In what follows, I address the mythology surrounding motherhood as the ostensible pinnacle of feminine identity and purpose by considering the *Terminator* franchise's founding principles, in which a mother's defense of her son both explicitly and implicitly serves as an allegory for her defense of democracy and freedom and the sanctity of human life. At the same time, the *Terminator* films and show sanction murder, torture, vigilante justice, and other forms of violent behavior in the name of motherhood and maternal desires to protect the vulnerable. Despite her initial misgivings about motherhood, Sarah turns out to be an imminently capable mother-warrior; she will destroy anything that threatens her son, who is coded symbolically as an embodiment of life, freedom, and prosperity—for the family, the nation, or the world. Revealed herein is a trend in contemporary U.S. social discourse that mythologizes mothers as a special class of citizen both burdened and gifted with a myopic dedication to their children, which I consider alongside discussions of the fraught relationship between women, femininity, and global conflict in the real world.

"DO I LOOK LIKE THE MOTHER OF THE FUTURE?": THE MYTH OF MOTHERHOOD AND THE ORIGINS OF THE HERO

Mothers and motherhood, as a group of people and a state of being, are bound up in a complex intersecting web of assumptions and assertions, most of which will be familiar to us regardless of whether we ourselves are mothers or whether we believe that individual mothers should or should not hew to these traits. Mothers may poke and pry and nag their children, who, in turn, may groan and roll their eyes, sighing "Oh, mom," but, in the end, cultural production and social norms assert that it is the mother's prerogative to police the behavior of her children. Eye rolls and grunts of protest are no match for a maternal stare. However, while the epitomic mother may have leave over her children, her position of privilege within the world at large, insomuch as she has any at all, is far more tenuous. The mother, writes Jane Gallop, is the "receiver of the child's discourse," and her engagement with the world thus reflects her motherhood.[4] By extension, in order for a mother's actions—especially those that tread outside the norms of proprietary—to be sanctioned by society, what she does must be for the good of her children. This myth of motherhood—that mothers are supposed to be nurturing, giving, self-sacrificing, caring, loving, and dedicated (to their children)—prevails through much of Western literature and popular culture and has been thoughtfully and tirelessly explicated by philosophers, sociologists, psychologists, historians, and other scholars. As with endemic topics like the nature of gender roles or feminist ideology in prior chapters, I have no intention of exhaustively rehashing the substantial work that has come before. Instead, I wish to emphasize a central component of these accounts as it pertains to the question of feminine knowledge and power: the role of the mother in relation to the child and the fostering of heroic, extraordinary action, whether in the child or in herself.

As Jennifer Baumgardner and Amy Richards astutely summarize in their third-wave feminist *Manifesta*, "A patriarchal society expects mothers to be totally giving and available, downplaying their own needs, ambitions, and desires, as well as fears and guilts."[5] Certainly, we can see this rhetoric play out anecdotally and in media representation, even if many individuals push back against this notion of altruistic self-effacement. Andrea O'Reilly, whose scholarly work focuses in myriad ways on the structural, social, and ideological frameworks of motherhood, elaborates further that "patriarchal motherhood causes motherwork to be oppressive to women because it necessitates the repression or denial of the mother's own selfhood; as well, it assigns mothers all the responsibility for mothering but gives them no real power. Such 'powerless responsibility,' to use Rich's term, denies a mother the authority and agency to determine her own experiences of mothering."[6] This concurring assertion of responsibility and denial of power underscores a vexing question for the relationship of the mother both to her child and to the systems at work in her life that affect her agency as person and mother. The ongoing and volatile debates over reproductive rights, abortion, and the rights of those who are pregnant versus the rights of (unborn) children in the United States only make these tensions more fraught.

The relationship between child and mother is structured around power and negotiations over how that power should be balanced. In the first few years, the mother has tremendous direct power over her child, often causing dissent in later years in relation to minor matters of bedtime and screen usage; she simultaneously has very little power over the child's future beyond that which she can immediately impact, a vanishingly small zone of influence as the child ages into public life. This push-pull of the mother-child relationship and its inherent fusion of love and cruelty take center stage in Jacqueline Rose's 2018 book-length essay, in which she articulates how "at the very moment a mother appears to be acquiring a new power she immediately has to cede it. She owns but does not own. She engenders a life only in so far as it escapes."[7] This begs the question, Rose explains, following a line of thought she gleans from philosopher Simone de Beauvoir, whether the mother would be better off without the child after all. To return to Beauvoir: "The relation of mother to child becomes more and more complex: the child is a double, an *alter ego*, into whom the mother is sometimes tempted to project herself entirely, but he is an independent subject and therefore rebellious; he is intensely real today, but in imagination he is the adolescent and adult of the future. He is a rich possession, a treasure, but also a charge upon her, a tyrant."[8] This imagined futurity in the mother-child relationship and the dynamic via which the mother projects herself onto his survival, according to Beauvoir, only to be eventually rejected or left behind, is something we see viscerally represented in the first two *Terminator* films and the television show. Furthermore, I argue that the mother-child dualism of the franchise offers an extended metaphor in which the social fabric of the nation—or even humanity writ large—must be protected from imagined destruction by precisely those subjects who do not cleanly fit into its present-day narratives of conformity.

Andrea O'Reilly and Marie Porter, in their introduction to a collection of essays on motherhood and power, consider that motherhood can function as "transformative power," as a "positive expression of power that seeks its own obsolescence."[9] Here, again, we have an emphasis on maternal power as a loss, as self-effacement or self-sacrifice. Mothers are also often configured as creators of life, as Adrienne Rich famously declares in *Of Woman Born*: "The power of the mother has two aspects: the biological potential or capacity to bear and nourish human life, and the magical power invested in women by men, whether in the form of Goddess-worship or the fear of being controlled and overwhelmed by women."[10] A clear example of this dichotomy jumps from the midpoint of *Terminator 2: Judg-*

ment Day, when Sarah herself asserts women's powers of creation only to be cut off by her own son. Lambasting scientist Miles Dyson for the unwitting part he will play in the coming apocalypse, Sarah rants, "Fucking men like you built the hydrogen bomb. Men like you thought it up. You think you're so creative. You don't know what it's like to really create something; to create a life; to feel it growing inside you. All you know how to create is death and destruction." Between the maw of the words *death* and *destruction*, John talks over Sarah, trying to pacify his mother in a way only the self-righteous innocence of the child could allow. Sarah is full of justified rage, but John—not yet beset by the horrors of adulthood—still believes in the ultimate worth of humanity.

In *Civilization and Its Discontents*, written in the first two decades of the twentieth century, Sigmund Freud binds women to the "family" and "sexual life" as a way to explain the "hostile attitude" he assigns women vis-à-vis civilization, which is "increasingly the business of men." While he offers the rather insulting claim that civilization confronts women "with ever more difficult tasks and compels them to carry out instinctual sublimations of which women are little capable," Freud's assessment that these circumstances find women "forced into the background by the claims of civilization" has a vein of truth to it.[11] Not, as Freud suggests, because women are incapable of sublimating the patriarchal demands of civilized society but because women, assumed subjugated to the family, must endure more than maintaining the social order; they must also negotiate a series of intimate relationships with children and are often outside the bounds of civilization, either as potential (expectant, thwarted, or refused) vessels or as caregivers (willing or unwilling). Whether a woman has had a child or not is somewhat immaterial when faced with the assertion that she has the *potential* to bear or care for children, that it is within her feminine nature to do so. What becomes especially compelling with the *Terminator* franchise, as we shall see, is that even in moments when other aspects of overt femininity have been stripped from its characters, Sarah Connor and other feminized subjects in these narratives still exhibit this central trait: myopic dedication to the child as symbol of the social order and human possibility.

In an essay on the role of motherhood in global conflict, Linda Ahall argues that "motherhood or maternalism is commonly used in nationalist discourses in which women's heroism is written through their roles as mothers."[12] Whether due to her life-giving capacities or assumptions around women's nurturing and caretaking natures, consigning the heroism of women to the maternal register is tempting, particularly when one wants to justify women's violence. Ahall emphasizes, as I have done earlier, that the myth of motherhood circumscribes the way "that unconscious ideologies write motherhood as natural, something we do not question, when it is in fact not natural, but a social and cultural construction."[13] Even under the auspices of actual ancient myth, as my example in the introduction from Euripides's Greek tragedy *The Trojan Women* illustrates but which has also been frequently examined by others, women are often conscripted into the hero's narrative as mothers, whether actual or de facto.[14] Maria Tatar's work on Joseph

Campbell's "hero's journey" specifically acknowledges this role but also links it to a coming into knowledge for the hero: "In the grammar of mythology, Campbell argued, women represent 'the totality of what can be known.' He correctly intuited that the mythical imagination links women with knowledge, often in insidious ways. The hero, he added, somewhat craftily and cryptically, is 'the one who comes to know.'"[15] Here we can see the now familiar invocation of women's intuitive knowledge, a totality contained *in* the woman, and the hero's *coming into* knowledge through "his" training and experiences. It also invokes the implied mastery of the subject-supposed-to-know: mothers are expected to understand what is best for their children; however, they are often constrained by society and destined to be surpassed or usurped by the child as they become adults.

Whether mothers or not, women are often framed as having the capacity for the maternal within them, another way in which they are subjects-supposed-to-know. This has the corollary effect that lack of knowledge or failure implies "bad motherhood." Rose posits that "mothers always fail," and that, while this failure is normal and necessary in lived reality, "because mothers are seen as our point of entry into the world, there is nothing easier than to make social deterioration look like something that it is the sacred duty of mothers to prevent—a type of socially upgraded version of the tendency in modern families to blame mothers for everything. This neatly makes mothers guilty, not just for the ills of the world, but also for the rage that the unavoidable disappointments of an individual life cannot help but provide."[16] Failure to meet the standards of the ideal mother is a built-in aspect of modern life and one explicitly expressed in the *Terminator* franchise. It is also echoed in a tremendous anxiety we can see in representations of the mother-child bond, one that reflects itself in both knowledge and fear of loss, as Jessica Benjamin elaborates in her psychoanalytic account of the fantasy of the "omnipotent mother": "The perfect mother of fantasy is one who is always there, ready to sacrifice herself—and the child is not conscious of how strongly such a fantasy mother makes him or her feel controlled, guilty, envious, or unable to go away. The child simply remains terrified of her leaving or of destroying her by becoming separate. In turn, the mother feels terrified of destroying her child with her own separation."[17] The pressure of imminent loss and fear of separation, for both the mother and the child, is vividly exemplified in the relationship between Sarah and John throughout the franchise. While Sarah's violence would seem to run counter to her status as a mother, the premise of *Terminator* and its sequels vividly renders Sarah's maternal instincts—not just for John, but for all of humanity through him—as justification for her extreme and reactionary behavior.[18]

The first film in the franchise, *The Terminator*, originated in the mind of director and cowriter James Cameron, who would become a household name after the film became a surprise hit. In oral histories of the film, Cameron and cowriter Gale Ann Hurd acknowledge how Sarah Connor was always meant to be an "unlikely hero." Hurd reminisces that behind the first film and its immediate sequel "was the idea that heroic people are the ones who [you] least expect to be heroes. There's a tradition of male characters who go to war, who are in the boxing ring, who rise to be the corporate titan, you name it. But Jim has always found women to be the more compelling parts to write. Culturally, they're the ones who feel less equipped, because that's what society tells them."[19] Subsequently, the Sarah we meet in the first film is a somewhat flighty and carefree waitress who is thrown into a horrifying fight for her life when a cybernetic assassin from the future, the Terminator (Arnold Schwarzenegger), is sent back in time to kill her before she can give birth to her son, John, who is destined to be a military leader and help turn the tide in the coming war against the machines. John of the future sends his own father, Kyle Reese, back in time to protect Sarah, and the one night the two spend together before Kyle is killed results in Sarah's pregnancy. Told she will be the mother of humanity's salvation, Sarah is immediately forced into a role of survivor and, eventually, warrior, although the first film mainly showcases her fortitude in the former capacity, especially as its generic allegiance aligns more closely to horror, with gruesome imagery and a high body count.

The premise of *Terminator* puts Sarah in the position of being coerced into motherhood, and while she tries to resist this role—protesting, as quoted in the heading for this section "Do I look like the mother of the future?"—she ultimately cannot. As Karen B. Mann astutely observes, Sarah is compelled to "say yes" to "fulfill[ing] her sexual role in a cultural plot" in three ways: "by threat of force (the terminator); by the ideal of motherhood (John Conner); and by emotional response (Kyle Reese). That culture cannot continue without the mother is clear."[20] The implication of Sarah's lack of choice in her own pregnancy, in the *necessity* of her motherhood, is further acknowledged in the narrative, when criminal psychologist Dr. Silberman (Earl Boen), in his patronizing and cynical response to Kyle's story about time travel, calls the Terminator's goal a "retroactive abortion." Here, Judith Butler's assertion that the maternal body can be understood as an "effect or consequence of a system of sexuality in which the female body is required to assume maternity as the essence of its self and the law of its desire" is also relevant.[21] Butler argues that women's bodies are presumptively maternal, which feeds into the supposition in the *Terminator* films that even Sarah as a not-yet mother will fight for her unborn child—that, in fact, any woman would do the same. This framing, and our knowledge as viewers that Kyle and Sarah's fear is very real, immediately underscores John's conception and birth as ordained and compulsory; Sarah must become a mother if humanity is to have any chance of survival in a foreseeable future. Donald Palumbo further acknowledges how this drives Sarah's narrative as a hero, effectively transferring her heroism onto John as embryonic ideal, since "what is exceptional about her is her 'destiny'" as both John's mother and a warrior who will teach him how to fight. However, "she has not yet become a warrior, nor given birth to John, by the film's conclusion," which means "she is somewhat like the hero's mother who is assumed into heaven or crowned a queen; yet if Sarah's status as a 'legend' is interpreted in this way, then her son John (who never appears in the film) would exhibit this

FIGURE 4.1. John and the T-800 break Sarah out of the mental institution where she has been held due to her so-called delusions about a nuclear apocalypse. *Terminator 2: Judgment Day*, directed by James Cameron (1991).

quality of the hero, not she."[22] While the foundation of the *Terminator* places Sarah in the role of a mother who engenders a hero, the second film more firmly renders her powerful in her own right but only insofar as her maternal capacity drives her to protect John and the world.

Set a decade after her encounter with Kyle Reese, *Judgment Day* finds Sarah locked away in a mental institution, having spent the intervening years "shacking up" with men (John's description) who can train her and John in all manner of survival skills from computer hacking to martial arts, marksmanship, and operating heavy artillery. Like a modern-day Cassandra, Sarah's outcries about the coming apocalypse read as psychosis to the authorities, leading to her institutionalization. In this installment, a new assassin is sent to kill ten-year-old John, and Arnold Schwarzenegger reprises his role as the Terminator, a T-800, who has been reprogrammed by future John to protect his child self. The T-1000 assassin (Robert Patrick), by contrast, is a technologically superior cyborg made of fluidic metal that can morph to take on the form of anything he touches. Sarah has transformed as well, developing into what Julie Baumgold terms, in an oft-quoted film review, a "hardbody"; she writes, "Linda Hamilton is one fighting mama! She can pick a lock, swing a broom handle and crush a skull, wire bombs, lug artillery. She strikes a pose, smacks those magazines in, shoots with two hands in the combat crouch. She is hung with hardware like jewelry."[23] Furthermore, Baumgold exalts, Sarah eschews the primacy of her role as mother, even deigning to leave John under the T-800's protection for a time, as he is a "better mother."

Linda Hamilton's physique in the sequel, unequivocally the most successful film of the franchise, not only was of great interest to critics and viewers but also ushered in a wave of scholarship about action heroines with masculinized physical characteristics.[24] Jeffrey A. Brown describes the way Hamilton's "muscular makeover" sparked interest in newspapers and magazines at the time.[25] He further acknowledges in a separate analysis how "this new hardbody is not offered up as a mere sexual commodity. While the well-toned, muscular female body is obviously an ideal in this age of physical fitness, it is presented in these films as first and foremost a functional body, a weapon."[26] Yvonne Tasker writes about Sarah as one in a series of "spectacular bodies" in films of the 1980s and 1990s, as a "masculinization of the female body, which is effected most visibly through her muscles, [and] can be understood in terms of a notion of 'musculinity,'" which "indicates the way in which the signifiers of strength are not limited to male characters."[27] Marc O'Day interprets this musculinity as one kind of "gender theft" perpetrated deliberately by action films, one that also accounts for the T-800's "softness" toward John: "In the action-adventure cinema, therefore, a series of gender transactions and, sometimes, gender thefts can be seen to take place, as qualities of masculinity and femininity, activity and passivity, are traded over the bodies of action heroes and heroines."[28] And yet, in her discussion of how *Terminator* "charts the developing toughness of Sarah Connor," Sherrie Inness also notes that *Judgment Day* illustrates a "link between her non-traditional tough actions and society's assumption that she is insane."[29] Interpreted variously as a kind of gender-swapped physicality in which masculine presentation (muscles, toughness) is the assumed province of action heroes regardless of gender or as a basis for her to be labeled "crazy" and a bad mother, Sarah's muscular frame in the second film of the franchise marks a notable deviation from her portrayal in the first.

Whatever there is to say about Sarah's body, her physical prowess, or her abilities as a fighter, there is no question that the second film frames her as protector of humanity's future via the survival of John. She is not an ideal mother in a traditionally gendered sense—she is not nurturing or emotionally present and, *Judgment Day* makes clear, has something to learn from the T-800's attentiveness to John—but she is unfailingly self-sacrificing. George Faithful reads this Sarah (and heroic contemporary Ellen Ripley from the *Alien* franchise) as "not content to save themselves alone. In the face of inhuman threats, they grew to become warriors, mothers, and saviors of humanity, revealing themselves to be the ultimate humans in the process."[30] While Faithful marks Sarah as emblematic of "humanism," we can see the function of the maternal as an intense, imperative aspect of Sarah's ethos. As defined by Barbara Creed in her germinal work *The Monstrous Feminine*, Sarah typifies the "archaic mother," whose primary trait is "her total dedication to the generative, procreative principle. She is the mother who conceives all by herself, the original parent, the godhead of all fertility and the origin of procreation. She is outside morality and the law."[31] It is through this assertion of motherhood and its protective impulses that Sarah can enact whatever violence necessary to protect her son.

Mark Jancovich asserts that characters like Sarah are "associated with the maternal while also performing activities usually restricted to men" such that they "erase or blur distinctions between masculine and feminine activities in ways similar to the female heroines in the slasher films."[32] This argument takes into account the franchise's alliance with certain dynamics of the horror and thriller genres, namely, the imperative to survive, constant fear, and a preponderance of blood and brutal destruction. Other scholars like Lisa Purse argue that Sarah's "hard-body" is allowable precisely because of the science fiction/fantasy context. Purse writes that the film's genre puts "the potentially culturally disturbing possibility of female agency and physical power at a distance from our everyday contemporary reality . . . providing a space in which female physical power is permitted, but in a fantastical setting that (with or without comedy) underlines its real-world impos-sibility."[33] While different genres, both horror/thriller and sci-fi/fantasy make allowances for extraordinary behaviors perhaps not typically "allowed" for women. However, it is Sarah's inherent maternalism that both makes her hawkishness discomfiting and renders it permissible within the context of her protection of John. As Sharon Willis asserts, Sarah's "physical and emotional resemblance to the terminator and the militaristic discipline she applies to her affective relationship with her son, along with her obsession with weapons technology, code her as a threat to conventional maternity and establish her as a figure who mobilizes vari-ous anxieties." Therefore, "the film needs to stress that Sarah Connor really is the 'good mother,' ever ready to give her life to preserve her child's."[34] The maternal protective instinct in the first films and the television show, especially, circulates around John's place in saving the word. We discover in the last film of the fran-chise, *Terminator: Dark Fate* (2019), that while the world does not need John specifically—new saviors will arise—Sarah still needs John. The maternal bond and its related protective instincts come from a conjoining of Sarah's desire to pro-tect her son at all costs and a presumptively feminine response to the coming apocalypse.

A grisly scene midway through *Judgment Day*, one Cameron deemed neces-sary despite its significant special effects expense when compared with its short duration, depicts Sarah's nightmare of a world wiped out by nuclear blasts.[35] In it, she observes a younger and more innocent version of herself playing with a tod-dler in a playground surrounded by other mothers and children. We might be tempted to see this scene as a memory of John's toddler years, and yet we know that John never experienced a "normal" childhood, and the Sarah we are shown—happy, carefree—has not existed since prior to her pregnancy. As the nuclear bomb detonates, and the city and park around them explode into light and flames, the families catch fire and burn in front of Sarah's eyes as she herself begins to burn, screaming and clutching the chain-link fence separating herself from the others. Gruesome and terrifying, the imagery in the dream layers nightmare atop nightmare as the bodies, charred to ash in protective poses huddled with their children like the mummies that remained after the destruction of Pompeii, are blown away in a second blast that sends the dust and bones of the fallen into the air around Sarah's screaming skeletal form. When she wakes from the dream, she has carved "NO FATE" into a picnic table and seems more determined than ever to do whatever it takes to defeat the threats she faces, both direct and existential. The iconography of the playground or schoolyard is echoed toward the end of

Dark Fate, under quite difference circumstances, but also addressed early in the television show *Terminator: The Sarah Connor Chronicles* (Fox, 2008–2009), as I elaborate in the next section.

WHAT MOTHERS KNOW: MOTHER PRIVILEGE AND PREEMPTIVE ACTION

A short-lived television show, thirty-one episodes over two seasons, *Sarah Connor Chronicles* takes up a few years after *Judgment Day* leaves off, following a haunted and hounded Sarah (Lena Headey) and fifteen-year-old John (Thomas Dekker).[36] The pilot episode utilizes a school shooting perpetrated by yet another would-be cyborg assassin (a terminator masquerading as a substitute teacher who tries to shoot John in the classroom), which only further cements the premise of the franchise as an allegory for U.S. political violence and Sarah's desire as a mother to protect her child. Along the way, the show presents a unique, dystopic reflection on the American family, with the mother as fierce, single-minded protector and the son as reluctant, self-pitying future hero. It also introduces another central woman character, Cameron (Summer Glau), a terminator reprogrammed and sent back in time by John's future self. As with the first two films, Sarah's need to protect her son is absolute: she breaks off an engagement at the beginning of the series, unable to sustain a romantic relationship when her sole concern is John. At the end of the pilot, Sarah, John, and Cameron time travel from 1999 to 2007, effectively excising the show from the timelines of the other sequels but also conveniently bringing the action into the present day. Motherhood for Sarah, in this installment as in the films, is not a choice but a duty, a calling.

As I referenced earlier, Beauvoir emphasizes the cultural expectations, social roles, and mythology of being a woman, treating motherhood as one of many categories through which women's roles are restricted and regulated. While she spends a good deal of time exploring the mother-daughter relationship—as one thought to be reflective of narcissism, among other things—her brief summation of the mother-son relationship is remarkably fitting for my analysis of Sarah as a mother-warrior even some seven decades removed from *The Second Sex*'s first printing. "Because of the prestige attributed to men by women, as well as the advantages they actually have, many women prefer to have sons," Beauvoir writes.[37] As enshrined in my epigraph, Beauvoir's invocation of the son as "hero" marks the mother's ostensible privilege in raising sons over daughters. *The Chronicles* makes this notion explicit, as Sarah's only power over John relies on his future status as a hero, as, quite literally, "a leader of men, a soldier, a creator"—and this power grows increasingly tenuous as John comes into his own and begins to learn how to protect himself.[38] Notably, the title of the show and Sarah's voice-over narrative threaded heavily through the first season (the use of voice-over lessens significantly in the second season) frame the series as her story, *Sarah's* chronicles—but the only stories she has to tell are about her son. In one such voice-over in the second episode, Sarah laments, "A wise man once said, 'Know thyself.' Easier said than done. I've had nine aliases, twenty-three jobs, spoken four languages, and spent three years in a mental hospital speaking the truth. At least when I was there I could use my real name. Through it all, I've always known who I am and why I'm here. Protect my son. Prepare him for the future."[39] Sarah's voice-over concedes that all her hardships, identities, and skills have been in service of John's upbringing, underscoring how her agency abuts against the limits of what must be done to safeguard John.

In the fourth episode of the show, "Heavy Metal," John temporarily becomes separated from his mother and Cameron. As they strategize how to find him, Sarah tells Cameron that it is "impossible for [her] to understand" what losing John feels like to her as his mother, and Cameron responds, "Without John, your life has no purpose." Cameron correctly intuits that Sarah feels she has no purpose at all without John and suggests Sarah must learn to give John more autonomy if he is to become the hero he is meant to be. Beauvoir asserts that, in order to have any power, the mother must "possess her son." Losing John, Sarah fears losing herself. It is notable, too, that this scene marks John's first real moment of independence, slipping away from his mother and Cameron to plant his phone-qua-tracking device on a shipment of Coltan, a special metal used to make terminators' endoskeletons. In doing so, he accidentally goes along for the ride, triggering a daring escape and a high-speed car chase, a series of scenes highlighting both John's impending manhood and his continual dependence on his mother's and Cameron's protection—for now. Sarah's "possession" of John is tenuous. While she is responsible for everything John knows—she trained him to fight, to shoot, and to protect himself in myriad smaller ways—Sarah is also beholden to the future-John, John-the-man, who sent his own father back in time to protect (and impregnate) his mother. John-the-man continues to send terminators and resistance fighters back in time to help his mother and his adolescent self stave off their horrific future. Sarah may have a modicum of control over teenage John's fate, but he has already, by way of his future self, taken possession of her and her entire life. As such, Sarah's power and her abilities only extend so far as they intersect with John's needs.

Motherhood is a fraught discourse within psychoanalysis, and far too complex to fully elaborate the implications of here, but its principles inform a number of crucial ways in which mothers are mythologized, even in contemporary cultural production. Freudian psychoanalysis gives us the Oedipal mother, an object of misplaced desire, and the castrating mother, who signals her own lack and threatens the boy-child (especially) by extension: cross her, and she might literally cut him down to size.[40] Most relevant for my current purposes, however, is the phallic mother, who functions alongside Lacan's subject-supposed-to-know; this is the mother as one whom the child speciously believes holds all the answers—the imagined phallus a placeholder for power. However, according to Gallop (in turn, channeling French feminist Luce Irigaray), the phallic mother in psychoanalytic discourse is always a fraud, a discovery the child eventually makes, all the better to establish his true power over her. The phallic mother, as such, has no actual power and compounds her folly by wading in the murky, shark-infested waters of male privilege for as long as her motherhood lends her this false authority.[41]

Instead of a perverted form of male privilege, *The Chronicles* presents a sort of "mother privilege." Sarah never shies away from a fight and can more than hold her own against assailants twice her size, but her power is tied intimately and explicitly to her motherhood. In her first words of the series, Sarah's voice-over intones:

> There are those who believe that a child in the womb shares his mother's dreams. Her love for him. Her hopes for his future. Is it told to him in pictures while he sleeps inside her? Is that why he reaches for her in that first moment and cries for her touch? But what if you've known since he was inside you what his life held for him? That he would be hunted. That his fate was tied to the fate of millions. That every moment of your life would be spent keeping him alive. Would he understand why you were so hard? Why you held on so tight? Would he still reach for you if the only dream you've ever shared with him was a nightmare? Would he know my love runs through him like blood?

These first words we hear from the new, televised version of Sarah serve as a backdrop to visuals of Sarah driving a car down an empty highway, hands tense on the wheel as she stares ahead with determination. There is a notable change in register just at the end of her voice-over, where she switches from third to first person, asking, "Would *he* know *my* love runs through him like blood?" effectively making her abstracted questions about motherhood into a personal meditation. On-screen, she squeals to a stop in front of a high school, marches into the school library to locate her son, and demands John come with her; when they emerge from the school, they are greeted by the police, who arrest them, shoving them into the backs of police cars. Moments later, a terminator finds them, opening fire on the police as Sarah frees herself and John. She shields his body with hers during the bloodbath, urges him to run, only to watch the terminator gun him down. During these moments, time seems to stand still and fray, reflecting Sarah's desperate horror; the camera goes in and out of focus, the frame jerking and staticky. Then, the focus snaps into clarity again and Sarah runs to kneel over her son's dead body, cradling his head in her lap like a pietà. She stares down the terminator, screaming at him to kill her, too, adding: "Nothing matters anymore." The terminator refuses, telling Sarah that "the future is ours," just before the landscape around them erupts in nuclear mushroom clouds and the sky darkens. In a callback to *Judgment Day*, the blast sears the flesh from the terminator's endoskeleton and flames surround Sarah but do not burn her, as he approaches and grabs her throat with his metallic hand. Sarah wakes up from her nightmare. This scene, the first in the pilot episode, succinctly highlights the premise of the new series: Sarah's actions are justified and protective, even though law enforcement would view

FIGURE 4.2. The pilot of the *Terminator* television series begins with a nightmare in which Sarah imagines John being shot by a terminator and then begs the terminator to kill her, too. *Terminator: The Sarah Connor Chronicles* (2008–2009), episode 1.1, "Pilot," Fox, aired 13 January 2008.

them as criminal; John, although closer to man than boy now, still relies on her protection; and Sarah feels her life is meaningless without him.

Later in the pilot, John tells Cameron, at first believing her to be a normal teenage girl at his new school, "I'm all she's got," referring to his mother's single-minded devotion to him. Without her son to protect, Sarah's sometimes criminal, always aggressive actions might founder under a gamut of accusations ranging from irrationally violent to overly masculine. Because she is a mother, Sarah is given special dispensation to act according to her son's best interest, regardless of concerns for propriety, society, or the law. "Mother privilege" may also account for some of the ways that women's violence becomes codified, particularly under the auspices of real political conflict and war. For example, in their book on women's violence in global politics, Laura Sjoberg and Caron E. Gentry explain, "Narratives of women's violence often centre around biologically determinist assumptions and arguments. In stories about violent women, their motherhood defines them—their inability/failure to serve as mothers is *so* dehumanizing (or de-womanizing) that it drives a woman to violence."[42] This sense that a denial or failure of motherhood may lead to violence abuts in compelling ways with the parallel, but speciously oppositional, notion that women are bastions of peace and nonviolence. In her oft-cited book on the subject, *Women and War*, Jean Bethke Elshtain clarifies this corollary connection: "We in the West are the heirs of a tradition that assumes an affinity between women and peace, between men and war, a tradition that consists of culturally constructed and transmitted myths and memories. . . . Man construed as violent, whether eagerly and inevitably or reluctantly and tragically;

woman as nonviolent, offering succor and compassion: these tropes on the social identities of men and women, past and present, do not denote what men and women *really* are in time of war, but function instead to re-create and secure women's location as noncombatants and men's as warriors."[43] It bears emphasizing Elshtain's point that these assumptions about masculine and feminine behavior do not necessarily drive individual actions—and certainly the ethos of the action heroine, as previously discussed, highlights significant representational exceptions to these conventions.

However, other well-known texts, such as Sara Ruddick's *Maternal Thinking: Towards a Politics of Peace*, do not just align women with peace but specifically designate the maternal mindset as a fundamental framework for peacekeeping. "Peace, like mothering," Ruddick explains, "is sentimentally honored and often secretly despised. Like mothers, peacemakers are scorned as powerless appeasers who are innocent of the real world. Just because mothering and peace have been so long and so sentimentally married, a critical understanding of mothering and maternal nonviolence will itself contribute to the reconception of 'peace.'"[44] By reclaiming peace and motherhood together, Ruddick hopes to reframe their relationship to each other and to critically assess the ways in which cultural ideas about motherhood might reflect on peace politics. In a retrospective discussion of her germinal work, Ruddick reiterates this interpretation, writing, "I believe I offer a model of Nonviolent Action to replace collective violence and tell alternative histories of human flesh that contrast both Reason's Body and War's Body with Love's Body as understood by maternal thinking."[45] As I have noted in prior chapters, the desire for nonviolence and a politics of love and hope is a laudable goal, but continually assigning these traits to women (in this case to mothers, specifically), and thereby binding their power to those gendered assumptions, only amplifies the precarity of women's agency.

In a similar vein, Ranjana Khanna questions how Ruddick "sees peace politics as resistant to the masculinist and as specifically feminist. Ruddick anticipates critics who may call her naive because the very tenets of maternal practice seem apt for nationalist and xenophobic preservation. But she does not enter into adequate discussion of the violence it often takes to maintain perpetual peace."[46] In other words, maintaining peace is not always a nonviolent activity and the maternal itself, as Rose explores in her recent work, is often bound up with the intersections of love, cruelty and failure.[47] As I explore more thoroughly in my discussion of *Dark Fate*, race and class politics only further complicate these understandings in the real world and in media representation. Stephanie Hartzell incisively states, for example, the "dominant cultural understandings of motherhood remain steeped in a history of racialized constructions of goodness/badness that continue to inform perceptions and experiences of mothers."[48] Although she is white, Sarah does not fit into the traditional ideals of the "good mother": she is violent, itinerant, a criminal, and cannot allow herself to nurture John because she is overcome with fear. She is also a single mother, a figure whom Rose points out is "the original 'scrounger,'" and placed socially, alongside immigrants, as "at the bottom of the social scrapheap."[49] And yet, Sarah still benefits from white privilege on a visual register—viewers may be more inclined to forgive her so-called transgressions because she looks the part of the "good mother" (white, straight, middle-class) even if she does not act it.

Two significant points of emphasis emerge from the dichotomy of women driven to violence by circumstance and women's so-called preference for peace. First of all, even within Elshtain's understanding of womanhood during wartime, the woman is deemed responsible for "the 'family claim' and the 'social claim,' for she is told, without her unselfish devotion to country and family each would be lost."[50] Again, we can see the eliding of the family with the social order, how the woman's role during political conflict is consigned to a protective impulse. Second, these circumstances present a pressing question: What is more important to maintain when the coherent family/society is threatened with annihilation, peace or the family? This returns us to Khanna's acknowledgment that sometimes peace or security cannot be obtained through nonviolent means. In *The Terror Dream*, Susan Faludi expounds on the ways post-9/11 rhetoric in the United States framed assumptions about gender and its relationship to power and sociocultural agency. She writes that the "intrusions of September 11 broke the dead bolt on our protective myth, the illusion that we are masters of our security, that our might makes our homeland impregnable, that our families are safe in the bower of their communities and our women and children safe in the arms of their men."[51] And while Laura Shepard emphasizes how political rhetoric at the time extolled feminine virtues as responsible for maintaining American "family values," Faludi notes that these threats of violence against the social order were and still are used to justify violent (sometimes preemptive) retribution against those deemed responsible.[52]

The Sarah of *Judgment Day*, for example, does not directly kill Dyson, the man unwittingly responsible for building the technology that allows the machine apocalypse to take place, but the death and destruction she leaves behind (including Dyson, who dies anyway, killed by police as he helps Sarah destroy his work) are justified by the ethos of the franchise. Without Sarah's violent actions, we would have nuclear annihilation, thereby justifying anything she must do to thwart Skynet and protect John. A similar philosophy undergirds *The Chronicles*, exemplified by the brutal streak of dead bodies both Sarah and Cameron leave behind in their quest to protect John; while Sarah hesitates to kill other humans outright, Cameron does not, and neither character questions the legitimacy of their actions. The first episode of season 2, "Samson and Delilah," picks up from the season 1 finale, in which Cameron was damaged in an explosion and Sarah and John were captured by criminal Margos Sarkissian (James Urbaniak), who is in possession of the computer program that will eventually become Skynet. A long opening sequence shot entirely without audible dialogue and in slow motion intercuts scenes of Cameron extracting herself from the wreckage of a car bomb while Sarah endures a beating from their captors and John attempts to break free from the zip ties that restrain him. Subverting our expectations of Cameron arriving to save mother and son, the bomb has reset her programming, and she now seeks to terminate John, who narrowly escapes when the house they are in explodes just as Cameron finds them. To undergird this betrayal from a loved companion, the opener plays out under a loud, nondiegetic cover of the Grateful Dead song "Samson and Delilah," sung by Shirley Manson. Recounting Samson's defeat of a mighty lion but also setting up Delilah's duplicity—"Delilah, she gained ground on Samson's mind / . . . Then she spoke so kind and she talked so fair / Till Samson said 'Delilah, cut off my hair / You can shave my head clean as my hand / And my strength becomes as natural as any man'"—the song positions John as Samson and Cameron as a potential Delilah, a metaphor that frames the remainder of the episode.

At the end of the explosive slow-motion opening, Sarkissian has been strangled to death, and it remains unclear whether mother or son committed the act, although the framing of John as Samson in the soundtrack and later conversations in the episode strongly imply that he is responsible. Sarah and John run from Cameron before eventually trapping her, to John's distress. Despite her betrayal, John wants Cameron back, impassionedly explaining, "She saved my life. She saves my life." This use of both past and present tense emphasizes a yearning for Cameron that goes beyond the mere practicality of safety and security. In a scene full of pathos and brutality, Sarah pins Cameron to a wall with her truck so that John can dig a computer chip out of the back of her head; Cameron begs for mercy, crying and declaring her love for John to convince him not to deactivate her. While John hesitates, moved by her pleas, he rationally understands that she is programmed to manipulate him in any way she can and removes the chip. Instead of destroying Cameron's chip and body as Sarah and his uncle, Derek, expect him to do, he reprograms the chip and gives Cameron another chance to prove her loyalty to him, handing her a gun when she reactivates.[53] She hands the gun back to him to show that she no longer wants to kill him and is redeemed. Of all the installments in the franchise, *The Chronicles* is the one most rife with biblical references, many of them overt. Besides the episode's title and the franchise's widespread allusions to John serving as a metaphor for Jesus Christ, Cameron's redemption in this episode is framed as a kind of rebirth, with John as the faithful subject who inspires faith and loyalty in return.

When John goes against the wishes of his mother, uncle, and cyborg protector, his act of teenage defiance in resurrecting Cameron demonstrates his shifting loyalties away from parental figures and toward his own morality and vision for the future, further degrading Sarah's agency. John's growing agency, on the other hand, becomes a central theme of the second season. Even though Sarah "drives the action" of the *Chronicles*, Marianne Kac-Vergne argues that "what looks like an ode to Linda Hamilton and radical second-wave feminism—notably its empowerment of women, its celebration of feminine subjectivity and imagination, and its challenge to patriarchy through the promotion of matriarchal structures—is fraught with joylessness and distress."[54] Kac-Vergne also exhorts viewers to consider the ways the character of Cameron functions as a postfeminist interlocutor inveighing against second-wave feminist methods and achievements.[55] The show plays Cameron as a combination of ingenue and protector; in the body of a teenage girl and frequently needing to mimic human behaviors to blend in, Cameron becomes a confusing presence in John's life. He recognizes she is a machine and yet still finds himself attracted to her romantically and sexually. In the show's final episode, she removes her top and asks John to climb on top of her in bed so he can cut into her body to check the integrity of her power source, requiring him to reach inside the skin of her half-naked torso.[56] Despite the apparent sexualized intimacy of this scene, especially from John's perspective—he looks for a moment like he might try to kiss her—Cameron seems physically unaffected. On an emotional register, as far as Cameron's protective programming may be considered a substitute for emotional attachment, Cameron cares for John, indicated later in the episode when she leaves a message behind apologizing to John after sacrificing herself to a greater cause: the undoing of Skynet.[57]

While it would take me too far afield to fully unpack here, another character who plays a prominent role in the second season, a T-1001 who uses her "mimetic polyalloy" composition to morph into any object she wants, and who has assumed the identity of tech entrepreneur Catherine Weaver (Shirley Manson), also seeks to combat Skynet and save humanity—for unknown reasons due to the cancellation of the show. Part of her scheme includes reprogramming and "raising" a T-800, John Henry, whom she attempts to teach about ethics and humanity. Calling John Henry her son, Weaver finally meets Sarah at the end of the season and insists that only together can their two sons save the world. When John Henry takes Cameron's chip and travels to the future, John and Weaver go after him, with Sarah, for the first time, letting her son go off on his own. Forced to choose between staying with his mother and trying to rescue "the girl" (Cameron), thereby forging his own path, John chooses Cameron—and even Sarah does not seem surprised.

The Chronicles asks questions about the power Sarah garners from her knowledge both of the future and of the importance of John, as well as the nature of morality and faith. A police detective in the final episode of the series tells Sarah, "I believe you have participated in the miraculous and the terrible and through it all you have maintained a moral and good soul," and while it is unclear whether he is attempting to manipulate her to gain her trust, the structure of the show frames Sarah in this way as well. Like Weaver and John Henry, Sarah has taught her son how to be a "good man"—that and his survival being her primary motivations— and, ultimately, she must let him become a hero in his own right. The other installments in the franchise handle the timeline differently and do not feature the connection between Sarah and John in the same ways, if at all.[58] However, the third, fourth, and fifth films, which I touch on briefly in the following discussion as a backdrop to my final analysis of *Dark Fate*, ask how expectations of these maternal narratives might be altered when the relationship between mother and son is severed or perverted.

In the most clear-cut example of this, *Terminator 3: Rise of the Machines* (2003) begins with Sarah dead, having succumbed to leukemia shortly after she was assured that the foretold apocalypse of 1997 had not occurred. John (Nick Stahl) is a twentysomething nomad, living off the grid, still wary—and with good reason. Through a series of events, he discovers that the apocalypse has only been delayed and an advanced T-X terminator (Kristanna Loken), this time in a woman's body clad almost exclusively in skintight leather, has been sent back in time to kill his "lieutenants," those who will aid John in the upcoming resistance, including the woman whom he finds out will be his future wife, Kate (Claire Danes). Over the course of the film, Kate and John struggle to stay alive, with the help of another reprogrammed T-800 (Schwarzenegger), and then try to forestall the apocalypse, only to find that their actions have no effect; at the end of the film, the nuclear annihilation wrought by the sentient machines begins, and they can do nothing but wait in their fallout shelter for the smoke to clear and the real war to begin.

Terminator Salvation (2009) presents a human cyborg, Marcus (Sam Worthington), a cybernetically enhanced man meant to be a sleeper agent for Skynet who ultimately disobeys his programming in order so save John, Kyle, and a host of human prisoners from the machines. There is little to parse out in *Salvation* in light of my argument in this chapter—as women are only tangential to the film—but it is worth noting that *Salvation* becomes about John saving the teenage Kyle (destined to be his father through time travel) in order to preserve his own place in the resistance. *Terminator Genisys* (2015)—like *Judgment Day* and *Salvation*, another biblical title, anointing John into a messianic role as with the references in *The Chronicles*—follows a much more convoluted premise, involving several intersecting timelines. But it also brings back Sarah Connor in a significantly different vein.

Genysis follows Kyle Reese (Jai Courtney) when he journeys back to 1984 to protect Sarah (Emilia Clarke), as in the first film. However, the Sarah he meets there is from an altered timeline, one during which her parents were assassinated when she was nine and the young Sarah was rescued, raised, and trained by a reprogrammed T-800, whom she calls Pops (still played by Schwarzenegger). In this alternate timeline, Sarah does not need Kyle's protection and resents the idea that she must fulfill her destiny as a mother; moreover, they eventually time jump to 2017 (when the apocalypse is now set to occur) and meet an adult John who has been captured and mechanized by Skynet. Unlike the geopolitical concerns refracted in the first three films, all of which play heavily on the anxieties of a nuclear apocalypse originating from weapons defense systems gone rogue, *Genisys* (in some ways like *The Chronicles*) highlights a more contemporary anxiety about technology quite literally "going too far" and the global interconnectedness of the internet age.[59] In a stark change from all four prior films and the show—but something we see echoed in the final film, *Dark Fate*—*Genisys* questions John's relevance, positing that perhaps Sarah and Kyle were the only necessary heroes all along.

Instead of a survival narrative about a mother trying to save her child and thereby save the future of humanity, *Genisys* follows a standard action film plot—with a budding romance between Sarah and Kyle thrown in, but divorced from the imperative to conceive John. The family drama of the other films remains in place, but subverted, with the T-800 still serving as a de facto father, this time to Sarah, and a twisted narrative of displaced matricide/patricide/infanticide wherein Sarah and Kyle must find a way to stop and destroy the son they have not yet conceived before John can destroy them. Unlike in the other films, the T-800, Pops, attempts to sacrifice himself to save Sarah but ultimately survives, leaving all three heroes (mother, father, and machine) alive at the end and the son dead. Despite Sarah's hardened and battle-ready demeanor in *Genisys*, she is not muscular like Hamilton in *Judgment Day*; instead, Clarke's Sarah is petite and lithe, sarcastic with Kyle at first but still ultimately falling in love with him several days into their meeting. One can imagine that, in this scenario, the man again becomes the protector—two men, in fact—willing to sacrifice himself for the family in order to safeguard Sarah; even though she is no longer destined to birth humanity's savior, she still must remain alive to defend the social order.

In *American Pietàs: Visions of Race, Death, and the Maternal*, Ruby C. Tapia makes explicit both the ways the maternal functions through religious metaphors and the ways it can stand in as a sociopolitical proxy for national identity. She describes an ephemeral idea of the maternal that "bears, hosts, and resurrects whiteness on behalf of the nation. This is the maternal we turn to, piece together, hide under, revere, disdain, erect when we want to recuperate ourselves as pure and proper citizen-subjects, as well when we want to protest our exclusion from this category."[60] By framing the maternal as a symbolic bearer of a system that centralizes white subjects and organizes political life around fantasies of the family, Tapia recognizes the importance of an imaginary and idealized democratic nation in which differences are elided in favor of normative citizenship. Although the patriotic messaging of the *Terminator* franchise never reaches the explicit register achieved by *Supergirl*, its films and show do articulate the body and idea of the mother as de rigueur protector of humanity—but a protector who is dispensable in the wake of her child's promise or, in the case of *Genisys*, who must make the impossible choice to sacrifice her child for the greater good.

In a curious way, the first four films follow machine logic: the terminators and their computational programmers believe that killing John Connor, his parents, or his lieutenants will stave off the human resistance—and the humans involved in these narratives also follow this logic religiously. Safeguarding first Sarah, then John, then Kyle, then Sarah again (round and round) becomes so central to the mission of each film and its protagonists that one can easily forget to question why John himself is so important except to the effect that he has said so. After all, it is future John who sends his own father back to protect Sarah in *Terminator*, and John who insists on saving Kyle in *Salvation* in order to guarantee his own birth, to name only a few instances of John's own preservationist instincts. Just because the machines believe that killing John will eliminate the resistance does not make it true; John happens to be the leader of the resistance in the timeline spawned by *Terminator*, but perhaps another leader would have come forward if not for him. As such, by preserving the life of his mother and father—and his past selves— throughout the films, John is only fulfilling the ultimate selfish desire of the child: that the mother and father serve his needs and desires in the absence of their own. In *Genisys*, these selfish desires are taken to their zenith with the son attempting to kill his parents literally, but also in a biblical and psychoanalytic sense, to guarantee his own destiny, evil though it may be. *Dark Fate*, however, begs the question of what happens to the mother-warrior who loses her child alongside a deeper meditation on what happens to the social order or the nation when it is no longer worth protecting.

APOCALYPTIC NIGHTMARES, DYSTOPIAN DREAMS: REWRITING THE MATERNAL NARRATIVE

The most recent installment in the franchise, *Dark Fate* immediately establishes its loyalty to the timeline created by the first two films, refusing the revisions of the *Chronicles*, the erasure of Sarah in *Rise of the Machines* and *Salvation*, and the reimagining of her girlhood and love affair with Kyle in *Genisys*. Instead, as the film studio logos flash on the screen in the opening minutes of the film, they are intercut with grainy recorded footage of Sarah in the mental institution from *Judgment Day* being interviewed by Dr. Silberman about what *he believes* are her paranoid delusions and what *she knows* to be dreams and nightmares of an imminent future. The Sarah of the pixelated past recalls the cataclysmic nightmare of the nuclear blast we see so vividly rendered in *Judgment Day*, describing in anguished and guttural rasps, "Children look like burnt paper. Black. Not moving. And then the blast wave hits them, and they fly apart like leaves." Merging this flashback with the studio logos means the film allows no distance between its production contexts outside the world of the film and its diegesis, immediately subjecting viewers to the pall of imagined future horrors. Unlike in the second film, we do not see the carnage of the blasted playground, but as the opening credits begin, we are given another familiar scene: a beach littered with broken skeletons and terminators rising from the water in their metallic frames, guns blazing and eyes glowing red. "There once was a future in which humankind was hunted by a machine that could think and terminators built to kill. A future without hope," Sarah's voice-over explains, before the scene transitions to a sunnier past. On a bright, warm beach in Guatemala, Sarah, two years after the events of *Judgment Day*, relaxes in a café with John, now approximately twelve.[61] Her voice-over continues—"That future

FIGURE 4.3. Enhanced human Grace protects future savior Dani from the terminators sent to annihilate her. *Terminator: Dark Fate*, directed by Tim Miller (2019).

never happened because I stopped it. To protect my son. To save us all"—only to have the reverie of this "happy ending" disrupted when a T-800 ambushes them, killing John without a second glance.

The opening moments of the film reestablish the parameters of the original timeline and do away with John's primacy with shocking and brutal efficiency. Sarah, too, vanishes from the next half hour of film, which takes place in the present day and does not deviate temporally with the exception of two flash-forwards (that actually serve as flashbacks for the character in question, who has come from the future). Following the basic premise of *Terminator*, with a twist, a Rev-9 terminator is sent back from the year 2042 to assassinate Dani Ramos (Natalia Reyes), a twentysomething Mexican factory worker. Her protector, Grace (Mackenzie Davis), a slim, tall, and muscular white woman with short-cropped hair who is also from the future, is a cybernetically enhanced human soldier whose sole mission is saving Dani at all costs. The two eventually encounter a much older Sarah (played faithfully by Linda Hamilton in her early sixties), who rescues them from the Rev-9 after their first car chase and reveals she has been destroying terminators for years, hunting each newly arrived machine based on coordinates sent to her by an encrypted number. That mysterious helper turns out to be Carl (Schwarzenegger), the same T-800 who killed John but is now reformed, having more or less reprogrammed himself after many years of masquerading as human once his murderous objective was fulfilled. This motley crew—two human women conscripted because of their unlived destinies and two cybernetic soldiers—eludes, fights, and eventually prevails against the Rev-9. Both Carl and Grace sacrifice themselves in the final battle, leaving Sarah and Dani to prepare for the unaverted apocalypse ahead.[62]

It perhaps goes without saying that, despite similarities in its premise, *Dark Fate* represents a significant deviation in characterization. The T-800, Carl, serves a crucial role in the film's fight scenes and has an interesting emotional backstory in that he is a machine who has become humanized by lived experience, but the core of the film circulates around Dani, Grace, and Sarah. Moreover, while Sarah initially assumes that Dani is also destined to be the mother of a future hero, a sentiment she expresses with audible bitterness and which Grace does not initially contradict, Grace eventually reveals that Dani herself is the hero she has been sent to protect. Contrary to Sarah's assumption that Dani is wanted merely for her "womb," Grace's flashback (to her experiences in the future) reveals that Dani saved her from certain death, rescuing a teenage Grace from marauding survivors and recruiting them and other scavengers to fight against the machines instead of merely killing other humans to survive. In an impassioned speech, given while the foursome attempts to escape the Rev-9 on a military jet, Grace kneels before Dani, her eyes misted and tone sincere: "You turned scavengers into militias and militias into an army. We rose up out of the ashes and we took our world back. You taught us there is no fate but what we make for ourselves. Dani, you are not the mother of some man who saves the future. You are the future." Like the reimagining of Sarah in *Genisys*, Grace's revelation shifts the classic narrative so that Dani becomes the hero, the leader of the future. During her initial misidentification of Dani's importance, Sarah grouses, "Fine, let someone else be Mother Mary for a while," firmly emphasizing both her consternation around her own coercive though ultimately thwarted role as mother-of-a-hero and her affirmation that John's role positioned him as a Christ-like savior. Upon discovering Dani's real purpose, Sarah admits, her tone amazed, "She's John."

While Sarah takes on a mentor role in her relationship with Dani, especially implied at the end of the film when they are the two remaining survivors of their ordeal, she does not fall into an obviously maternal position relative to this new hero. This in spite of the fact that she patronizingly tells Dani early on that "sometimes mommies and daddies have to have grown-up discussions," in reference to herself and Grace, and implying that Dani is like a helpless child who must be protected from things she cannot understand.[63] Regardless of this framing, however, it is Dani who becomes ensnared in the maternal plot; despite Dani's lack of present or future offspring, *Dark Fate* still manages to establish her as a mother-warrior, with all the attendant privileges and losses—not least of which is Grace's aforementioned assertion that Dani assembles a new sort of human family from the ruins of civilization. I will return to the complexities of Dani and Grace's relationship but first wish to mention a few related aspects of the dynamic between Sarah, Grace, and Carl vis-à-vis their protection of Dani. Whereas Grace asserts Dani's importance to her and to the future, Sarah explains that she feels invested in helping Dani "because I was her, and it sucks." This identification, then, may also explain Carl's relevance; while he admits to a skeptical Sarah that he sent her the coordinates for each terminator attack to give her purpose after the death of John, he clearly also finds purpose in protecting Dani seemingly of his own volition. Although Carl functions in the film as a kind of absolute "brawn," insomuch as he cannot feel pain or be incapacitated due to wounds or fear, Grace and Sarah are not far behind, throwing themselves unquestioningly into fights with battle-hardened readiness and muscled efficiency.

Dani treats Carl as if he were human, speaking frankly with him about his ability to comprehend human emotion and expressing sympathy when he has to leave his wife and adoptive son; she similarly manages to draw out Sarah's humanity, as the older woman recounts her devastation over John's death to Dani in a rare moment of vulnerability. Though somewhat tangential to my central analysis, Dani's nurturing quality and her inherent kindness and empathy—also her refusal to abandon either Sarah or Grace regardless of danger to herself—establish the character as one with the potential to be a "good" mother, a potential that Grace actualizes. Grace's behavior toward Dani initially defies easy interpretation; she single-mindedly protects her charge in the film's first fight sequence, a brutal brawl at the automotive factory where Dani works, and gruffly demands Dani escape with her much like the protective terminators in other films who operate based on programming rather than emotional connections. However, during a crucial moment, cornered after a grueling car chase and shielding Dani from the blast of an exploding car, Grace gathers Dani into her arms, wrapping her taller body around the young woman in a way suggestive of either a child or a lover. In fact, the first half of *Dark Fate* allows the implication of a possible romance between the women, not only through the metareferential ghost of Kyle Reese as lover/father/protective savior in *Terminator* and *Genisys*. Grace's first embrace is echoed in several others throughout the film, including grateful hugs from Dani and similar shielding holds initiated by Grace. In a telling yet unclarified moment as the three women ride in the back of a pickup truck on their way to cross the U.S.-Mexico border, Sarah scrutinizes her younger counterparts while they are unaware. Dani lies asleep, head cradled in Grace's lap while Grace watches her softly, eyes downcast (a reversal of an earlier moment in the film in which an injured Grace lies in Dani's lap in the back of Sarah's car). Sarah's eyes flick first to Grace and then to Dani, observing them with unspoken suspicion before she turns away. And yet, *Dark Fate* ultimately refuses (or at least complicates) this reading, as the maternal bond is used once again to underscore Grace's unflinching loyalty toward Dani and Dani's rapid fondness for Grace.

The noticeable height difference between Grace's wiry five-foot-ten frame and Dani's diminutive five-foot-one, emphasized in two-shots with relative frequency, alongside Grace's protective impulse, might suggest that, if anyone is to be a mother figure in this film, it would be Grace. And yet, it is the Dani of the future who will rescue a teenage Grace, and Grace characterizes their bond as, if not exactly maternal, one of nurturing adoption. "You saved me and raised me and you taught me to hope," she tells Dani. This moment comes to bear at the end of the film during the final confrontation with the Rev-9. Using the last of her energy, Grace wedges a chain between the terminator's teeth and rips his face in half with a primal scream of rage and exertion before forcing his body into a rapidly rotating turbine.[64] When Dani finds Grace's failing body after the resulting explosion, Grace hands Dani a jagged shard of metal and begs her to cut out her power source to kill the Rev-9 once and for all. Dani, weeping as she kneels over the dying Grace, hesitates, but Grace reminds her, "You saved me; let me save you." Dani relents, cutting open Grace's torso and reaching her hand inside her body to draw out the power source as Grace groans. This echoes the aforementioned scene in *The Chronicles* in which John cuts open Cameron's body to check her power source; in *Dark Fate*, the moment resonates with an even stronger depth of affection, but without the overt sexualization. While the imagery of this scene evokes both the intimacy of bodily penetration and a caesarean birth, the implications reverse the ethos of maternal protection. Here, Dani must choose to sacrifice the child/woman whom she will one day nurture, so that she herself can survive and help untold millions. When the fight is over, Sarah kneels beside Dani over Grace's dead body and wraps a supportive arm around the younger woman's shoulders. Weeks later, the two unobtrusively observe present-day Grace (who knows nothing of her future) as a child, Dani lingering behind the chain-link fence of a playground in an explicit echo of Sarah's apocalyptic nightmare. Dani vows she will not allow Grace to die for her again.

Like Sarah in the film's opening flashback, future Dani must endure the loss of a beloved companion whom she has sheltered and trained (whether we interpret adult Grace as adoptive daughter or lover or comrade in arms) by sending her back in time in favor of Dani's own survival. In their similar experiences of threatened and actual loss, all the Sarahs and, now, Dani exemplify narratives of maternal loss as a precursor to violence, echoing my earlier assertion that even the potential of loss justifies violent preemptive action on the part of mothers and the social order they signify.[65] Sjoberg and Gentry explain how "a conservative interpretation of gender sees women as peaceful and apolitical, a liberal view understands women as a pacifying influence on politics, and feminists who study global politics often critique the masculine violence of interstate relations. Women's violence falls outside of these ideal-typical understandings of what it means to be a woman."[66] The *Terminator* franchise presents violence as necessary due to maternal thinking or a mother's privilege to act for her children and humanity, unwittingly echoing Khanna's assertion that violent means are sometimes necessary to achieve peace. Nevertheless, as we see starkly in *Dark Fate*, while the narrative supports the agency of its women characters, they are still all presented as "others" in some way, with mainly Dani, the most explicitly feminine and implicitly maternal character, emerging as the future hero.

While they are tangential to my central claims throughout the majority of this chapter, by way of conclusion, I will take a moment to draw connections between the ways *Dark Fate* engages in intersectional feminist signposting similar to that reflected by all contemporary installments of the franchises I have explored so far, from *Charlie's Angels* and *Wonder Woman* to *Supergirl*. Not only does the latest film feature three heroic women, none of whom are explicitly bound to any male characters, but *Dark Fate* also employs Dani and Grace to make statements of varying subtlety regarding the masculine/feminine binary as well as U.S. border politics and whiteness. Grace's androgyny is made explicit by the film in several ways, including clear parallels drawn between Grace and Carl in their no-holds-barred physicality and their affinity for close-contact fighting (whereas Sarah, although tough, still prefers guns and distance from her target). Unlike the Sarah of *Judgment Day*, who faces harsh consequences for her "musculinity," including a notable rift between her and John before she is reminded to be nurturing by the T-800, Grace faces no significant consequences for her masculinized appearance or demeanor. In fact, while all three women eventually change into combat attire, Grace wears explicitly men's clothes from the start of the film, highlighted in two separate incidents: when she first arrives naked due to the time travel, she steals a young man's clothes; when she escapes the border patrol facility, she steals the clothes of male guard. In both instances, women's clothes are available—in the form of the young man's girlfriend and a female agent, respectively—and the shots of the half-naked men she leaves in her wake emphasize Grace's choice of attire as deliberate.[67] The preapocalyptic girl version of Grace we see in flashbacks and at the end of the film, however, appears more obviously feminine, with long hair and delicate features, which could suggest that her androgynous appearance is less about preference than the battle-weary efficiency of a soldier.

Dani, although not as strong as Grace or Sarah, overcomes her initial fear and panic quite rapidly, taking charge when necessary and eventually taking up arms despite her diminutive stature and lack of training. Even early in the film, when Grace's human metabolism begins to shut down due to her exertion against the Rev-9, Dani takes over the robbery of a pharmacy to get the medication Grace needs. Using a combination of threatened violence (a gun in her hand) and desperate explanation, Dani not only secures the medication but receives compassion from the pharmacist, who helps her support Grace's sagging body. By midway through the film, she proves herself a competent member of the trio, arranging for their passage through the Mexican desert without hesitation. Perhaps remarkably, Dani is never explicitly Othered by the narrative of the film, neither for her relative physical weakness nor her race/nationality. As a Mexican woman, Dani speaks primarily in Spanish for several minutes after her initial introduction on-screen, slipping in and out of English with her brother and finally speaking only English with Dani and Sarah. At the end of the film, Dani again reverts to a combination of Spanish and English in her final attack on the Rev-9, marking herself as a bilingual subject, one located literally and figuratively outside of the explicit Americanization of all the previous films. She even jokes that their clandestine passage across the U.S.-Mexico border to seek Carl's help would be simpler if Grace and Sarah were not "so white." While Dani is light-skinned and speaks English fluently, her complexion and Mexican accent still mark her explicitly as Latinx, just as a long border crossing set piece in the middle of the film emphasizes the implications of casting Reyes as the first non-American, protagonist of color in a quintessentially U.S. franchise dominated by white characters.[68] The institutions at the border may mark her as "illegal," but none of the central characters question her position as future savior of humanity.

As illustrated in previous chapters, these nods toward diversity and inclusion—and fulfillment of the need for more dynamic women characters in later installments of a franchise—may reframe but ultimately do not diminish the *Terminator* franchise's reliance on a central maternal narrative. In fact, Yvonne Tasker's analysis from 1998 remains relevant: "Distanced from a classed and raced 'femininity' which is defined by passivity and hysteria, the female action hero offers a fantasy image of (proletarian) physical strength showcased within narratives that repeatedly seek to explain her (and to explain her away). Female action heroes are constructed in narrative terms as macho/masculine, as mothers or as Others: sometimes even as all three at different points within the narrative."[69] Accordingly, motherhood has long offered one notable way in which female action heroes might be differentiated from typically feminine subjects. While Dani is neither coerced into motherhood nor bound to its logics in literal ways, the film attempts to reframe the qualities previous installments mark as maternal (rescuing a young Grace, empathizing with Sarah and Carl, and refusing to leave her companions behind despite threats to her own life) as human qualities unique to a particular feminized mode of power. In a similar vein, Barbara Gurr contends in her introduction to a collection of essays on postapocalyptic media that these stories "ask us to consider what it means to be truly human, particularly in the context of survival horror and genocide, by testing not only our physical survival skills, but also our values, our morals, and our beliefs."[70] Fantasies of the end of the world would seem an obvious place for doing away with gendered presumptions and implicit roles. And yet, the closer the narrative world comes to the complete degradation of civilization, the closer it seems to hew to norms that help maintain some semblance of the social order. An implied "master" of her children, the mother and her corollaries in the *Terminator* franchise and beyond are repeatedly asked to bear the burden of responsibility for our global future, birthing new heroes and sacrificing their power to choose how to lead their own lives at the cost of the greater good.

5 · AT THE END OF THE WORLD
Apocalyptic Bodies and the
Feminine Sublime

Two edges are created: an obedient, conformist, plagiarizing edge (the language is to be copied in its canonical state, as it has been established by schooling, good usage, literature, culture), and *another edge*, mobile, blank (ready to assume any contours), which is never anything but the site of its effect: the place where the death of language is glimpsed. The two edges, *the compromise they bring about*, are necessary. Neither culture nor its destruction are erotic; it is the seam between them, the fault, the flaw, which becomes so.
—Roland Barthes, *The Pleasure of the Text* (author's emphasis)

If woman is culturally defined as the one at the margin between culture and chaos, order and anarchy, reason and the abyss, then she typifies abjection. She is the deject on the brink always of losing herself; but for culture she represents that dangerous zone against which culture must struggle to retain itself. Hence, women are sometimes reviled as too close to chaos, as outside of culture; but may then be idealized and elevated as supreme defenders against the wilderness that would envelop man.
—E. Ann Kaplan, *Motherhood and Representation*

When we speak of trauma, in psychoanalytic, physical, or even lay terms, we tend to articulate a rift between the moment and the subject, an incomprehensibility, an inarticulable gap between what the subject once knew and the often horrifying—or otherwise inexplicable—reality that they never could have imagined and that has now been irrevocably revealed to them. The disfiguring car crash. The ravages of war. The unexpected death. The violation of body or soul. There is no going back to the world as it was before: safe, whole, and unassailable. The filmic representation of such a paradigm shift offers an additional layer in that trauma must be visualized, an unimaginable abyss bridged. How these intractable experiences of loss, radical change, horror, and violence manifest themselves on the screen, with all the potential offered by twenty-first-century technologies, and the terms through which they are offered to the viewer vary widely, ranging from gut-wrenching dramatic realism to high-fantasy wish fulfillment. As I explore in this final chapter, women have often been starkly rendered against this backdrop of unspeakable loss, whether through the outlook of their bodies as sites of violent abuse or through their desperate attempts to protect the boundaries of the family, home, or even human civilization itself. In the *Terminator* franchise, the traumatic rift between the social order and the horror of humanity's annihilation is a future possibility but not an absolute; through the machinations of time travel, this ultimate loss of civilization and human life may be preventable, and the women in the films strive to find ways to change their fates. The nuclear nightmare of bodies reduced to ash and dust that haunts Sarah in *Judgment Day* and *The Chronicles*—and which is revisited in Dani's observation of a young Grace at the end of *Dark Fate*—is not a certainty but a threat of annihilation, rendering sharply the role of the mother as one who must remain vigilant to even perceived threats to the safety of her children-qua-humanity.

The locus of my final chapter, the *Resident Evil* franchise, takes this sword of Damocles and brings it down. The franchise's framing renders loss no longer a threat but an absolute, and one that is repeated flagrantly. With films, games, and a television show that oscillate between survival horror, body horror, and apocalyptic action adventure, *Resident Evil* offers viewers a nightmare of a radically destroyed version of reality, with just enough of a resemblance to our own world to be recognizable but with salient differences rendering it unsettling, distressing, and grotesque. For the characters in the franchise, there is no going back, no redemption or reclamation of an unmarred past; there is only barren land and ruin, blood and dust and darkness, and desperate attempts to navigate an impossible future. In the film series on which I focus, the axis of loss and destruction rests in the body of Alice (Milla Jovovich), a martially gifted warrior who navigates the continuously terrifying landscapes of each film with felicitous precision. In the first film, Alice is a cipher, an amnesiac who believes that she is an operative of the Umbrella corporation who tried to stop her employer's unethical biomedical experimentation and failed. The main villain in these films is not the zombies but rather the corporation, which functions across the franchise as a creator of all kinds of horrors, from giant, ax-wielding behemoths to grisly hounds with faces that distort into gaping tooth-filed *vagina dentata* maws and horrendous, hulking creatures capable of wielding advanced weaponry and taking orders. In a fight to the death to save a burned-out, overrun, wasted world, the survivors are a not-so-ragtag group of former military operatives and mercenaries with civilians only serving as background characters or zombie fodder and children cast strategically to ramp up the pathos of evasion and escape.[1]

Throughout the films, Alice is given powerful telekinetic abilities by Umbrella only to have them later taken away; she is cloned by the corporation in the thousands, only to eventually liberate or destroy her remaining copies. By the end of the series, she is one of few survivors of a devastating global zombie apocalypse orchestrated by the corporation's wealthy elite. The final film reveals the shocking secret that Alice has been a clone all along: "born" on the day of her awakening at the start of the first *Resident Evil*, Alice is a true "motherless child," a copy of a young girl whose progressive disease inspired the creation of the T-virus, the powerful pathogen also to blame for the world's undead.[2] Like the zombies she slays, Alice is a hybrid, an impossibility, a boundary creature; the only human ever to successfully bond with the T-virus, she is also not, in some ways, human at all. To Umbrella, she is Project Alice—an object, not a person—its most successful experiment. She is also a thorn in Umbrella's side, a loose cannon the corporation is constantly trying to manipulate and control. As such, Alice evinces an intriguing mix of nature and culture: both primal mother and father, creator of life and destroyer of worlds. And it is not insignificant that it is her body (more so than her *self*) around which most of the narratives circulate. We are told her blood, her miraculous genetic structure, can cure the ailing planet and bring back humanity, and yet she is both indirectly responsible for the virus being released in the first place and spends six films killing, or rekilling, everything in her path from the undead to the living Umbrella operatives.

Resident Evil began in the mid-1990s as a video game and has since spawned an additional eight games (and several remakes), a few computer-animated films, comic books, and, most notably, a series of six interrelated films, a reboot film prequel, and a streaming television show. The storylines and characters change notably in each iteration, the franchise's one constant being its representation of an apocalypse set in motion and perpetuated by zombies, bioengineered mutants, and corporate greed. I focus here on the film series—*Resident Evil* (2002) and its sequels, subtitled *Apocalypse* (2004), *Extinction* (2007), *Afterlife* (2010), *Retribution* (2012), and *The Final Chapter* (2016). A combination of horror and action-adventure, the *Resident Evil* films offer Alice as a constant, with a loose though mainly coherent narrative through line and a rotating cast of other survivors, many of whom reappear in several films and some of whom appear in the games.[3] Although I touch on the two most recent installments in the franchise in the conclusion of this chapter, the 2021 prequel *Welcome to Raccoon City* and the 2022 Netflix show *Resident Evil* are not central to my analysis. Both the prequel and the streaming show completely reboot the franchise and have little connection to the games or the earlier film series beyond the premise and some shared characters (not inclusive of Alice).

Investigating the six-film series allows me to plumb the depths of Alice's character as symbolic of the divide between nature and culture via feminine structures of knowledge and power. While the films are broadly considered B movies, they do constitute one of the highest-grossing horror film series to date, to say nothing of the extensive popular success of the video games, comics, and merchandise.[4] The films are formulaic, involving a steady stream of zombies and monsters, gory imagery, startling reveals and jump scares, and extended action sequences. In all but one, Alice begins the narrative in a place of ultimate vulnerability (with no memory, captive, sometimes nude, unarmed, alone). In two of the films, Alice is brutally killed in the opening moments, only for it to be revealed that the dead Alice is a clone and not *our* Alice. Then, Alice finds allies and sets herself on a mission involving escape, revenge, or the protection of other survivors; to do so, she obliterates as many zombies and monsters as possible and confronts the machinations of Umbrella and its operatives. By film's end, she has succeeded at her task, although many of her companions have died. However, in the final moments of each film (except the last), Alice's victory is tainted by a new assault or devastating turnabout. With the possible exception of the first and last, the films hew more closely to the action-adventure genre than horror, despite their endless parade of zombies. With jump scares no longer surprising after the first film and the threat to lasting harm against Alice mitigated by progressive sequels, *Resident Evil*—like its diegetic corporate villains—invests in the body of Alice at the core of its ideology. Moreover, the series emphasizes the frisson between the abject zombie bodies and the violent, bloody beauty of scenes of their destruction through the employment of heavy-handed cinematography and sound, including slow motion, freeze frames, pumping techno scores, and, in the final three films, an acute reliance on stereoscopic 3D.

In some ways, Alice represents the most explicit example of one of my tenets in this book: that women protagonists whose power stems from some aspect of their feminine embodiment or knowledge are most vulnerable to having that power stripped from them. Alice quite literally is a creation of a patriarchal corporation that not only gave her life but also endowed her with superpowers only to take them away, who make her believe she has won only to incapacitate her anew. She is framed as a fundamentally intuitive person, frequently waking up without any memory but somehow still instinctually knowing how to fight, escape, and survive—a notable assumption of innate mastery. And yet, the films suggest that there is something unique to Alice, something uniquely human and uniquely more than human, that allows her to overcome the repeated manipulations of Umbrella, demonstrating her resilience and her ultimate altruistic heroism. While Alice does exemplify my claims in these clear ways, I contend that there is something more insidious happening with how she is represented in the films—not only in obvious terms (her occasional nudity or the actress's conventional beauty) but in ways that have to do with aesthetic philosophy and its relationship to gendered notions of power. As such, this chapter takes on Alice in the *Resident Evil* franchise by bringing into stark relief some of the undergirding assumptions and principles defining the employment of the woman's body as symbolic vessel. I begin by considering the films' use of repetition in their enactment and reenactment of trauma, particularly in their aesthetic mimesis of video game ideology and the relationship of repetitive failure to mastery. This segues into a discussion of theories of abjection, beauty, and the sublime as they pertain to ideals of the feminine alongside a closer analysis of the third and fourth films in the franchise, *Extinction* and *Afterlife*, including the notable use of stereoscopic 3D technology and other cinematographic techniques endemic to the franchise like slow, fast, and stop motion. In the final section, I return to my exploration of trauma and repeated deaths and, in doing so, reflect further on the epigraphs for this chapter and woman's symbolic role in media as the erotic seam between culture and chaos, as well as desire and horror, and the role of Alice's body (the woman's body) in safeguarding social relations beyond language.

ET IN ARCADIA EGO: FANTASIES OF DESTRUCTION AND REBIRTH ON THE ROAD TO NOWHERE

While it may be a cliché to say that death is the ultimate unknowable frontier, it is upon this idea that much of the apocalyptic horror genre rests, particularly representations of the undead. On the boundary between life and death, the undead speak to viewers' fears of both the loss of life and the loss of an afterlife; what terrors await us on this threshold? Arguably the most grotesque of the undead, zombies render questions of mortality in literal flesh, blood, and viscera. They are also remarkably popular, having become increasingly ubiquitous on the small and large screen in the years since *Resident Evil*'s first release, with portrayals varying widely from dark comedies (*Shaun of the Dead*, 2004; *Zombieland*, 2009; *Santa Clarita Diet*, TV: 2017–2019) and gritty survival horror (*The Walking Dead*, TV: 2010–2022; *World War Z*, 2013) to crime procedurals (*iZombie*, TV: 2015–2019) and romance (*Warm Bodies*, 2013). *Resident Evil* fits snugly into this pantheon and can arguably be credited as part of the revival of interest in zombies and zombie media in the last two decades, although recent forays into the genre like HBO's *The Last of Us* (2023–present), also based on a video game franchise started in 2013, arguably have more cultural cachet.[5]

While the *Resident Evil* films exist in a fictional dystopia that is similar to that of the games, their narrative structure reads as markedly divergent, unsurprising given the differences between the user experience of interactive gameplay and the experience of cinema viewers, even when it may be immersive and reactive.[6] Nevertheless, the films do employ similar aesthetic devices to pay homage to their origin and to mimic the haptic and spatial dimensions of gameplay, while they are arguably less viscerally frightening than the video games.[7] For example, the use of maps, schematic diagrams, and satellite recordings, a staple of the films used in congress with (or sometimes in lieu of) establishing shots, marks the location of Alice and her companions in buildings and natural environments while simultaneously emphasizing how they are being constantly surveilled. These schematics not only mimic the use of maps during gameplay, helping the player orient themselves, but, according to Nick Jones, also "calculate and smooth out whatever friction and ambiguities might be found in real material space and replace them with constructed mathematical space."[8] In resolving incongruities, the maps further remind viewers that many of the environments Alice and others navigate are constructed, monitored, controlled, or deeply manipulated by Umbrella directly or via the results of their viral experimentation. The corporation and its environments are significantly Alice's most fervent antagonists, surpassing the terror of the zombies on myriad levels. Perhaps this is one of the reasons some scholars, such as Thomas M. Sipos, argue that the *Resident Evil* films may be "mistaken for horror," but their "protagonists lack the vulnerability necessary to be threatened by an unnatural threat." Sipos continues that films like *Resident Evil* invoke "the emotional pleasures of the action film," with Alice operating as a "female Rambo," who seems indestructible and not at risk.[9] However, I would argue that it is precisely the effects of corporate domination and the part it plays in another central facet of video game experience—repetition—that mark the *Resident Evil* franchise and explicitly the body of Alice as sites of horror even if the films themselves straddle the generic boundaries of horror and action cinema.

Perhaps the most notable similarity between the films and the games is the reliance on repetition, especially the repeated deaths of the central character and the conceit of cloning as a vehicle for emphasizing the uncanny experience of witnessing one's own gruesome and repeated death. In video games, repetition has several purposes. One is to provide players of game franchises familiar mechanics, characters, and settings to appeal to fans of the franchise's world. A second, and the one on which I will focus, is to allow the player to develop a sense of mastery during a particular course of action in a game; their avatar may die but can be revived (often infinitely) to attempt the action again until the player is able to succeed. Most action/survival games—in fact, even ones in fairly benign genres like casual time management or puzzle games—employ the mechanic of "health" or "lives." The films, despite their lack of direct interactivity, employ a similar technique, one marked by the body of Alice and the place of the character in the films' narratives. Daniel Müller argues that "Alice's amnesia is key to translating the concept of survival into the context of narrative film," in the sense that it creates "an intra-diegetic excuse" for explaining each film's premise while also "satisf[ying] the classical need for a movement towards knowledge and a more contemporary interest in the effects of trauma."[10] Her amnesia often literally puts her in viewers' shoes—or us in hers—as we also enter the narrative with little to no knowledge of what happened in the intervening time between sequels. In fact, rarely does the viewer have insight beyond what Alice knows; we gain knowledge alongside her, experiencing each of Umbrella's betrayals or revelations through Alice's narrative point of view. Thus, when each film ends in a triumph that is undone, viewers have the potential to feel as shocked or disappointed as Alice herself, as we are thrust into a state of looming conflict in anticipation of the subsequent sequel. In addition to this form of repetitive continuity, Alice's cloned bodies (and those of many of the franchise's recurring characters) are literally used by Umbrella as living avatars to test out its simulated environments. Even though the "main" Alice does not die (as far as we know), her constant replication through clones and the way in which she is inserted into manufactured or controlled environments to test her abilities clearly pay homage to the function of video game avatars.

FIGURE 5.1. Alice encounters one of her "unborn" clones in an amniotic bubble. *Resident Evil: Extinction*, directed by Russell Mulcahy (2007).

The lure of salvation embedded in Alice's continued attempts to survive, seek revenge against Umbrella, and undo the ravages of the virus is exemplified by the narrative undertow of *Extinction* and *Afterlife*, in particular. Just before Alice comes upon a large caravan of survivors led by Claire Redfield (Ali Larter), who may be the only recurring character in the franchise besides Alice who does not die or vanish by the end, Alice finds an abandoned journal detailing a potential safe haven called Arcadia that is rumored to have "no infection," offering "safety and security . . . food and shelter."[11] She convinces Claire's convoy, including many children, to seek out Arcadia, and by the end of *Extinction*, Alice has delivered Claire and a handful of survivors into a helicopter bound for Alaska, its rumored location. After seeking revenge against Umbrella with an army of Alice clones at the beginning of *Afterlife*, Alice flies to Alaska herself, finding only abandoned vehicles and no sign of human life except an amnesiac Claire, who attacks her until Alice is able to remove a strange mechanical scarab from Claire's chest. Searching for other survivors, Alice takes Claire with her, and the two fly down the western U.S. coastline, under the impression that Arcadia was either a dream or a ruse. When the women encounter a few people in an embattled former prison in Los Angeles, they discover that Arcadia is, in fact, a ship making its way down the coastline broadcasting its message about "safety and security" and gathering survivors. However, when they finally make it to the ship at the end of *Afterlife*, this Arcadia is also a trap, luring survivors into a mobile facility operated by Umbrella in which they are put in stasis to be the subject of more gruesome experiments. Even the seeming triumph over the villain Wesker (Shawn Roberts) on the Arcadia ship is undone in a midcredits scene during which Umbrella operatives in military aircraft attack the just-freed survivors. This attack carries over into the opening of *Retribution*, with Alice and her fellow survivors recaptured or killed by Umbrella once again. The telling use of the name Arcadia in these films signifies the seeming hopelessness of any real or lasting victory. In Greek mythology, Arcadia is an idyllic landscape of romantic beauty and harmony; it is also famously a utopia, unreachable and unreal. Like all the locations in the films, and its narrative moments of respite, Arcadia is both there and nowhere, its promise of safety ultimately rendered impossible. Like the Latin idiom used in this section's heading implies—borrowed from two famous baroque memento mori paintings—even in paradise, there is death.[12]

The films' emphasis on a cycle of victory against a horrifying foe followed by a failure or reframing of the terms of engagement so that the characters must ultimately try again invokes the mechanics of video games and their concomitant implication of eventual mastery. It also calls to mind the place of repetition as a symptom of trauma. Freudian notions of trauma as a "working through" dovetail aptly with the loss and return of the video game avatar—dead, alive, dead, alive, until mastery is achieved. Jacques Lacan emphasizes how traumatic repetition constitutes not just *Wiederholung* (to repeat) but a *Wiederholungszwang* (a compulsion to repeat).[13] This compulsion haunts the *Resident Evil* franchise, since Alice must fight and live in order to ensure humanity's survival. While there is an implication of her mastery, like the Lacanian subject-supposed-to-know, Alice is never completely in control of that which she ostensibly knows or the power she wields. In the films, knowledge and power intersect through trauma: the repetitive violence of the narrative, the body of Alice, and the uncanny bodies of its abject subjects, including Alice and the undead abominations she combats. All of these sites of trauma underscore the films' reliance on the apocalyptic imaginary and the reiteration of both real and fictional disruptions to sociocultural integrity. As with the *Terminator* franchise, the woman is charged with safeguarding the remnants of the social order, but it is too late for Alice to save the world as we know it. Instead, her body figures as a symbolic and real boundary beyond which lies humanity's complete annihilation; this manifests, as I will discuss further in the final section, first, through the supposition that Alice's body itself will generate a cure for the virus and, second, through the possibility that only if she risks or even sacrifices herself can humanity survive.

In *Apocalyptic Dread: American Film at the Turn of the Millennium*, Kirsten Moana Thompson also identifies trauma and repetition as staples of apocalyptic narratives. Trauma, in Thompson's estimation, is not only "the product of repetition, but also of the ways in which the subject repeats or represents an event to themselves, and is therefore symptomatic of this memorial violation of the ego."[14] The primary violation in *Resident Evil* originates with the decimating effects of the T-virus and its role in rending civilization from its mooring—a trauma intimately connected to both Alice and Umbrella. But, for Alice, the primary violation erupts from her "birth" as a clone, beginning with her awakening in the first film and many subsequent reawakenings in which she reenacts the primal trauma of being born fully formed and forced to survive unspeakable horrors. As with many forms of trauma, Alice does not remember what happened to her or where she came from; hence, her actions manifest as responses to this lack of knowledge. These traumatic rifts, and their attendant iterations, open further sites for revelations into the uncanny, the abject, and, perhaps more surprisingly, a dichotomy of the beautiful and the sublime heavily emphasized in the mise-en-scène and cinematography of the franchise. Thompson, though not discussing the *Resident Evil* films specifically here, articulates a further connection between apocalyptic imagery and the uncanny, which "makes visible the repressed, and is characterized by certain elements like burial alive, dismembered limbs, animism, magic and sorcery, omnipotence of thoughts, the fear of death, involuntary repetition, and castration. The figure of the double or doppelganger is a privileged form of the uncanny and one that foregrounds the thematic relationship between self and monster with which horror is concerned."[15] The decaying visages of the films' zombies, Umbrella's aberrant mutants, the constant threat and reality of death for most of the characters besides Alice, the infinitely duplicated and frequently mutilated bodies of Alice's copies, and even the fearsome power of Alice's intermittent telekinesis all point to ways in which the *Resident Evil* franchise illustrates precisely what Thompson outlines in her broader discussion of apocalyptic film.

Thompson further claims that films in the late 1990s and early aughts evince a certain "apocalyptic dread" presaged by "social anxieties, fears, and ambivalences about global catastrophe."[16] I would argue, however, that the *Resident Evil* franchise takes us far beyond dread and into the milieu of ecstatic actualization, with acknowledgment of how the films seem to glory in the wanton destruction of their abhorrent antagonists and the almost serene ferocity of Alice's martial abilities. Certainly, the films also dovetail with cultural anxieties about war and conflict, environmental catastrophe, global pandemics, and widespread fear of the "other." Some scholars, like Stephen Harper in his discussion of race and sexuality in the first two films, explicitly link the start of the cinematic franchise to "an anxious cultural climate in which the imagining of otherness is particularly attenuated. In this connection, it seems significant that some of the imagery in these films recalls television images of the World Trade Center attacks of September 11, 2001."[17] Andrea Harris similarly undergirds her argument about the films' feminism by noting how the franchise and perhaps all zombie films offer a compelling allegory for real-world threats of destruction, in which "we cannot help but see terrorist attacks and health epidemics."[18] These assertions extend beyond *Resident Evil* and the zombie flick to encompass much post-9/11 media and, I would argue, take on a different valence now in the wake of the COVID-19 pandemic.[19] At their heart, the spectacle of postapocalyptic media evinces a twofold rift and reflection on our contemporary age, what Todd A. Comer and Lloyd Isaac Vayo describe as "a rending, a tear or, perhaps, a separation or perforation, a line already scored and awaiting parting, a world in which terror is rule, not exception, a state of acceptance reigning in which terror, unless paradoxically exceptional, is more a bore than boring."[20] This persistent and endemic terror of the postapocalyptic in the *Resident Evil* franchise, indeed the impossibility of escape or a return to "normalcy," further reaffirms the films' focus on the body of Alice as locus of its true horrors. While the first two films entice characters with the possibility of containment, by the third film, aptly subtitled *Extinction*, the T-virus has overrun the world, shifting the stakes of the franchise to survival against overwhelming odds and revenge against corporate megalomania that is responsible for the almost total annihilation of human life.

Victory, in the form of healing the rift in the social order, is not possible for Alice or her companions; as such, Alice occupies a contentious position between the pain of continued loss and the pleasures of retributive violence. Like theories of the unrepresentable abyss traumatized subjects nonetheless insist on revisiting again and again, the films return repeatedly to the sites of Alice's vulnerability and the Pyrrhic inevitability of her instances of mastery and survival. W.J.T. Mitchell writes, "Trauma, like God, is supposed to be the unrepresentable in word and image. But we incorrigibly insist on talking about it, depicting it, and trying to render it in increasingly vivid and literal ways."[21] How often do these representations of trauma figure in the body of a woman? In the case of Alice, her body also serves a symbolic function as corollary to her environments and, as we have seen before, humanity as a whole. And yet, Alice herself is only a copy; her body is a repetition itself, a clone of a girl who grows up to be a different woman. Alice is both someone and not-one, just like the simulations within Umbrella's facilities of cities and suburban environments whose real-life corollaries have been lost to the ravages of the virus and humanity's collapse. Alice, then, becomes a perfect embodiment of the symptom of trauma—an embodiment of an unknowable and unrepresentable future. While he is writing more broadly about representations of terror and trauma in art and literature, Mitchell's discussion of cloning correlates remarkably well with Alice's function within the franchise: "The clone is, in short, the living image of the unimaginable in our time, and it is very difficult to speak of it without lapsing into the same tones of metaphysical and moral certainty that inform discussions of terrorism. The clone and the terrorist personify twin anxieties about the production and destruction of living images respectively: the clone incarnates the horror of the biological simulacrum, the uncontrolled proliferation of organisms associated with cancer, viruses, and plagues. The terrorist is the figure of iconoclasm and suicidal self-sacrifice, the destruction of living images."[22] Alice is, after all, an archetypal simulation.[23] She is also symbolic of both the destruction and (re)birth of humanity. She is not only beset upon by the traumas of an apocalypse that coincides with her own creation but also, one might argue, is symbolic of trauma itself, especially if we hew to Slavoj Žižek's assertion that "trauma has no existence of its own prior to symbolization."[24] By this, he seems to mean that trauma cannot exist without a symptomatic body in which to manifest. Without an effect, there can be no free-floating cause. However, I do not mean to suggest that Alice is an object or a nonagentic subject, despite the ways in which she is manipulated by Umbrella. There is little question that Alice is a resistant figure, a consummate fighter, and an oppositional cog in the corporate machine attempting to shape her and humanity to its will. While she may be constantly reenacting her trauma—à la Freud's grandson who works his way through a "*passive* situation" (his mother's departure) by taking an active part and turning unpleasure into pleasure via the *fort-da* game—Alice is also a reenactment of the self, an embodiment of the split subject who troubles our distinction between body and world.[25]

Nick Jones contends that "to use words like clone and replica presumes the existence of originals that the franchise does not provide."[26] This is marginally true, although there is an "original" Alice, even if she is not actually the Alice we come to know over the course of the six films. Cloned from the DNA of Alicia Markus, a girl whose father created the T-virus as a way to combat her degenerative illness—only to have his invention stolen and corrupted by Umbrella—Alice exists somewhere in an imaginary between the girl of the past and a woman who would never be. The real Alicia, whom we meet in *The Final Chapter*, is a woman ravaged by disease and wheelchair bound—emotionally fierce but a far cry from the nimble, hardened Alice. In one of many allusions to Lewis Carroll's *Alice in Wonderland*, the relationship between Alicia and Alice (and even that between Alice and her clones and Alice and the Umbrella computer program tellingly named the Red Queen) echoes Alice's declaration in the children's book that "I could tell you my adventures— beginning from this morning . . . but it's no use going back to yesterday, because I was a different person then."[27] In *Resident Evil*, there is no original Alice except what she has made of herself after each rebirth. More to the point, Alice is forced to operate in liminal spaces like her undead antagonists with no history or community to fall back on. Her life has only ever been lived against a backdrop of death. As Margo Collins asserts, "In order to function effectively in the posthuman world as depicted in these films, Alice—or rather, Project Alice—must become all of these: cyborg, corporation, clone, mutation, revenant. In doing so, she becomes the answer to the question of what it means to be humane in a posthuman world."[28] Alice is fundamentally humane in spite of everything. While initially only trying to survive, even by the end of the first film, Alice evinces concern for those around her insomuch as she helps her companions when possible, even as she accepts the inevitability of some deaths. Along similar lines, and in concert with my discussion of the function of repetition and trauma in apocalyptic narratives, the next section locates Alice within discourses of the abject, beauty, and the sublime. She is, after all, a preeminent example of what Žižek calls a "sublime body," a physical body that does not obey the laws of nature because it is, at heart, unnatural.[29] Žižek likens this sublime body to the way cartoon characters experience unending violence without permanent harm and the repetitive death of video game characters, but also to the Sadeian fantasy of the tortured woman who remains beautiful despite traumatic violations.[30]

ABJECTION, BEAUTY, AND THE APOCALYPTIC SUBLIME

Resident Evil and its immediate sequel, *Apocalypse*, are set in somewhat enclosed environments: the former in the underground labs of an Umbrella facility below

Racoon City and the latter in the streets and buildings of the same fictional U.S. metropolis itself under lockdown conditions via which citizens and the growing undead horde cannot theoretically escape. Unlike these contained settings, the third and fourth films, *Extinction* and *Afterlife*, offer Alice and her companions more mobility; *Extinction* is set almost entirely in the desert wasteland of the abandoned U.S. Southwest, and *Afterlife* features travel from Alaska to Los Angeles, where Alice comes upon survivors in a fortified former prison before their eventual escape to the Arcadia. Combining the constraints of the first two films with the expansive desolation of the middle two, *Retribution* is set almost entirely within the simulated city and suburban environments of an Umbrella testing facility as Alice attempts to escape back to the "real world." In *The Final Chapter*, Alice navigates both terrifying outdoor environments—urban and rural—and an Umbrella facility rife with literal death traps and the franchise-typical undead monstrosities. As such, the first two films and the fifth emphasize the need to escape (the facility, the city, the facility made up of simulated cities); the third and fourth highlight mobility as a form of survival (running, hiding, fighting, seeking shelter); and the final film brings Alice back to the origins of both her own trauma and the world's, when she must infiltrate Umbrella, presuming she will not survive, in order to give humanity another chance at life.

I present the films' settings and the trajectory of Alice's movements within them to underscore how both become associated with the traumas inflicted on the world at large and on Alice's body. Just as zombie bodies mimic the "sometimes contested, sometimes fluid" boundaries of public and private in urban space, they also replicate narratives around the fear and revulsion toward otherness to which we cannot help but return.[31] Jones considers how Alice "is herself a product of this space," and her amnesia "speaks to the character's embodiment of Umbrella's abstracting operations: like the spaces she moves within, she has no memory or history, merely a specific set of functions."[32] Jones's assertions should remind us of the films' indebtedness to the games and their mimicry of game mechanics, but also how Alice continually signifies how trauma and the uncanny play out on and in the body of women. Along these lines, Jenn Webb and Sam Byrnand explore zombies through a Lacanian understanding of the split subject, something "unacknowledged yet frightening and obscene" that "also exists as something alluring."[33] This push-pull between disgust and desire, articulated further in theories of the abject, runs rampant through the body of Alice and her virtuosic, violent forms of retribution. Webb and Byrnand argue further that "the likeness between zombies and humans, along with the terrifying otherness of zombies, is pitched . . . at the unendurable, unending story of otherness, the underside of our symbolic order that is posed by the three weird sisters: death, the Sublime and the Real."[34] Somewhat a cipher who follows her survival instincts and operates under the auspices of an intuited set of abilities and power(s), Alice epitomizes the role of the captivating subject from whom we cannot look away despite the disturbing nature of her creation and iteration. Likewise, the films themselves mirror the contradictions of their heroine: the world is a wasteland, a desolate horror, but its frightening beauty is amplified through the films' cinematography and mise-en-scène.

Afterlife, in particular, thrives on the common tension between a desire to watch and a desire to hide. By this fourth film, the *Resident Evil* franchise can no longer rely on horror or suspense to keep viewers engaged. Instead, *Afterlife* heightens the pleasures of viewing violence and gore beyond the cathartic and into the aesthetic, a calculated shift we can see even in its first scene. The film opens with a beautiful, unnamed young Japanese woman motionless on a busy Tokyo street. The rain pours down on the city's inhabitants; the throngs of people bustling around her carry umbrellas, but she stands drenched. In *Afterlife*, the first of the film series shot and screened in 3D, the cinematography revels in the raindrops forming rivulets of water glistening down the woman's legs, her fingers, her eyelashes, as the camera takes its time tracking up her body. When we reach her face, time stands still: the woman arrests the narrative, the camera's gaze, our gaze, the gaze of the man who approaches her looking on curiously, and our gazes linger on her, waiting. She lunges at the camera, no longer a passive object, now a feral, primal force, and the shot cuts to show her attacking not the viewer but the businessman who had cast his gaze her way. This cheat emphasizes how viewers are rendered inside and outside of the narrative through the emergent properties of 3D. When she tears into his face with her teeth, this action registers as both a shocking act of speed and violence and a familiar jump scare endemic to the franchise, games and films alike. Blood spatters the street; the camera, like the other witnesses, surges away in horror.

This slow-moving, indulgent teaser marks the film as a visual narrative reliant on two prominent tropes: the unexpected viciousness of a seemingly innocent subject and the halting movement of the camera and its arrested gaze on women (often dripping with water), a gaze that is continuously shattered by action sequences or zombie attacks. This opening scene also highlights the film's investment in digital 3D. In an essay on *Avatar* (2009), Miriam Ross discusses how films shot in 3D draw the audience into the space of the film, such that, "Rather than finding distance from the screen and a sense of mastery over the images, we consider and reconfigure our bodily placement in relation to the screen content.... The proximity of objects in the field screen threatens to engulf the audience, and this affects both vision and other senses."[35] All the *Resident Evil* films, in one way or another, concern themselves with enticing the viewer into intimate and immersive settings, often only to disrupt the boundary between the screen and the viewer through visceral disruptions, the sudden emergence of a threat, or shocking scenes of gore. All the films also employ a mix of slow motion, stop motion, and speed ramping in order to heighten the visual effects of the action. But *Afterlife*, as the first 3D film in the franchise, takes this a step further by evincing an exceptional attention to aesthetic detail, thereby providing an exemplary foundation for exploring the relationship between gendered power, knowledge, and the body (of Alice) found in all the films but particularly emphasized in this one.

In *Powers of Horror*, Julia Kristeva describes the abject as that which "disturbs identity, system and order. What does not respect borders, positions, rules . . . that which defines what is fully human from what is not."[36] Barbara Creed takes up this call, clarifying that "the concept of the border is central to the construction of the monstrous in the horror film; that which crosses or threatens to cross the 'border' is abject. Although the specific nature of the border changes from film to film, the function of the monstrous remains the same—to bring about an encounter between the symbolic order and that which threatens its stability."[37] Lastly, Isabel Cristina Pinedo articulates the relationship of horror film to rational discourse, such that "horror exposes the limit of rationality and compels us to confront the irrational. The realm of rationality represents the ordered, intelligible universe that can be controlled and predicted. In contrast, the irrational represents the disordered, ineffable, chaotic, and unpredictable universe, which constitutes the underside of life. In horror, irrational forces disrupt the social order."[38] This triumvirate of analyses of horror's emotional power and valence expresses a set of interlocking questions that bring us to a consideration of how the sublime might function as an aesthetic in these narratives: Kristeva and Creed interrogate the abject as something that disturbs both our sensibilities and our understanding of boundaries (between human and nonhuman, life and death, pleasure and disgust, love and terror). Pinedo gestures at the way horror disrupts rational discourse and destabilizes the faculty of Reason, a pathway via which I will segue into a brief outline of why the sublime functions as a useful lens for my analysis of *Afterlife* and the way in which its 3D-enhanced and enhancing cinematic techniques, abject zombie bodies, and destroyed landscapes come to bear on and around the body of Alice.

An eighteenth-century aesthetic term discussed at length by Edmund Burke, Immanuel Kant, and Friedrich von Schiller, among others, the sublime is taken up again in the twentieth century by Jacques Derrida, Jean-François Lyotard, and Jean-Luc Nancy. Burke's *Philosophical Enquiry into the Sublime and the Beautiful* (1759) associates the sublime with a kind of delighted terror. He makes an important distinction, however, between the delight experienced because of the *idea* of terror, such as the distant threat of a horrible, yet magnificent, thunderstorm, and terror or pain as such, which do not generate any sublime feelings because the body is too overwhelmed by the instinct for self-preservation. Kant takes this idea further, proposing that the sublime is a kind of "negative pleasure."[39] Cornelia Klinger elaborates, "Conflict, disharmony, struggle and violence are the predominant features of the sublime and yet, there is also a strange kind of attraction, a 'negative pleasure' connected to it."[40] The awe or astonishment elicited by an experience of the sublime is in part "negative" because of its intractability, manifested in the impossibility of the subject's desire for a harmonious resolution of the tension between the Imagination's aesthetic judgment of the sublime object's vastness or intensity and Reason's attempt to circumscribe that same magnitude. The dichotomy between pleasure and pain evinced by Kant's sublime—wherein pain and pleasure either occur simultaneously or emerge from each other—stems, in turn, from the paradox of trying to represent an inapprehensible object or event. Or, as Lyotard explicates, the sublime "occurs when the imagination in fact fails to present any object that could accord with a concept, even if only in principle. We have the Idea of the world (the totality of what is), but not the capacity to show an example of it."[41] Hence, a rift develops between observation and one's ability to interpret what one is seeing.

Kant articulates the difference between the sublime and the beautiful around an associated tension. Beauty is straightforward, it is either inherent to the object or not, whereas the sublime only emerges when nature and culture intersect. The sublime is not inherent in the object but instead stems from the (cultivated) viewer. He writes, "We must seek a ground external to ourselves for the Beautiful of nature; but seek it for the Sublime merely in ourselves and in our attitude of thought which introduces sublimity into the representation of nature."[42] Therefore, the sublime exists almost completely in the eyes of the beholder. The object only excites the possibility of sublimity, and each individual subject must approach and experience the object in her own fashion. Klinger writes of Kant that "the female principle is identified as immersion in nature whereas it is a male prerogative to surmount nature's confines and to attain the autonomous moral law."[43] This is particularly compelling if we think of the function of the abject as a kind of perversion of nature (or culture) and feminine subjectivity, in Kristeva, as concomitant with an understanding of abjection. Helga Geyer-Ryan describes how "in Kant's conception of the dynamic sublime, the subject seems to be overwhelmed by too much nature—lightning and thunder, water, wild animals, ravines. For Burke, on the other hand, it is precisely a lack of nature that horrifies the human being: a 'universe of death,' as he calls the horror of emptiness."[44] Here, we can see how the abject and the sublime abut interrogations of death and the trauma of the unspeakable/unknowable. It is this same slippage that comes to the fore so strongly in *Afterlife*, as a film that struggles to find its place in the franchise alongside the relatively new visual language of 3D. While Kant's formulations suggest the sublime operates in the position of masculine knowledge (Reason), I argue that the function of the sublime in *Afterlife* is fundamentally feminized as an intuitive form of women's embodiment and power in a world in which social boundaries have dissolved.

About the relationship between the abject and the sublime, Kristeva writes, "The abject permeates me, I become abject. Through sublimation, I keep it under control. The abject is edged with the sublime. It is not the same moment on the journey, but the same subject and speech bring them into being. . . . For the sublime has no object either."[45] *Afterlife* completes this transition from abject to sublime, taking the ostensibly horrific, the unspeakable, and legitimizing its presence as sublime. The sublime is one way viewers can distinguish themselves and their pleasures from those of a world that has become grotesque and undesirable, but it also serves as a mode for Alice to emerge, once again, in a position of embodied and intuitive mastery, on full display through her expert and aesthetically gratifying fight choreography. While Alice's body *is* a vessel and an object to Umbrella—weapon, genetic laboratory, and blemishless host for the T-virus—she is also something more. The other infected literally fall apart around her, but Alice's body bonds with the virus without succumbing to its effects. We can lean a bit on Kristeva here to walk us through this conundrum; she writes, "It is thus not a lack of cleanliness or health that causes abjection but what disturbs identity, systems, order. What does not respect borders, positions, rules. The in-between, the ambiguous, the composite."[46] Zombies are clearly abject; they violate everything our culture urges us to be, oozing and decaying visibly with torn and eviscerated flesh. But is Alice the more unspeakable horror, or is it that her body holds the abject at bay? To return to this chapter's epigraph, Barthes writes in his discussion of another kind of unspeakable pleasure that "neither culture nor its destruction are erotic; it is the seam between them, the fault, the flaw, which becomes so."[47] I take that idea just a step further with Alice as the locus of this boundary, where the edges fray. If there is eroticism in Alice's power, it is of a deadly variety, one both beautiful and inapprehensible within the context of her destroyed world.

In addition to the opening teaser, which vividly exposes the new stakes of the film and its aesthetic pretensions vis-à-vis 3D, two fight scenes offer glimpses into the complex relationship between the cinematography, knowledge, power, and Alice's body. After the woman's attack in the film's opening causes the crowds to surge away from her, the camera zooms out rapidly as well, and an extreme high-angle shot takes us away from Tokyo into the Earth's atmosphere, all the better to see blackness seep out from the epicenter of the violence we just witnessed. The lights of global cities go dark as the plague spreads from Tokyo around the world. This scene is overwhelmed by the thumping beat of techno music endemic to the films, before being overlaid with Alice's voice-over matter-of-factly describing the events that led to the T-virus's escape and then ominously intoning that the "men responsible for this disaster . . . felt secure in their high-tech fortress, but they were wrong." Having discovered a trench-qua-mass grave of her own dead clones and a facility full of yet-to-be-"born" living clones at the end of *Extinction*, Alice has spent the six intervening months mobilizing an army of Alices. Some of these clones seem in possession of telekinetic powers like those bestowed upon Alice by Umbrella just prior to the events of *Apocalypse*.[48] All of them are remarkably capable warriors, fighting harmoniously alongside each other with seemingly instinctive felicity. In an action sequence rife, as always, with syncopated slow motion and moves choreographed to match the ubiquitous techno beat, the first Alice on-screen—depicted alone, a feint prior to the reveal of the other clones—is shot in the back after easily besting dozens of armed guards while wielding only two katanas and clad in a skintight black suit and body armor. This Alice's death can only register as a shock briefly before three more arrive to take her place (one of them quipping, "Hey boys, is that any way to treat a lady?"). Evincing no obvious fear, the Alices overwhelm the remaining guards, infiltrating the facility further, fighting precisely and in sync with each other. As each Alice dies, more arrive to take her place. It is only when Wesker initiates a self-destruct sequence on the facility and escapes in a helicopter that we meet the primary Alice, whose hair is loose and shorter than that of her clones with their identical long, slicked-back ponytails. Despite Alice ambushing Wesker, he manages to inject her with an antivirus serum that functionally robs her of her extraordinary powers, making her mortal once more.

On an aesthetic level, this scene serves as a rousing showcase of the possibilities of the 3D environment and the intersection of fast-paced action with what director Paul W. S. Anderson refers to as "from a 3D point-of-view."[49] In these first sequences, viewers are offered two variations on the theme of 3D aesthetics: one arresting and rain-soaked, emphasizing form over function, the other fast-paced and precise, emphasizing Alice's (all of the Alices') power, strength, and dexterity. A later scene combines these two approaches, in an example Jones argues "accentuates the acrobatic physicality and bodily capability of the protagonists, doing so partly through staging, partly through slow motion, and partly through stereoscopic depth information, all of which emphasize the shifting spatial relations of the scene."[50] This scene takes place once Alice and Claire have been reunited and flown together to Los Angeles searching for survivors. They land on the roof of an old prison facility, eventually meeting Claire's brother Chris (Wentworth Miller), even though she does not remember him, and a cast of other survivors, most of whom will be killed by the end of the film as they attempt to flee for the presumed safety of the Arcadia visibly anchored just off shore.[51] When this fight sequence occurs, Alice's plane has been stolen by one of the survivors, and the exit to the prison is blocked by a thousands-strong horde of zombies and a giant wielding a double-headed weapon, part axe and part meat pounder; this monster, referred to in the credits as the Axeman, appears faceless, wearing nail-studded burlap, an executioner's hood, and a butcher's apron complete with enormous meat hooks attached to his back. Alice urges her charges to follow her underground, escaping the prison through a series of sewers and tunnels under the shower block. Before Alice and Claire can follow their companions into the tunnels, however, they are attacked by the Axeman, who has now made his way into the prison and announces his appearance by cleaving survivor Kim Yong (Norman Yeung) in half, slicing his oversize axe cleanly through the young man's head and shoulders at a diagonal. In the spectacular fight scene that follows, the arresting qualities of water rendered in 3D layer onto the heavy-handed yet effective use of slow motion, precise choreography, and martial prowess to present a complex mélange of effects. Alice and Claire are certainly arresting objects of desire, but they are also violent subjects who take clear satisfaction in their aptitude for destruction.

Perhaps in an homage or reclamation of the classic, prurient prison shower scene, the Axeman's bursting of the surrounding pipes—causing cascades of water droplets to dominate the screen—augments the effects of the 3D while simultaneously showcasing the bodies of Alice and Claire through their wet, clingy clothing and glistening hair and skin. Throughout the scene, the women strike intense, forced poses of martial readiness punctuated by audible gasps and groans of surprise and exertion that explicitly reveal both their graceful physicality and their sexual objectification. Alice begins the scene as primary aggressor, attacking the Axeman with a flying kick that does little damage besides incurring his wrath before she is knocked unconscious against a tile wall. The fight then focuses instead on Claire, who has proved herself as fierce a contender as Alice—even without bioengineering—as she steps in to defend her comrade. Claire takes Alice's place momentarily as vehicle for the film's immersive display of stunts and acrobatics. In slow motion, which encompasses almost the entirety of the scene, she runs from the Axeman, leading him away from Alice's supine body. Each time she looks over her shoulder, he swings his axe, practically as large as she is, bursting pipes as Claire ducks his strikes and triggering the cascading spray of water that soaks Claire's body. The camera angles shift to accommodate various perspectives on the action: from the side, so we can see the athleticism of Claire's sprint; from behind Claire, where we can see her look back to avoid the swinging axe; and from a bird's-eye-view that emphasizes the hulking height and size of the Axeman in contrast to Claire's petite form. In each case, the 3D cinematography sends different elements into the space of the audience, from the Axeman's weapon and his head and shoulders high above Claire's in the high-angle shot to Claire's own running body from several vantage points.

Approaching the far wall of the shower block, Claire catapults herself off it and leaps over the Axeman's head in a backward somersault before landing in a crouched pose markedly punctuated by the score just as her head snaps back in readiness. Then, she and the Axeman run toward each other, once again emphasizing his exceptional size and her superlative dexterity and grace; she slides between his legs at the last moment, grabbing Alice's dropped gun to blast a hole through his neck. As he collapses, the music goes silent, emphasizing the sound of the still spraying water; a medium shot on Claire, haloed by light from the shower block's windows, accentuates her chest heaving with exertion and her slick skin as she pants out several attenuated breaths. The techno music resumes as the Axeman, not yet defeated, rises to his knees and tosses his axe at Claire. At the last moment, Alice appears from out of the frame, grabbing Claire's shoulders as she gasps in surprise. In the following shot, the axe whirs toward the camera (and the viewer) seeming almost to collide with it, before a cut to an extreme low-angle shot from under Alice and Claire as they duck one final time, together, and the axe whizzes close over their heads. They rise in tandem in a two-shot, with water spraying so intensely around them that they are practically obscured by it; Alice raises her double-barreled pistol and fires directly at the camera; there is a flash of gunpowder

FIGURE 5.2. Claire fights the Axeman while Alice is unconscious amid the burst water pipes of a prison shower block. *Resident Evil: Afterlife*, directed by Paul W. S. Anderson (2010).

and then a wide shot shows the monster on his knees, his head exploding in a blast of blood and gore. A ground-level shot focuses on his body as it falls, and dozens of quarters—Alice uses these to load her guns for maximum damage—spill from the gaping hole in his neck onto the concrete shower block floor with musical clinks. It is only after the Axeman is dead that the scene resumes normal speed, with Alice and Claire looking up to marvel in relief at the axe embedded in the wall above them.

This scene is instructive for several reasons, not least of which because it merges elements of both the Tokyo teaser and Alice's invasion of the Umbrella facility with her clone army. Like the woman in the film's opening, Alice and Claire are surrounded by pelting water, their bodies on display, but in feats of athleticism rather than in arresting beauty-turned-horror. The visual parallels with the woman in Tokyo—the water glistening on skin and dripping from hair, the focus on drops hitting the women's bodies and soaking their clothes—toe a line between an objectifying gaze and the sharp attention paid by the camera in the early scene of the Alices' invasion of the Umbrella compound. Unlike the Tokyo woman, Alice and Claire are dressed in more or less practical attire, pants and tightly fitted shirts, not so dissimilar to athletic male counterparts like Luthor West (Boris Kodjoe) and in stark contrast to women in other installments of the franchise like Jill Valentine (Sienna Guillory) and Ada Wong (Li Bingbing). While neither woman is distinctively muscular, despite their apparent physical skill, they are athletic and dexterous. They manifest shock and some fear, but not terror, both fiercely launching into their respective attacks without hesitation. There is little question this fight scene relies on a spectacle of aesthetic mastery rather than horror conventions or even fast-paced action. The fight is unnaturally slow, calculated, and well lit, with the peril stylized rather than visceral. Jones notes, however, that despite the explicit exploitation of the 3D technology to its zenith, the scene still resonates as a consummate and functional part of the narrative, with moments when "the sequence sends various objects into theater space in an assaultive manner . . .

clearly integrated into the action and motivated by the situation—a threatening and disruptive attack by a monster leads to the occasionally aggressive use of excessive emergence."[52] I would argue that Jones's observations hold for most of the action sequences in the films, 3D or not. Even when the camera lingers somewhat gratuitously on moments of fear, revulsion, or horror—or on the beautiful bodies of its heroine(s)—the scenes serve a function to the diegesis. Rather than merely portraying fear or beauty, the camera draws attention to remarkable displays of finesse and skill in the face of otherworldly monsters. The Axeman is no ordinary zombie; he is an abomination set loose on the world to destroy—not driven by a compulsive hunger for flesh but rather by a willful desire to annihilate the living, especially Alice, who threatens both Umbrella's plans to manipulate the apocalypse in their favor and typically sacred boundaries between life and death.

Alice epitomizes in many ways the myth of feminine survival and resilience, all while her body functions as a "seam," to reference Barthes, between culture and chaos. I tend to agree with critics of the first two films that Alice reads, at times, as a sexualized object. In the most literal way, there is no question that Alice, while a formidable protagonist, spends notable moments vulnerable and naked in most of the films (although, in some of these cases, the naked bodies are those of her clones). She is, in fact, naked when we are first introduced to her in *Resident Evil*, passed out in the shower of a house stationed above the Umbrella lab she will eventually descend into. Alice also experiences myriad physical violations—many, but not all, perpetrated on her clones. James Stone's assertion that the films "betray a fascination with sexual violence," despite the fact that no explicit acts of sexual violence occur in any of the films, rings true given Alice is frequently subjected to invasive and cruel experiments while she is unconscious (although these happen largely off-screen).[53] While Stone casts Alice as "the wayward daughter to the decidedly patriarchal Umbrella Corporation," these suppositions of filial loyalty, contention, and Alice's so-called childishness shift over the course of the franchise. Laura Wilson notes how Alice's body "is a character in itself; dressed in tight and revealing clothes, her body's clean hard lines and stark White skin, often enhanced with lighting, is striking to behold."[54] Both Wilson and Stephen Harper further consider the way Alice contrasts with characters like Rain Ocampo (Michelle Rodriguez), who is Latinx and far more masculine-presenting than Alice, with her head-to-toe combat gear, tough posturing, and soldier's attitude that matches that of her male counterparts on the Umbrella special ops team. Primarily featured in the first film, where she survives almost to the end before turning into a zombie and needing to be killed, Rain later appears as cloned versions of herself, both good and evil, in *Retribution*. Wilson argues that Rain is active and aggressive in contrast to Alice's quiet passivity in the first film.[55] Harper challenges the race and gender stereotypes present in the first two films, observing that "while Alice and Rain are both 'strong women,' they are consciously differentiated on the basis of a time-honoured goodie girl/tough girl dyad."[56] In *Resident Evil*, Rain, a butch woman of color, is ultimately sacrificed so the feminine white woman can survive.

But we also see this happen with hyperfeminine characters like Jill Valentine (*Apocalypse* and *Retribution*) and Ada Wong (*Retribution*), with Jill's outfit in *Apocalypse*, short-shorts and a cleavage-exposing shirt, reading as a high femme version of Alice's own "Lara Croft–style wardrobe."[57] Ada's red dress in *Retribution* visually marks her as a femme fatale, a role that carries over from the game version of her character.[58]

In *Extinction*, however, when Alice meets Claire, who similarly straddles the boundary between androgynous and feminine, both women wear clothes that are practical for their desert environment: rugged fabrics and layers to protect themselves from the sand and sun. In alignment with this change in costuming, the focus on Alice shifts from one of objectification—a pretty, innocent cipher turned reluctant warrior—into one of sublime power. In *Extinction* and *Afterlife*, Alice's agency is at its height despite the intrusive pursuit of Umbrella and its attempts to control her telekinesis and eventual success in depowering her. The events of *Afterlife*, however, prove Alice does not need bioengineered abilities to be the most powerful person in the room, and both Alice and Claire prove against the Axeman that they are capable of extraordinary acts of athleticism and skill despite being merely human. The stakes shift yet again by the last two movies, *Retribution* and *The Final Chapter*, homing in once more on Alice's body as a locus point for the franchise—but not in the sense, I argue, of an objectified body subjected to the will of the corporation. Alice's body is resilient, unbreakable, and essential to human salvation, prompting scholar Andrea Harris to argue, for example, that "through Alice, a new notion of biological essentialism is presented—the possibility that woman, by virtue of her DNA, may in fact be superior to man. Such a possibility is empowering not as a reality—which would only serve to reverse the order of an oppressive hierarchy—but as a possibility because such a possibility denaturalizes the notion of male superiority."[59] Throughout the series, with the possible exception of the first film, great pains are taken to establish Alice as more than eye candy or a passive victim. While in *Resident Evil* we may assume that her fighting skills were acquired in some former special ops training and in *Apocalypse* she is literally given supernatural powers and strength by Umbrella to test her as a new kind of monstrous killing machine, *Extinction* makes clear that there is something intrinsic to Alice that makes her more than a feat of bioengineering or a passive body.

Although not shot in 3D, *Extinction* resonates with several extravagant displays of Alice's power, ones that become even more frequent in the latter films. Here, we can see evidence that the franchise was moving beyond the survival horror emphasis of the first film and the action-horror ambience of *Apocalypse* toward its third installment, which alternates quiet moments of trepidation and existential dread with spectacular visual effects far beyond the grotesque makeup and body horror of the undead and their mutant cousins. By the time Alice encounters Claire's convoy in the desert in *Extinction*, they are under attack by undead crows, an homage to Alfred Hitchcock that results in several adults being pecked to death or eaten alive and children screaming and fleeing into the convoy's vehicles. The film has followed the convoy for several scenes to develop viewer empathy and affinity with this new set of survivors, and two of the characters in Claire's group are returning ones we first met in *Apocalypse*: Carlos Olivera (Oded Fehr) and L.J. (Mike Epps). Alice arrives on the scene just in time to shield Carlos and a young girl from a wayward flamethrower with her telekinesis. She erects a mental shield around them, visibly blocking the flames in a concave arc, before blasting them up and away, filling the sky above the convoy with fire and brimstone and killing all the birds. Like the herald of a miniature apocalypse all Alice's own, the sky burns red and black, swirling with ash and sparks, and this hellish cloud takes up the entirety of the screen around Alice, who is shot from below in a wide, slow circle to fully capture her display of power. A scene representing Alice's formidability, both fearsome and arresting, it may stall the action of the narrative, but not to objectify Alice's body as sexualized or desirous. Rather, the moment invests her with awesome power, power that renders members of Claire's convoy both grateful for Alice's aid and deeply wary of who she is and what she can do. Far beyond her body as beautiful, Alice is a fearsome amalgamation of the effects of bioengineering, loss, and human subjectivity. Her abject bonding with the T-virus and the devastation it has wrought nevertheless bestow on her terrible and unimaginable power, both literal and symbolic. As such, her character may read as parallel to other ways women are imagined in horror and grimly dramatic action films, while emphasizing an essential difference grounded in her feminine embodiment and intuitive existence on the boundaries between nature and culture, as well as pleasure and pain.

DEATH BECOMES HER: NEITHER FEMME FATALE NOR FINAL GIRL

"All human societies have a conception of the monstrous-feminine, of what it is about woman that is shocking, terrifying, horrific, abject," Barbara Creed writes in her germinal analysis of women in science fiction and horror.[60] A few pages later she adds, "Although the specific nature of the border changes from film to film, the function of the monstrous remains the same—to bring about an encounter between the symbolic order and that which threatens its stability."[61] I have already demonstrated a number of ways in which Alice does just this, as so many women in horror have done before her. However, I will take this claim a step further, beyond the framing of the abject and into an understanding of Alice as a sublime body. An arresting image from *The Final Chapter* sets the stage for this last facet of my analysis of Alice's broader function as symbolic of how feminine knowledge and power manifest in representations of the frisson between death and desire. At the end of the film, Alice escapes Umbrella's headquarters just before it explodes, destroying the cryogenically stored bodies of thousands of Umbrella employees (their complicity in the destruction of the world is meant to offer narrative justification for killing them). She faces the coming horde of zombies and shatters the

FIGURE 5.3. In the final moment of the last film, Alice (right) receives the childhood memories of Alicia Markus from the Red Queen computer program, as she and Claire (left) stand among the rotting bodies of thousands of undead who have finally been defeated by an airborne antivirus. *Resident Evil: The Final Chapter*, directed by Paul W. S. Anderson (2016).

vial of antivirus, assuming that she will die too. The undead crumple to the ground in a giant wave, finally vanquished. The music swells in heroic melancholy and then Alice, too, falls. The screen fades to black. A moment later, flashes of sunlight and Claire's face interrupt the blackness of Alice's point of view. "You did it," Claire marvels, as Alice blinks herself to consciousness. Alice turns on a small holographic projector given to her by Alicia, and a triplicate image of the Red Queen flickers to life. Together, Alice and Claire stand bathed in the cool light of day and the red aura of the projection. At their feet lie thousands of dead bodies, a shallow grave of the undead who serve as a macabre frame for the two, live women standing alone together on this unconventional battlefield. Claire's hair blows lightly in the breeze as she stands, leg propped on a rock, in the pose of an explorer or conqueror surveying their kingdom; Alice, an upright soldier, listens solemnly to the Red Queen's explanation. The war has been won, but with unimaginable loss— and yet the thousands of bodies littering the ground barely seem to register for the two women who rise above them having experienced so much death that they can coolly converse in a field full of the results of a viral genocide.

This short scene, the penultimate in the film, reaffirms Alice's position as a harbinger of death herself, a grim reaper who offers hope of survival through the annihilation of ubiquitous, abject "others"—an archetypal feminine position between "culture and its destruction."[62] Alice laments that she was just an instrument for Umbrella, made by the corporation, but the Red Queen rejoins, "No. You became something more than they could ever have anticipated. The clone became more human than they ever could be." She bestows upon Alice memories from Alicia's childhood, giving Alice a semblance of her humanity, and the swelling score punctuates Alice's tears as they run down her face, Claire standing supportively nearby. In the first *Resident Evil*, the Red Queen, a computer program that takes the holographic form of a young girl, hunts Alice and her companions as they try to escape the Umbrella facility. "You're all going to die down here," the computer menaces, explaining that her directive is to keep infection from reaching the surface; she cannot allow any survivors of the "accident" in the laboratory to leave. The Red Queen "fails," and Alice and journalist Matt (Eric Mabius) escape the facility, only to be captured by Umbrella operatives immediately and fall victim to their experiments. In *The Final Chapter*, Alice discovers that the Red Queen was made in the image of Alicia as a girl; the program is also, then, a differentiated copy like Alice herself. In this film, the Red Queen helps Alice navigate Umbrella's headquarters instead of stymying her progress, as far as her programming will allow under the watchful eye of a sadistic, mutated Wesker and evil corporate virologist Dr. Isaacs (Iain Glen), who stole Alicia's father's serum in the first place and serves as a villain throughout the franchise.[63] Now, in these final moments surrounded by the fallen undead, the Red Queen admits to her older flesh-and-blood counterpart that, as a test, the adult Alicia and the Red Queen told Alice she would die when she released the antivirus to make sure she had not been corrupted by corporate greed like those at Umbrella. While Alice's genes have bonded with the T-virus, she possesses more healthy cells than infected ones and, thus, survives, unlike her fully undead kin.

In alignment with her motives throughout the prior films—survival but also the altruistic protection of other survivors—Alice operates in self-sacrificial and retributive terms. It is through her body, after all, that humanity has been both lost and found. For much of the franchise, Alice believes that she is at least partly to blame for the T-virus's escape from the facility; by the final film, she learns that Umbrella had plans to release the virus all along as a form of biological warfare, leaving only a handful of resilient survivors and the protected, cryogenically frozen "chosen ones" to repopulate the world once the metaphoric smoke had cleared. Umbrella, however, did not count on Alice working against it every step of the way: escaping Racoon City after being experimented on and given extraordinary powers (*Apocalypse*), resisting its mind control and freeing many of her clones (*Extinction*), surviving despite the extraction of her telekinetic and self-healing powers and freeing survivors on the Arcadia (*Afterlife*), escaping and destroying the Umbrella testing facility (*Retribution*), and infiltrating and destroying its headquarters after liberating the antivirus (*Final Chapter*). Resistant to Umbrella's continuous schemes despite being originally made to serve its purposes, Alice proves to have will beyond the corporation's attempts to infuse her with certain memories and motivations. While Alice is not personally culpable for the release of the T-virus, her body becomes a vessel for it; young Alicia, after all, was the impetus for the creation of the virus, and her blood holds the key to its creation and destruction. Alice is both a survivor and an ambivalent product of the corporation's systemic infiltration into human and animal biology, rendering her monstrous. It might be tempting to locate Alice in other familiar roles for women who disrupt the processes of institutions for their gain or those who survive horrific ordeals—but a deeper look should reassure us that Alice is no femme fatale or final girl.

A stock character of film noir, the femme fatale has been amply theorized as a character who seduces, manipulates, or otherwise disturbs the equilibrium of the (male) protagonist. In her germinal work on the subject, Mary Ann Doane describes a figure who "never really is what she seems to be. She harbors a threat which is not entirely legible, predictable, or manageable."[64] This threat has, at least in noir and crime film, much to do with the femme fatale's body, often excessive in its sexual allure and display; along these lines Doane notes that "if the femme fatale overrepresents the body it is because she is attributed with a body which is itself given agency independently of consciousness. In a sense, she has power *despite herself.*"[65] On paper, these distinctions would seem to fit Alice; she is, after all, a body created in a laboratory for a specific use, although ultimately she refuses to hew to her expected utility. Žižek also asserts that femme fatales seem to "suffer immensely" from the oscillation of their pleasure and pain in acts of seduction and manipulation, over which they have only tenuous control: "When she seems to be the victim of some horrible and unspeakable violence, it suddenly becomes clear that she enjoys it. We can never be quite sure if she enjoys or suffers, if she manipulates or is herself the victim of manipulation."[66] Alice, too, may fear her powers (she expresses relief when they are taken from her) and resent that she can never rest in her bid for revenge and salvation, but she also relishes her martial mastery, athletic dexterity, and flawless aim. Žižek further suggests that the peril embodied by the femme fatale figure is not her control over the man but her relationship to the death drive; the femme fatale is an "'inhuman partner,' a traumatic Object with whom no relationship is possible, an apathetic void imposing senseless, arbitrary ordeals."[67] Here is where the connection to Alice begins to fray; while we might recognize her as inhuman and even a symptomatic vessel of apocalyptic trauma, she is unerringly humane and far from apathetic. Rather than imposing ordeals on the hero, she is the hero who must bear the brunt of Umbrella's machinations; the world is a traumatic object, and Alice is the only subject who seems capable of navigating it. She aligns more closely with Julie Grossman's recent definition of the femme fatale as a character who "critiques social structures and resets power relations," although this model is also not ideal as it elides the way Alice is tested, hunted, and abused by Umbrella.[68]

We might try to better align Alice with another stock character, one from horror: the final girl. Once again, by basic definition Alice's position in the films dovetails with the term coined by Carol Clover to identify the women at the end of slasher films who survive. Clover writes that the final girl "is the one who encounters the mutilated bodies of her friends and perceives the full extent of the preceding horror and of her own peril; who is chased, cornered, wounded; whom we see scream, stagger, fall, rise, and scream again. She is abject terror personified."[69]

While Clover's analysis aptly applies to many such characters in horror, besides Alice's literal, repeated position in the narrative as the last woman standing, she does not issue forth screams of terror or falter at the sight of her fallen comrades. Likewise, Janet Staiger's exploration of the final girl as a "castrating woman" aligns marginally with Alice. Staiger writes that in fighting back against the killer, "the Final Girl also becomes non-normal, a monster and, while adult, contradictorily associated with the abject, the other side of 'now,' a terrible place of loss and death."[70] Alice illustrates these connections—monstrous, aligned with the abject, and supranormal—but she also evinces something more profound in the sum of her role as a subject who, despite being literally born of trauma, is not a victim.

In *The Gift of Death*, Jacques Derrida muses how "death is very much that which nobody else can undergo or confront in my place. . . . It is from the site of death as the place of my irreplaceability, that is, of my singularity, that I feel called to responsibility. In this sense only a mortal can be responsible."[71] Alice is neither irreplaceable nor, in conventional terms, mortal. She is a liminal subject, caught between life and death. She cannot be infected by the undead, since she already carries the T-virus in her blood. She was never actually born, and the logics of the franchise do not allow her to die. She is not disposable like her other clones, ones even she willingly sacrifices as casualties of the war against Umbrella. The investment placed in Project Alice by Umbrella and as a subject in the films circulates around her distinctiveness (the idea that she is the original Alice) even once we discover she is an iterative subject, unique only in the specific sequence of experimentation she endured alongside the succession of world-destroying traumas. Alice functions symbolically as the primal feminine, creator and bringer of death, resistant to the forms of biopower Michel Foucault identifies as belonging to modern society. "One might say," Foucault writes, "that the ancient right to *take* life or *let* live was replaced by a power to *foster* life or *disallow* it to the point of death."[72] Rather than a biopower that organizes the living into fields of regulation through a process of norming that restricts human sexuality, among other things, Alice operates along these ancient principles more and more as civilization unravels.[73] Freud, too, states that the "replacement of the power of the individual by the power of a community constitutes the decisive step of civilization. . . . The first requisite of civilization, therefore, is that of justice—that is, the assurance that a law once made will not be broken in favour of an individual."[74] And yet, no laws constrain Alice because there are no laws that remain; the confrontations she faces operate "between the primal instincts of Eros and death."[75] This is the feminine position Alice takes up, then, something beyond sexualized object or vengeful victim. Aligned with primal nature via her biological superiority, while simultaneously serving as the last bastion of hope for human civilization, Alice represents feminine knowledge as both lack and excess, a fundamentally intuitive position.

I stress this here not to invalidate critiques of Alice's objectification or affirmations of the ways the film series "disrupts patriarchal ideology," which I would agree it does in many ways.[76] As with my previous chapters, I wish to articulate something deeper at work in the way Alice, no matter her strength, prowess, or resilience, still serves a role "safeguarding social relations beyond language," to borrow Kaplan's phrase from this chapter's epigraph.[77] Alice's labor, then, actualized in her body, becomes translated from traumatic erasure to an ecstatic pleasure, sublime in that it decodes what should be painful as a kind of retributive gratification. Regardless of the companions she has lost and the life she has not been allowed to live, one of the defining features of Alice's screen presence—emphasized both through Jovovich's acting and through the films' cinematography—is her fervor for combat. This zeal is echoed by other characters, male and female, but it is primarily Alice, as protagonist but also linchpin of Umbrella's maneuvering, whose skills remain the camera's dedicated focus. Alice is not only beautiful in conventional terms but also defies understanding and exceeds the boundaries of her body in the Symbolic, just as she is bound deeply to the effects of her physical body in the Real. She is feminine because of this excess, a jouissance Lacan, for one, aligns with the idea of God as "the immobile sphere from which originates all movements, translations or whatever, [which] is situated in the place, the opaque place of the *jouissance* of the Other—that Other which, if she existed, the woman might be. It is so far as her *jouissance* is radically Other that the woman has a relation to God greater than all that has been stated in ancient speculation."[78] If nothing else, Alice's place in the narrative is one of a radical Other, a quintessential place of the feminine in the cultural imaginary no matter how dedicated we are to equal representation. In our repeated encounters with her, she only becomes more removed, betraying a growing intuitive knowledge and a power that comes from within her body in enigmatic ways. She is a subject-supposed-to-know who does not know who she is and yet can preserve the self while enacting intuitive, retributive justice for humanity as a whole. The films frame Alice as a subject who should elicit awe, not terror, despite her fearsome abilities and unimaginable origins. As a paradigm of the sublime feminine, the boundary between life and death, Alice exemplifies a subject whose power stems from something dramatically primal, embodied, and unknowable.

It is telling that Alice vanishes from the narratives of the two most recent installments in the *Resident Evil* franchise. *Welcome to Raccoon City* (2021) a prequel that rewrites the backstory of the T-virus outbreak, focuses on Claire (Kaya Scodelario) and her brother Chris (Robbie Amell), and includes a few other familiar characters from the games and prior films, such as Wesker (Tom Hopper) and Jill Valentine (Hannah John-Kamen). In the prequel, Umbrella has been experimenting for years on children, and its experiments are one part of the equation that eventually leads to the contagion and subsequent destruction of the city. Incorporating elements of action, *Welcome to Raccoon City* still fits more firmly into the survival horror genre, much like the first two *Resident Evil* films, and privileges gruesome imagery of bloody victims, disfigured children, and grotesque undead monsters, as well as the building of fear and suspense, above the martial abilities of its protagonists. The prequel leans on two popular characters from the games and film series in order to draw in fans of the franchise, but it also reimagines these characters and their origins so as not to hew too closely to their roles in Alice's films. Notably, *Welcome to Raccoon City* still stars Claire, who became known in the films as a consummate fighter, which carries over the franchise's emphasis on the necessity of women to amplify the stakes of the survival horror genre.

The 2022 Netflix series, another reboot that bears no relationship to the original six films, but references events we see in *Welcome to Racoon City*, similarly highlights experimentation on children but creates two new characters, Wesker's adoptive twin daughters, Jade (Ella Balinska, who also starred in 2019's *Charlie's Angels*, which I discuss in chapter 2) and Billie (Adeline Rudolph). Taking a tack that may seem familiar from *Terminator*, the show oscillates between the present (2022) and the future (2036), employing a mix of deepening suspense and eerie visuals in the present scenes to heighten tension before shifting to high-key survival action horror in the future. In the present day, Umbrella is a suspicious organization running secret experiments young Jade and Billie investigate before being caught up in the corporation's schemes. In the future, Jade has become a warrior, hunted by Umbrella, as she navigates an embattled landscape with the surviving human populations constantly trying to keep the overwhelming majority of undead monsters at bay. This shift in timeline allows the series to play on both the innocence of the teenage Jade and the sharp skill and perseverance of her as an adult—and develops tension in the gap between these two versions of the same subject. How does the world devolve into chaos? How does a curious girl become a powerful survivor pursued by a corporation?

While the series is too recent for me to tackle in full here, I will conclude by saying that the creation of Jade, a new character not from the games or prior films—and a cast that is majority characters of color, including the two mixed-race actors playing Jade and Billie and the recasting of Wesker as a Black man—only further undergirds my assertions throughout this book. While Jade, in many ways, is handled in fundamentally different ways in the streaming series than Alice was in the films, she is also a child born via genetic experiments, created ostensibly to supply blood to her adoptive father, Wesker, who is himself an augmented clone. When Billie is infected with the T-virus, she does not succumb to the disease in the same way as those who become zombies. Like Alice, Jade and Billie have superior strength, skill, and immunity; they are products of the corporation created for a purpose that negates their subjecthood, but which they are then challenged to resist. Jade, breaking free from Umbrella as an adult, must decide where her loyalties lie: to family, to humanity, or to her own survival. Thus, even in this updated reboot, one that foregrounds a racially diverse cast and emphasizes the strength and intelligence of its women protagonists, it is a deep knowledge, the primal knowing inherent to bodies and blood, that ultimately holds the key to humanity's salvation.

CONCLUSION

On November 7, 2020, after Joe Biden had been officially declared the winner of the harrowing and protracted 2020 U.S. presidential election, the *Washington Post* ran a headline announcing that Vice President–Elect Kamala Harris "made history with quiet, exquisite power."[1] Both the first woman and the first woman of color to be elected vice president, Harris emphasized in her victory speech how her position signaled future potential as well as present progress: "While I may be the first woman in this office, I will not be the last. Because every little girl watching tonight sees that this is a country of possibilities."[2] Moments later, she advised viewers, "Dream with ambition, lead with conviction and see yourselves in a way others may not, simply because they have never seen it before." A month prior, former U.S. secretary of state Hillary Clinton penned a missive for *The Atlantic* titled "Power Shortage," with the subheading "Women's rights are human rights. But rights are nothing without the power to claim them."[3] In it, she similarly expresses how women's ability to succeed in positions of power, or to attain them at all, rests on a precarious axis where the existing cultural order intersects with optics. "So, what's holding us back?" Clinton asks rhetorically, then answers, "Although sexism and structural barriers are in many places no longer legal, they're still very much with us. Today, instead, they're cultural. . . . We all have images in our head of what a leader looks and sounds like. That image has been white and male for centuries and changing it will take deliberate effort."[4] This question of power, how women claim and wield it, alongside the challenge of visualizing women in powerful roles when, in many cases, they have "never been seen [there] before," undergirds the foundations of this book. While Harris and Clinton are, in large part, reflecting on the need to see actual women in positions of power, the prescient and progressive fantasies of fictional narrative media have been exploring these representations for decades.

For now, in the arena of U.S. politics, Clinton and Harris are both *firsts* and *onlys*. Clinton is the first and only woman to win the popular vote in a presidential election, barred from the presidency due to the complexities of the electoral college. Harris is the first and only woman, as well as the first and only woman of color, to be voted into office as vice president. As even a casual observation of popular media reveals, the fanfare of gendered exceptionalism teases at the boundaries of most conversations about women in political power.[5] Beginning around 2018, a wave of firsts have dominated headlines about political women: Stacey Abrams was the first Black woman to be nominated as a major party gubernatorial candidate in Georgia; Representatives Rashida Tlaib (D-IL) and Ilhan Omar (D-MI) simultaneously became the first two Muslim women elected to Congress; Ayanna Presley (D-MA) was the first Black woman to represent Massachusetts in Congress; and Representatives Sharice Davids (D-KS) (also the first LGBTQ member of Congress from Kansas) and Deb Haaland (D-NM) were the first Native American women to serve. These candidates are touted as success stories by progressives of many stripes, and yet it is hard to deny that much of the initial media fervor surrounding them extended in part from their status as remarkable, exceptional, or novel. This is not to suggest that Abrams, Tlaib, Presley, and the rest are, in fact, unremarkable; instead, I mean to underscore how the media portrays their *firstness* and their gendered exceptionalism in male-dominated positions as central to their power and ability within the political arena. Even a figure like Representative Alexandria Ocasio-Cortez (D-NY), who was not a first within her state, was branded as preternaturally extraordinary due to her youth, her social media acumen, and her rapid ascendancy to political power. Sometimes characterized by opponents as "just a girl" or a "fluke," by virtue of her race and gender, Ocasio-Cortez is marked as divergent from the many white male politicians who have similarly taken on the mantle of power relatively young. These assertions and others are immortalized in an October 2020 *Vanity Fair* cover story on Ocasio-Cortez: "[The white, male] demographic of politico are allowed to be wunderkinds—Joe Biden was 29 when he first won his Senate seat; Mayor Pete Buttigieg launched a presidential bid at 37, the same age as Tom Cotton when he ascended to the Senate. But 'we are not used to seeing young women of color in positions of power,' says journalist Andrea González-Ramírez, an early chronicler of AOC's rise."[6] While Clinton's essay emphasizes the cultural barriers still in place for women, long cemented by historical precedents that are being slowly chipped away, the tendency to attribute the status of women in elite and powerful positions to their gender and other exceptional aspects of their identity remains.

As Simone de Beauvoir astutely observed over seventy years ago, men are largely still considered in neutral and universal terms—whereas women, especially women of color, are *other than*, Others with a capital "O."[7] The *Vanity Fair* feature offers an easy illustration of this idea in its emphasis on how young male politicians are not as frequently questioned about their youth as young female politicians. Similarly, the way the taglines of "first" and "only" are added onto the accomplishments of influential women, as if exceptionalism alone affords them specialized knowledge and power, provides further supporting evidence. This emphasis often inspires congratulatory excitement, adulation that is not entirely misplaced. Women *should* have equal representation and footing in all fields of human accomplishment, and so celebrations of moments that bring them closer to this goal are understandable. Likewise with fictional media: As I enumerated in the introduction to this book, there have been extensive gains for women's roles in film and television over the last two decades. More and more networks, studios, and streaming services are putting out content many consider diverse and inclusive, with characters spanning the gamut of belonging from heretofore underrepresented communities: characters of color, queer characters, trans and nonbinary characters, and disabled characters. While women, broadly writ, have always featured in film, television, and other media, the representation of female characters is also shifting to accommodate more dynamic and nuanced portrayals vis-à-vis gender roles and expression.

However, as I contend in this book, just as there has been an increase in women's representation, there is also a temptation for self-congratulatory signposting regarding the ways in which female characters are exceptional—and these models often fall back on well-worn tropes of femininity, not least of which is an emphasis on intuitive knowledge and power born out of traits and abilities culturally coded as feminine. This has not necessarily dwindled even as more efforts have been made to be inclusive in intersectional ways, as I discuss alongside the most recent installments of franchises like *Charlie's Angels*, *Supergirl*, *Terminator*, and even *Resident Evil*.[8] Assertions of "girl power" and "women's empowerment" or even an insistence on "strong female characters" harbors built-in self-destruct mechanisms wherein qualifying power as feminine lays out a blueprint for that power's potential destabilization regardless of other identity markers along the lines of race or sexuality. Gendered exceptionalism also reasserts gender difference, leaving little room for nonbinary characters, androgyny, and/or representations of men and women who do not fit into masculine or feminine molds. The solution is not to have female characters who "act like men" but to create characters whose power or specialized knowledge is not based on their gender expression or on gendered norms, while still allowing those characters to embody and acknowledge gender difference. This aspiration, however, is a difficult one to achieve, particularly when there have always been fewer female protagonists than male ones on film and in television shows—a trend that is only recently on the upswing—necessitating the urge to exult every first and only as a triumph of achievement for women's media representation.

Focusing on transmedia franchises has allowed me to bracket my analyses through a consideration of how repetition breeds familiarity and assumptions of mastery, further cementing the notion that women's power stems from a deep, unknowable, timeless place. This is not the case for every media representation of women today, and there are certainly many exceptions to my claims; however, I would argue that the tendency to lean into gendered notions of knowledge and power remains strongest with narratives that purport to showcase exceptional women. We can see this with the updates to *Charlie's Angels* and *Wonder Woman*, where beloved characters are given new life but under similar terms of engagement. Or in *Supergirl*, where an explicit attempt to forefront social justice issues and intersectional feminism means the characters falter under the weight of expectations around empowerment and service to the community. When human civilization is at risk, the mothers and nurturers of the *Terminator* franchise are expected to safeguard the social order and the family as proxies for democratic values of life and liberty, without being allowed their own pursuit of happiness. Finally, even after the end of the world and far beyond the reaches of civilization's mandates, the *Resident Evil* films reify the notion that women's bodies are primal conduits for pleasure, pain, and the possibility of rebirth. There may be more women than ever in contemporary media representations—and increasingly more women in politics, industry, business, and beyond—but I challenge us to think what these roles, these representations, would look like without presumptions of feminine intuition and without expecting women to continue to carry the weight of gendered exceptionalism and its attendant vulnerabilities.

ACKNOWLEDGMENTS

Even though this book has very little to do with my doctoral dissertation, my gratitude reaches at least as far back as graduate school, if not further. In one of my first classes in my PhD program in visual and cultural studies at the University of Rochester, the late, great Douglas Crimp encouraged my early forays into writing about television even though it was far from his area of expertise and, frankly, I was not yet terribly good at it. Over the two years of my coursework there, I would have the privilege of working with many wonderful scholars, professors and peers alike, all of whom variously shaped my strengths as a writer and thinker and fostered in me a spirit of intellectual discovery that I still cherish. Members of my dissertation committee, Sharon Willis, Rachel Haidu, and Timothy Scheie, recommended books and other resources to me that I have returned to time and time again over the years, and my dissertation chair, A. Joan Saab, gave me the single best piece of writing advice I have yet to receive. "Sometimes you just need to start writing," she told me, meaning that there was a time when one had to put the research aside and actually put pen to paper and begin those daunting first paragraphs. It may sound like simple advice, but I cannot quantify how many times I have relied on it to get myself moving forward on a project, including this one.

The ideas that shaped this book were formed over the course of the last decade, taking the form of myriad conference papers wherein I explored the germinating principles that I flesh out here. While they may not remember these exchanges, conversations with and questions from scholars such as Diane Negra, Yvonne Tasker, Mary Celeste Kearney, Rhea A. Hoskin Bambi Haggins, Barbara Klinger, Linda Mizejewski, Corey Creekmur, Miriam Kent, and Suzanne Leonard have helped guide my thinking in key areas that intersect with this book. I am also extremely grateful for the continued support of Chris Holmlund, whose work and friendship helped buoy me throughout this project. I spent many years working alongside the board of directors of the Society for Cinema and Media Studies, and although that work was not directly related to my scholarship, the relationships I formed during that time have been instrumental to my career and have motivated my writing in unquantifiable ways. I cannot possibly name everyone whose scholarship and professional support inspire me, but I hope that will in no way signal that the effects of their collegiality have diminished.

I am especially indebted to my colleagues in Film and Media Studies at Arizona State University, particularly Julia Himberg and Aaron Baker, who were instrumental in helping me with my book proposal and in finding a publisher. This book was written with the support of the Department of English and through a Faculty Fellowship from the Institute for Humanities Research at ASU; special thanks should go to members of my fellowship cohort, Patricia Webb and Ilana Dann

Luna, whose comments on some of my drafts shifted my line of thinking in fundamental ways. In the final year of writing this manuscript, I had the great fortune to join a writing group for faculty women of color; it is not an overstatement to say that being part of this group got me through some of the thorniest sections of the book and helped me focus on my writing in ways that would have been impossible to do alone. I want to acknowledge the role played by the members of that group, particularly Angie Bautista-Chavez, who recruited me, as well as Xing Zhang and Christian Dyogi Phillips, among others, who were there nearly every day over Zoom with words of encouragement. I also could not be happier with my editor at Rutgers University Press, Nicole Solano, as well as the rest of the publishing team at RUP and beyond, especially my production editor Michelle Witkowski and copy editor Susan Ecklund. I owe a special debt of gratitude to my thoughtful and thorough reviewers, whose comments were instrumental in the shaping of the final manuscript.

Finally, I want to thank my family, including my parents, Rita Dove and Fred Viebahn, who endured hours of phone calls during which I rambled about various films and television shows while trying to foment the arguments that eventually found their way into this book; my wife, April Miller, an excellent scholar in her own right; and my child, Saoirse, for their continuous support of me and this project. While Saoirse is still too young to watch most of the films and shows I discuss here, I wrote much of the first draft while supervising their virtual schooling during the COVID-19 pandemic and hence they are inextricably tied to the book's germination. I also dedicated this book to them because their questions and insights have challenged me to think beyond the laudatory ideology of "representation matters" and toward a broader critique of gendered exceptionalism that considers lived experience alongside its translation into popular media.

NOTES

INTRODUCTION

1. Martha M. Lauzen, "It's a Man's (Celluloid) World: On-Screen Representations of Female Characters in the Top 100 Films of 2011" (Center for the Study of Women in Television and Film, 2012).

2. Katherine L. Neff, Stacy L. Smith, and Katherine Pieper, "Inequality across 1,500 Popular Films: Examining Gender and Race/Ethnicity of Leads/Co Leads from 2007 to 2021," Annenberg Inclusion Initiative (University of Southern California, 2020), 1.

3. The researcher's definition of "major character" includes those with significant impact on narrative and may not necessarily be limited to a show's protagonist. Martha M. Lauzen, "Boxed In: Women on Screen and behind the Scenes on Broadcast and Streaming Television in 2021–22" (Center for the Study of Women in Television and Film, 2022), 1–2.

4. This earlier report assesses the 2019–2020 television season. It is worth noting that streaming services were leading this change, with women leading 43 percent of their shows, whereas only a quarter of broadcast and cable channel shows had female protagonists—these numbers averaged out to approximately a third overall. Martha M. Lauzen, "Boxed In 2019–20: Women on Screen and behind the Scenes in Television" (Center for the Study of Women in Television and Film, 2020), 6, 9–12.

5. Kristen Warner's discussion of the diversity fallacy on streaming platforms offers one example of this. Visibly including more diversity in content and advertising one's inclusion efforts do not necessarily lead to greater diversity or inclusion in the C-suite or in programming over the long term. See Kristen Warner, "Blue Skies Again: Streamers and the Impossible Promise of Diversity," *Los Angeles Review of Books*, 24 June 2021, https://lareviewofbooks.org/article/blue-skies-again-streamers-and-the-impossible-promise-of-diversity/.

6. There are many franchises that are not included in this book for a host of reasons, including space, genre, and relevance. The primary delimiting factor, however, remains this book's focus on franchises that have historically focused on one or more female protagonists. For example, while the Marvel Cinematic Universe (MCU) comprises one of the most popular and massive recent transmedia franchises and has many women characters, it cannot be said to have historically focused on female protagonists. It does not follow that there is nothing compelling to say about women in the MCU—see, for example, Miriam Kent, *Women in Marvel Films* (Edinburgh: Edinburgh University Press, 2021)—just that the MCU does not fit my particular criteria.

7. *Empowerment* is neither a neutral term nor one that has a universally agreed-upon definition, although it is often bandied about in popular media in a way that suggests it is universally understood. Popularly, empowerment typically describes a subject's ability to act in agentic ways and control their own choices/life/destiny. I invoke it here as a placeholder for a further and more nuanced discussion of its use and meaning in later chapters.

8. Sarah Banet-Weiser's *Empowered: Popular Feminism and Popular Misogyny* (Durham, NC: Duke University Press, 2018) offers a thorough discussion of the ways popular feminism comes across in culture more broadly and in some forms of media culture, specifically. The published discussion in Sarah Banet-Weiser, Rosalind Gill, and Catherine Rottenberg, "Postfeminism, Popular Feminism and Neoliberal Feminism? Sarah Banet-Weiser, Rosalind Gill and Catherine Rottenberg in Conversation," *Feminist Theory* 21, no. 1 (2020), https://doi.org/10.1177/1464700119842555 also offers valuable insight into this subject. Other relevant discussions about the intersections of "girl power" and popular culture include Susan J. Douglas's *The Rise of Enlightened*

Sexism: How Pop Culture Took Us from Girl Power to Girls Gone Wild (New York: St. Martin's Griffin, 2010) and Peggy Orenstein's *Cinderella Ate My Daughter: Dispatches from the Front Lines of the New Girlie-Girl Culture* (New York: Harper, 2012).

9. See Carol Cohn, ed., *Women and Wars: Contested Histories, Uncertain Futures* (Cambridge, UK: Polity, 2012); Jean Bethke Elshtain, *Women and War* (New York: Basic Books, 1995); Christina Lamb, *Our Bodies, Their Battlefields: War through the Lives of Women* (New York: Scribner Books, 2020); Laura Sjoberg, *Gender, War, and Conflict* (Cambridge, UK: Polity, 2014); and Ann E. Towns, "'Diplomacy Is a Feminine Art': Feminised Figurations of the Diplomat," *Review of International Studies* 46, no. 5 (2020): 573–593.

10. Some popular news articles and a few studies have questioned whether women in positions of political power are actually more or less likely to be hawkish than their male counterparts or if these ideas have to do with gender roles, political party affiliation, or both. See, for example, William Bendix and Gyung-Ho Jeong, "Gender and Foreign Policy: Are Female Members of Congress More Dovish Than Their Male Colleagues?," *Political Research Quarterly* 73, no. 1 (March 2020): 126–140, and Mark Landler, "How Hillary Clinton Became a Hawk," *New York Times*, 21 April 2016, https://www.nytimes.com/2016/04/24/magazine/how-hillary-clinton-became-a-hawk.html.

11. See, for example, Michel Foucault, *Power*, vol. 3 of *The Essential Works of Michel Foucault, 1954–1984* (New York: New Press, 2001).

12. Jacqueline Rose, "Introduction II," in Jacques Lacan, *Feminine Sexuality: Jacques Lacan and the école freudienne*, ed. Juliet Mitchell and Jacqueline Rose, trans. Jacqueline Rose (New York: W. W. Norton, 1985), 43.

13. See Luce Irigaray, *The Sex Which Is Not One*, trans. Catherine Porter (Ithaca, NY: Cornell University Press, 1985), and Judith Buter, *Gender Trouble* (New York: Routledge, 1990).

14. See Jeffrey A. Brown, *Dangerous Curves: Action Heroines, Gender, Fetishism, and Popular Culture* (Jackson: University Press of Mississippi, 2011); Carolyn Cocca, *Superwomen: Gender, Power and Representation* (London: Bloomsbury, 2016); Chris Holmlund, *Impossible Bodies: Femininity and Masculinity at the Movies* (New York: Routledge, 2002); Catriona Miller, *Cult TV Heroines: Angels, Aliens and Amazons* (London: Bloomsbury, 2020); and Yvonne Tasker, *Spectacular Bodies: Gender, Genre, and the Action Cinema* (New York: Routledge, 1993).

15. See Linda Mizejewski, *Hardboiled and High Heeled: The Woman Detective in Popular Culture* (New York: Routledge, 2004); Diane Negra, *What a Girl Wants: Fantasizing the Reclamation of Self in Postfeminism* (New York: Routledge, 2009); and Yvonne Tasker, *Working Girls: Gender and Sexuality in Popular Cinema* (New York: Routledge, 1998).

CHAPTER 1   WHY FEMININE INTUITION?

1. Agatha Christie, *The Murder of Roger Ackroyd* [1926] (New York: HarperCollins, 2009), 106.
2. Isaac Asimov, "Feminine Intuition," in *Robot Visions* (New York: Penguin, 1990), 239.
3. Margaret Mead, "Why Do We Speak of Feminine Intuition?," *Anima* 8 (1981): 50.
4. For the Greeks, see Sarah Pomeroy, *Goddesses, Whores, Wives, and Slaves: Women in Classical Antiquity* (New York: Schocken Books, 1975); the introduction and supplemental material in Ruby Blondell, Mary-Kay Gamel, Nancy Sorkin Rabinowitz, and Bella Zweig, trans. and eds., *Women on the Edge: Four Plays by Euripides* (New York: Routledge, 1999); and Deborah Lyons, *Gender and Immortality: Heroines in Ancient Greek Myth and Cult* (Princeton, NJ: Princeton University Press, 1997). Also, Greek plays themselves, such as Euripides's *Medea* and *The Trojan Women*, Sophocles's *Antigone* and *Elektra*, and Aristophanes's *Lysistrata*, to name a few. For Shakespeare, see, for example, Ayanna Thompson, "Shakespeare's Female Icons: Doing and Embodying," *The Upstart Crow: A Shakespeare Journal* 31 (2012): 115–120; Penny Gay, *As She Likes It: Shakespeare's Unruly Women* (New York: Routledge, 2002); Carolyn Ruth Swift Lenz, Gayle Greene, and Carol Thomas Neely, eds., *The Woman's Part: Feminist Criticism of Shake-*

speare (Champaign: University of Illinois Press, 1983); and Phyllis Rackin, *Shakespeare and Women* (Oxford: Oxford University Press, 2005). For Buddhist scripture, see Susan Murcott, *The First Buddhist Women: Translations and Commentary on the Therigatha* (Berkeley, CA: Parallax Press, 1991), and Rita M. Gross, *Buddhism after Patriarchy: A Feminist History, Analysis, and Reconstruction of Buddhism* (Albany: State University of New York Press, 1992). For the Catholic notion of sex complementarity, see especially that of Hildegard von Bingen, as discussed in Sister Prudence Allen's first volume of her comprehensive theological analysis of women's philosophy and religion, *The Concept of Woman*, vol. 1, *The Aristotelian Revolution, 750 B.C.–A.D. 1250* (Grand Rapids, MI: William B. Eerdmans, 1997).

5. A minuscule sampling of texts that consider long-standing mythological, sociological, and/or historical articulations of women's gender roles: Simone de Beauvoir, *The Second Sex* [1949], trans. H. M. Parshley (New York: Vintage Books, 1989); Gayle Rubin, "The Traffic in Women: Notes on the 'Political Economy' of Sex," in *Women, Class, and the Feminist Imagination*, ed. Karen Hansen and Ilene Philipson (Philadelphia: Temple University Press, 1990), 74–113; and Joan W. Scott, "Gender: A Useful Category of Historical Analysis," *American Historical Review* 91, no. 5 (December 1986): 1053–1075.

6. Jean-Jacques Rousseau, *Emile, Or Treatise on Education* [1762], trans. William H. Payne (New York: D. Appleton and Company, 1909), 262. Only one chapter in the treatise pertains to women, who Rousseau deems significant only insomuch as they should be suitable companions to his imagined male pupil.

7. Rousseau, 260.

8. Immanuel Kant, *Observations of the Beautiful and the Sublime* [1764], trans. J. T. Goldthwait (Berkeley: University of California Press, 1960), 78.

9. Kant, 95.

10. Mary Wollstonecraft, *A Vindication of the Rights of Woman: With Strictures on Political and Moral Subjects* [1792] (London: T. Fisher Unwin, 1891), 33.

11. "Indeed the word masculine is only a bugbear: there is little reason to fear that women will acquire too much courage or fortitude; for their apparent inferiority with respect to bodily strength, must render them, in some degree, dependent on men in the various relations of life; but why should it be increased by prejudices that give a sex to virtue, and confound simple truths with sensual reveries?" Wollstonecraft, 36.

12. See Virginia Sapiro, *A Vindication of Political Virtue: The Political Theory of Mary Wollstonecraft* (Chicago: University of Chicago Press, 1992), and Lyndall Gordon, *Vindication: A Life of Mary Wollstonecraft* (London: Virago, 2005).

13. See Louise Michele Newman, *White Women's Rights: The Racial Origins of Feminism in the United States* (Oxford: Oxford University Press, 1999), particularly chapter 2, "The Making of a White Female Citizenry: Suffragism, Antisuffragism, and Race," 56–85.

14. Anna Julia Cooper, *A Voice from the South* [1892], electronic edition, published online in *Documenting the American South* (Chapel Hill: University of North Carolina at Chapel Hill, 2000), https://docsouth.unc.edu/church/cooper/cooper.html, 56.

15. Cooper, 60.

16. Cooper, 133.

17. Beauvoir, *Second Sex*, xix.

18. "He is the Subject, he is the Absolute—she is the Other" (Beauvoir, xxii). A page earlier she writes: "The terms *masculine* and *feminine* are used symmetrically only as a matter of form, as on legal papers. . . . A man is in the right in being a man; it is the woman who is in the wrong."

19. Beauvoir, 49.

20. See, for example, Judith Butler, "Performative Acts and Gender Constitution: An Essay in Phenomenology and Feminist Theory," *Theatre Journal* 40, no. 4 (December 1988): 519–531; Luce Irigaray, *Speculum of the Other Woman* [1974], trans. Gillian Gill (Ithaca, NY: Cornell

University Press, 1985); and Mary Ann Doane, "Film and the Masquerade: Theorizing the Female Spectator," *Screen* 23, no. 3–4 (September/October 1982): 74–88.

21. Joan Riviere, "Womanliness as a Masquerade," *International Journal of Psychoanalysis* 9 (1929): 306.

22. Betty Friedan, *The Feminine Mystique*, 4th ed. [1963] (New York: W. W. Norton, 1997), 43.

23. Bonnie Thornton Dill, "Race, Class, and Gender: Prospects for an All-Inclusive Sister-hood," *Feminist Studies* 9, no. 1 (Spring 1983): 135.

24. bell hooks, *Ain't I a Woman: Black Women and Feminism* (New York: Routledge, 1981), 191.

25. Dill, "Race, Class, and Gender," 134.

26. Koa Beck, *White Feminism: From the Suffragettes to Influencers and Who They Leave Behind* (New York: Atria Books, 2021), 104.

27. Yvonne Tasker and Diane Negra, "Introduction: Feminist Politics and Postfeminist Culture," in *Interrogating Post-feminism*, ed. Yvonne Tasker and Diane Negra (Durham, NC: Duke University Press, 2007), 2.

28. Sarah Banet-Weiser, *Empowered: Popular Feminism and Popular Misogyny* (Durham, NC: Duke University Press, 2018), 30.

29. See Amy Allen, "Rethinking Power," *Hypatia* 13, no. 13 (Winter 1998): 21–40.

30. Patricia Hill Collins, *Black Feminist Thought: Knowledge, Consciousness and the Politics of Empowerment*, 2nd ed. (New York: Routledge, 2000), 274–275.

31. Michel Foucault, *History of Sexuality: An Introduction, Volume 1* [1978] (New York: Vintage Books, 1990).

32. See Collins's work, particularly in *Black Feminist Thought*, but also more recent discussions on rethinking normative femininity (sometimes referred to as hegemonic femininity, which is a somewhat narrower and more contested term, which is why I am not using it) such as Berna-dette Barton and Lisa Huebner, "Feminine Power: A New Articulation," *Psychology and Sexu-ality* 13, no. 1 (2022): 23–32, https://doi.org/10.1080/19419899.2020.1771408, and Hannah McCann, "Is There Anything 'Toxic' about Femininity? The Rigid Femininities That keep Us Locked In," *Psychology and Sexuality* 13, no. 1 (2022): 9–22, https://doi.org/10.1080/19419899 .2020.1785534.

33. See, for example, Banet-Weiser, *Empowered*; Rhea A. Hoskin, "Femme Theory: Refocusing the Intersectional Lens," *Atlantis* 38, no. 1 (2017): 95–109; and Julie Serano, *Whipping Girl: A Transsexual Woman on Sexism and the Scapegoating of Femininity*, 2nd ed. (Berkeley, CA: Seal Press, 2016).

34. Mary Beard, "Women in Power," *London Review of Books* 39, no. 6 (16 March 2017), https:// www.lrb.co.uk/the-paper/v39/n06/mary-beard/women-in-power, n.p.

35. Euripides, *The Trojan Women*, trans. Alan Shapiro (Oxford: Oxford University Press, 2009).

36. Euripides, 54.

37. Cassandra: "Agamemnon, marrying me, will make a marriage more disastrous than Hel-en's. Our wedding night will be a night of death and devastation for his house; I'll kill him, I'll avenge my father and my brothers' blood" (Euripides, 43). Cassandra does not kill Agamem-non herself, but instead foresees how her presence in is home will give his disloyal wife, Cly-temnestra, the last push she needs to murder her husband, setting into motion the events chronicled in another trilogy of plays, Aeschylus's famous *Oresteia* (458 BCE).

38. Helen appears in book 4 of Homer's *The Odyssey* (eighth century BCE).

39. These forms of trauma are feminized not because only women experience rape, grieve lost children, or are forced into marriage but because these experiences happen far more frequently to women, both historically and now.

40. See the work of Mary Ann Doane, bell hooks (especially *Reel to Real: Race, Class, and Sex at the Movies* [New York: Routledge, 1996]), Teresa de Lauretis, and Laura Mulvey, to name only a very few.

41. See Beauvoir, *Second Sex*; Rubin, "Traffic in Women," and Kate Millett, *Sexual Politics* [1970] (New York: Columbia University Press, 2016).

42. Juliet Mitchell, "Introduction I," in Jacques Lacan, *Feminine Sexuality: Jacques Lacan and the école freudienne*, ed. Juliet Mitchell and Jacqueline Rose, trans. Jacqueline Rose (New York: W. W. Norton, 1985), 3.

43. Jacqueline Rose, "Femininity and Its Discontents," in *Sexuality in the Field of Vision* (East Peoria, IL: Verso, 1986), 91.

44. Jacques Lacan, *The Seminar of Jacques Lacan, Book XI: The Four Fundamental Concepts of Psychoanalysis* [1973], ed. Jacques-Alain Miller, trans. Alan Sheridan (New York: W. W. Norton, 1998), 224.

45. Lacan, 253.

46. Sigmund Freud, *Beyond the Pleasure Principle*, ed. and trans. James Strachey (New York: W. W. Norton, 1961), 15.

47. The *objet petit a* is short for *petit autre*. This "little other" is not the same as the "big" Other (usually designated in the figure of another person or even a more general presence of something outside or other than the subject); rather, the *petit a* signifies those objects that are not the subject but are not completely detached from the subject either. Lacan, *Four Fundamental Concepts*, 62.

48. Lacan, 239.

49. Teresa de Lauretis, *Technologies of Gender: Essays on Theories, Film, and Fiction* (Bloomington: Indiana University Press, 1987), 18.

50. Jeffrey A. Brown, *The Modern Superhero in Film and Television: Popular Genre and American Culture* (New York: Routledge, 2017), 14. See also Brown's other analyses of action heroines, such as in *Dangerous Curves: Action Heroines, Gender, Fetishism, and Popular Culture* (Jackson: University Press of Mississippi, 2011).

51. Although her emphasis is on representation and the need for more of it, as the title of her book implies, Carolyn Cocca's volume on superwomen also assesses some of these explicitly gendered traits for heroines. Carolyn Cocca, *Superwomen: Gender, Power, and Representation* (London: Bloomsbury, 2016).

52. Mark Gallagher, *Action Figures: Men, Action Films, and Contemporary Adventure Narratives* (London: Palgrave Macmillan, 2006), 45.

53. Yvonne Tasker, "Introduction," in *Action and Adventure Cinema*, ed. Yvonne Tasker (New York: Routledge, 2004), 9.

54. Mark Cooper, "Pearl White and Grace Cunard: The Serial Queen's Volatile Present," in *Flickers of Desire: Movie Stars of the 1910s*, ed. Jennifer M. Bean (New Brunswick, NJ: Rutgers University Press, 2011), 174–175.

55. Hillary Clinton, "Power Shortage." *The Atlantic*, October 2020. https://www.theatlantic .com/magazine/archive/2020/10/hillary-clinton-womens-rights/615463.

56. Luscombe, Belinda. "12 Questions with Patty Jenkins, Director of *Wonder Woman*." *Time*, 15 June 2017, https://time.com/4819569/patty-jenkins-wonder-woman-director-interview/.

CHAPTER 2   SERIALITY AND "STRONG FEMALE CHARACTERS"

1. The film was directed by Elizabeth Banks (2019; Sony Pictures, 2020, DVD); the original television series (ABC, 1976–1981) was created by Aaron Spelling.

2. Anna Gough-Yates, "Angels in Chains? Feminism, Femininity and Consumer Culture in *Charlie's Angels*," in *Action TV: Tough-Guys, Smooth Operators and Foxy Chicks*, ed. Bill Osgerby and Anna Gough-Yates (New York: Routledge, 2001), 91.

3. The term *jiggle television* was coined by NBC executive Paul Klein to criticize ABC's mid-1970s programming lineup, which included *Charlie's Angels*, *Three's Company*, and *Wonder Woman*. See Elana Levine, "Sex as a Weapon: Programming Sexuality in the 1970s," in *NBC: America's Network*, ed. Michele Hilmes (Berkeley: University of California Press, 2007), 229.

4. See, for example, Carina Chocano, "Tough, Cold, Terse, Taciturn and Prone to Not Saying Goodbye When They Hang Up the Phone," *New York Times Magazine*, 1 July 2011, https://www.nytimes.com/2011/07/03/magazine/a-plague-of-strong-female-characters.html; Sophia McDougall, "I Hate Strong Female Characters," *New Statesman*, 15 August 2013, https://www.newstatesman.com/culture/2013/08/i-hate-strong-female-characters; Tasha Robinson, "We're Losing All Our Strong Female Characters to Trinity Syndrome," *The Dissolve*, 16 June 2014, http://thedissolve.com/features/exposition/618-were-losing-all-our-strong-female-characters-to-tr/; Kelly Faircloth, "'Strong Female Characters' Aren't Enough, Goddammit," *Jezebel*, 17 June 2014, https://jezebel.com/strong-female-characters-arent-enough-goddammit-1592135553; and Rachel Wayne, "Fierce Femmes: The Problem with Strong Female Characters," *Medium*, 9 August 2018, https://medium.com/@rachelwayne/fierce-femmes-the-problem-with-strong-female-characters-6c4e23847b8f.

5. When I use the phrase "real women" or "real feminized subjects," I draw a distinction between fictional and real/living people and emphatically *not* a distinction along a sex/gender binary.

6. The concept of decoding comes from Stuart Hall, "Encoding/Decoding," in *Culture, Media, Language*, ed. Stuart Hall, Dorothy Hobson, Andrew Lowe, and Paul Willis (New York: Routledge, 1980), 117–127.

7. It is also not a coincidence that these franchises' recent installments are all directed by women.

8. Linda Mizejewski, *Hardboiled and High Heeled: The Woman Detective in Popular Culture* (New York: Routledge, 2004), 60.

9. Sumiko Higashi, "Hold It! Women in Television Adventure Series," *Journal of Popular Film and Television* 8, no. 3 (1980): 28.

10. See, for example, Lee Winfrey, "'Charlie's Angels' as Bad as Its Stars Are Beautiful," *Chicago Tribune*, 26 November 1976, A14.

11. According to ratings listings in the *New York Times*, *Charlie's Angels* was fairly consistently listed in the top-fifteen programs each week for at least its first two seasons.

12. Cecil Smith, "ABC's High-Flying Hit Charlie's Angels," *Los Angeles Times*, 2 January 1977, R4.

13. Interestingly, this article appears in the Beauty section of the newspaper. Lydia Lane, "Frills Delight This 'Angel,'" *Los Angeles Times*, 24 October 1976, F22.

14. Gough-Yates, "Angels in Chains?," 91.

15. Gough-Yates, 88.

16. Most major outlets published reviews of the show, many of them quite similar. A couple representative others I do not directly quote: Jessica Johnson, "TV Review: Charlie's Angels," *Time Out Chicago*, 22 September 2011, https://www.timeout.com/chicago/tv/tv-review-charlies-angels, and Ken Tucker, "'Charlie's Angels': Minka Kelly, Rachel Taylor and Annie Ilonzeh Fought Crime in a Silly Hour," *Entertainment Weekly*, 22 September 2011, https://ew.com/article/2011/09/22/charlies-angels-minka-kelly-rachel-taylor/.

17. Linda Holmes, "The New 'Charlie's Angels': The Depressing Spectacle of a Project No One Loves," NPR, 22 September 2011, https://www.npr.org/2011/09/22/140700388/the-new-charlies-angels-the-depressing-spectacle-of-a-project-no-one-loves.

18. Alessandra Stanley, "Female Detectives Revived: One Tough, Others Stylish," *New York Times*, 21 September 2011, https://www.nytimes.com/2011/09/22/arts/television/prime-suspect-and-charlies-angels-tv-review.html.

19. Stanley.

20. See Hilary Radner, *Neo-feminist Cinema: Girly Films, Chick Flicks, and Consumer Culture* (New York: Routledge, 2011).

21. In the 1970s version of the episode, the Angels discover prisoners are being forced to take part in a prostitution ring, but no one explicitly mentions rape, which would have disrupted the show's action comedy ethos and probably not have passed FCC muster.

22. Like many things in both films, but especially *Full Throttle*, Natalie's mascot costume is played up for its sexual innuendo, not to mention the calf-birthing scene that follows. This becomes especially obvious later in the film when she attends her boyfriend's high school reunion and discovers he was also his school's mascot: a cock.

23. Dylan's concern has precedence within the franchise. In the 1970s, the producers' solution to writing Sabrina off the show was to have her marry during the summer hiatus. At the beginning of season 4, Sabrina's marriage functions as the unquestioned reason for her departure; naturally, a married woman would no longer be interested in the life of a private eye.

24. Mariana Mogilevich, "Charlie's Pussycats," *Film Quarterly* 55, no. 3 (2002): 41.

25. Angie Manzano, "Charlie's Angels: Free-Market Feminism," *Off Our Backs* 30, no. 11 (December 2000): 10.

26. Manzano, 10.

27. For an overview, see Sarah Banet-Weiser, Rosalind Gill, and Catherine Rottenberg, "Postfeminism, Popular Feminism and Neoliberal Feminism? Sarah Banet-Weiser, Rosalind Gill and Catherine Rottenberg in Conversation," *Feminist Theory* 21, no. 1 (2020), https://doi.org/10.1177/1464700119842555. Also Sarah Banet-Weiser, *Empowered: Popular Feminism and Popular Misogyny* (Durham, NC: Duke University Press, 2018); Yvonne Tasker and Diane Negra, eds., *Interrogating Post-feminism* (Durham, NC: Duke University Press, 2007); Rosalind Gill, *Gender and the Media* (Cambridge, UK: Polity, 2007); and Catherine Rottenberg, *The Rise of Neoliberal Feminism* (Oxford: Oxford University Press, 2018).

28. I will henceforth refer to each of the Bosleys in this film by their first name in parentheses before "Bosley." Bosley is a rank and a code name within the Townsend Agency, so first names are generally not used or even known by the Angels. Jane, for example, only learns her Bosley's name was Edgar after his death; (John) Bosley refers to (Rebekah) Bosley by her first name because he knew her as an Angel (and, presumably, to undermine her authority). Given the plot of the film, it is necessary to distinguish them somehow; therefore, I have resorted to this unusual stylistic device.

29. Further evidence at the end of the film implies that Jaclyn Smith's character Kelly may, in fact, be the new Charlie.

30. Callisto in Greek myth is a forest nymph exiled by the virgin goddess Artemis when she is impregnated by Zeus, who disguises himself as Artemis in order to seduce and rape her. Rather than have sympathy for her former follower who was tricked and assaulted, Artemis shuns Callisto because she is no longer a virgin. Callisto is further punished by Zeus's wife, Hera, who turns her into a bear. Ultimately, just before Callisto's own son, now a hunter, unknowingly sets out to kill his bear-mother, Zeus "saves" her by changing Callisto and her son into the constellations Ursa Major and Ursa Minor. A tale of victimization and betrayal between women, it is unclear what, if any, relevance the name of the product has to the myth, but it remains an interesting parallel nonetheless.

31. Chris Azzopardi, "Elizabeth Banks Talks Queering 'Charlie's Angels' & How Kristen Stewart Is 'Definitely Gay' in the Movie," *Pride Source*, 12 November 2019, https://pridesource.com/article/elizabeth-banks-talks-queering-charlies-angels-how-kristen-stewart-is-definitely-gay-in-the-movie/.

32. The 2019 film features a short scene after Elena is brought to a safe house, where she marvels at the extensive walk-in closet full of gorgeous designer clothes, only to be even further wowed by the "second closet," a hidden cache of guns, spy gear, and fancy tech.

33. Inkoo Kang, "The Dutiful Feminism of the New *Charlie's Angels* Made Me Miss the Sleazy Camp of the Old Ones," *Slate*, 14 November 2019, https://slate.com/culture/2019/11/charlies-angels-2019-movie-reboot-kristen-stewart.html.

34. Peter Travers, "Elizabeth Banks' Crew of Woke Angels Rescue Latest 'Charlie's Angels' Reboot," *Rolling Stone*, 14 November 2019, https://www.rollingstone.com/movies/movie-reviews/charlies-angels-review-elizabeth-banks-910689/.

35. Clarisse Loughrey, "Charlie's Angels Review: A More Daring Film Lurks beneath the Surface of This Toothless Sequel," *The Independent*, 28 November 2019, https://www.independent.co.uk/arts-entertainment/films/reviews/charlies-angels-review-film-sequel-cast-kristen-stewart-elizabeth-banks-a9221116.html.

36. Rachel Charlene Lewis, "In 2019, 'Charlie's Angels' Isn't Just about Girl Power—It's a Critique of Male Leadership," *Bitch Media*, 27 November 2019, https://www.bitchmedia.org/article/charlies-angels-reboot-feminist-review.

37. See, for example, Banet-Weiser, *Empowered*, and Rhea A. Hoskin, "Femme Theory: Refocusing the Intersectional Lens," *Atlantis* 38, no. 1 (2017): 95–109.

38. A few of the book-length works on *Wonder Woman* include Noah Berlatsky, *Wonder Woman: Bondage and Feminism in the Marston/Peter Comics* (New Brunswick, NJ: Rutgers University Press, 2015); Les Daniels, *The Life and Times of the Amazon Princess Wonder Woman: The Complete History* (San Francisco: Chronicle Books, 2000); Tim Hanley and Jonathan Hahn, *Wonder Woman Unbound: The Curious History of the World's Most Famous Heroine* (Chicago: Chicago Review Press, 2014); and Jill Lepore, *The Secret History of Wonder Woman* (New York: Alfred A. Knopf, 2014).

39. See Carolyn Cocca, "Negotiating the Third Wave of Feminism in Wonder Woman," *Political Science and Politics* 47, no. 1 (January 2014): 98–103, and Kelli E. Stanley, "'Suffering Sappho': Wonder Woman and the (Re)Invention of the Feminine Ideal," *Helios* 32, no. 2 (2005): 143–171.

40. Mogilevich, "Charlie's Pussycats," 41; Berlatsky, *Wonder Woman*, 3–4.

41. "Wonder Woman Director Interview—Patty Jenkins," *YouTube*, uploaded by Flicks and The City Clips, 23 May 2017, https://www.youtube.com/watch?v=uTT-v8TvuQg.

42. Alyssa Rosenberg, "'Wonder Woman' Is a Beautiful Reminder of What Feminism Has to Offer Women—and Men," *Washington Post*, 5 June 2017, https://www.washingtonpost.com/news/act-four/wp/2017/06/05/wonder-woman-is-a-beautiful-reminder-of-what-feminism-has-to-offer-women-and-men/.

43. Jill Gutowitz, "Dear Men: You Should Absolutely Feel Excluded from 'Wonder Woman,'" *DAME*, 6 June 2017, https://www.damemagazine.com/2017/06/06/dear-men-you-should-absolutely-feel-excluded-wonder-woman/.

44. Angelica Jade Bastién, "The Strange, Complicated, Feminist History of Wonder Woman's Origin Story," *Vulture*, 8 June 2017, https://www.vulture.com/2017/06/wonder-woman-origin-story-the-strange-feminist-history.html.

45. See Marc DiPaolo, *War, Politics, and Superheroes: Ethics and Propaganda in Comics and Film* (Jefferson, NC: McFarland, 2011).

46. William Moulton Marston, *Wonder Woman (Archives, volume 1)* (Burbank, CA: DC Comics, 1998).

47. William Moulton Marston "Why 100,000,000 Americans Read Comics," *American Scholar*, Winter 1943–1944, 42–43, https://theamericanscholar.org/wonder-woman/.

48. See, for example, Hannah McCann, "Is There Anything 'Toxic' about Femininity? The Rigid Femininities That Keep Us Locked In," *Psychology and Sexuality* 13, no. 1 (2022): 9–22, https://doi.org/10.1080/19419899.2020.1785534, and Julie Serano, *Whipping Girl: A Transsexual Woman on Sexism and the Scapegoating of Femininity*, 2nd ed. (Berkeley, CA: Seal Press, 2016).

49. Joanne Edgar, "Wonder Woman Revisited," *Ms.*, July 1972, 54–55.

50. See Bernadette Barton and Lisa Huebner, "Feminine Power: A New Articulation," *Psychology and Sexuality* 13, no. 1 (2022): 23–32, https://doi.org/10.1080/19419899.2020.1771408, and Mary Beard, *Women and Power: A Manifesto* (New York: W. W. Norton, 2017).

51. See Ann Matsuuchi, "Wonder Woman Wears Pants: Wonder Woman, Feminism and the 1972 'Women's Lib' Issue," *Colloquy* 24 (2012): 118–142, and Katie Kilkenny, "How a Magazine Cover from the 1970s Helped Wonder Woman Win Over Feminists," *Pacific Standard*, 22

June 2017, https://psmag.com/social-justice/ms-magazine-helped-make-wonder-woman-a
-feminist-icon.

52. Michelle R. Finn, "William Marston's Feminist Agenda," in *The Ages of Wonder Woman: Essays on the Amazon Princess in Changing Times*, ed. Joseph J. Darowski (Jefferson, NC: McFarland, 2014), 15.

53. Aggregated ratings data, like that held in a database such as *The TV Ratings Guide*, puts *Wonder Woman* firmly in the lower middle of the pack in terms of rankings/ratings for network shows in the late 1970s before its cancellation after season 3. "1977–78 Ratings History," *The TV Ratings Guide*, accessed 1 February 2023, http://www.thetvratingsguide.com/2020/02/1977-78 -ratings-history.html.

54. Cory Albertson, "The New Wonder Woman," *Contexts* 15, no. 3 (2016): 68.

55. Joss Whedon, *Wonder Woman* [unproduced screenplay], 7 August 2006, PDF, 4, accessed 1 October 2020, https://indiegroundfilms.files.wordpress.com/2014/01/wonder-woman-aug7 -07-joss-whedon.pdf.

56. Christopher Rosa, "This Unfinished 'Wonder Woman' Script by Joss Whedon Is Getting Crucified on Twitter," *Glamour*, 19 June 2017, https://www.glamour.com/story/unfinished -wonder-woman-script-joss-whedon-twitter.

57. It bears mentioning that a few discussions of Jenkins's film in both popular and scholarly contexts critique the casting of Gadot on the grounds of her Israeli heritage and former training as an Israeli soldier, arguing that her personal views about Palestine invalidate her ability to represent a feminist icon. While this is a compelling line of critique, and several countries banned screenings of *Wonder Woman* at least in part because of Gadot's affiliation with the Israeli Defense Forces, it takes me too far afield from the goals of this project to delve into here, especially as I am more interested in the character of Wonder Woman than in the women who have portrayed her. For more, see Salam Al-Mahadin, "Wonder Woman: Goddess of Fictional and Actual Wars," *Journal of Middle East Women's Studies* 14, no. 2 (2018): 246–249, and Rachael Krishna and Rose Troup Buchanan, "Here's Why a Muslim Editor Called Out a Company for Working with Gal Gadot," *BuzzFeed News*, 22 January 2018, https://www.buzzfeednews.com /article/krishrach/heres-why-a-muslim-editor-criticized-a-company-for-working.

58. In a similar vein, accents play a large role in *Black Panther* (2018) in order to differentiate between Black Americans, like the villain Killmonger, and the Black African Wakandans, who are the film's heroes. See, for example, Aisha Harris, "*Black Panther*'s Dialect Coach on Wakanda's Regional Accents and Prepping Actors," *Slate*, 21 February 2018, https://slate.com/culture /2018/02/an-interview-with-black-panthers-dialect-coach.html.

59. For more on Wonder Woman and American patriotism/nationalism, see Mitra Emad, "Reading Wonder Woman's Body: Mythologies of Gender and Nation," *Journal of Popular Culture* 39, no. 6 (2006): 954–984.

60. Aviva Dove-Viebahn, "Peace Strength Wisdom Wonder," *Ms.*, Fall 2017, 31.

61. Rose McNulty, "The Badass Real Women Playing Amazons in 'Wonder Woman,'" *Muscle and Fitness*, accessed 1 October 2020, https://www.muscleandfitness.com/muscle-fitness-hers /hers-athletes-celebrities/badass-real-women-playing-amazons-wonder-woman/.

62. As a relevant aside, this exchange echoes a motif in the HBO series *Game of Thrones* (2011–2019) around the High Valyrian saying "Valar Morghulis," which translates to "all men must die" and circulates around two central women in the show, the runaway-turned-assassin Arya Stark and the forced bride turned dragon queen Daenerys Targaryen. During a notable exchange midseries, the latter verbalizes, "All men must die, but we are not men" to her adviser Missandei (episode 3.3, "Walk of Punishment"), explicitly acknowledging an undertone to the series' framing of some of its women characters. This exchange carries a similar tone to *WW*'s No Man's Land scene, asserting a subversion of the linguistic convention in which "men" are meant to stand in for all humans.

63. This may also be related to the film's rating (PG-13) and Jenkins wanting to make sure it would be accessible to older children and teenagers, as well as adults.

64. Soldiers would almost certainly die from some of the wounds inflicted by Diana during these battles, but the camera does not linger on fallen soldiers or offer any specificity in terms of how she wounds them. We do not see her slash soldiers with her sword, and even deflected bullets do not seem to enter the bodies of the soldiers; the men are just knocked away by the force of the blow. Meanwhile, the bullets from the guns of Steve, their comrades, and the German soldiers all make notable contact with bodies, even if blood is still absent.

65. Berlatsky, *Wonder Woman*, 100.

66. Marston, "Why 100,000,000 Americans Read Comics," 44.

67. Elsewhere, I argue that the relationship between Barbara and Diana in *WW84*, juxtaposed with the film's insistence on Diana as "other," symbolically renders the latter into a queer stand-in without allowing any kind of explicit queer expression and deliberately insisting on the character's heterosexuality at every turn. Building on this argument here would take me too far afield, but it does seem worth mentioning how Diana and Barbara's friendship both toys with and denies the possibilities of queer romance for Diana. See Dove-Viebahn, "How Much Longer Will Straight White Women Be Our Queer Superhero Stand-Ins?," *Xtra*, 18 June 2021, https://xtramagazine.com/culture/tv-film/straight-white-women-queer-superhero-203171.

68. Aviva Dove-Viebahn, "Despite a Promising Beginning, 'Wonder Woman 1984' Falls into the Same Old Traps," *Ms.*, 28 December 2020, https://msmagazine.com/2020/12/28/wonder-woman-1984-ww84/.

69. Dove-Viebahn.

70. Dove-Viebahn, "How Much Longer."

CHAPTER 3   FROM GIRL POWER TO INTERSECTIONAL SISTERHOOD

1. The Arrowverse is DC Comics' television arm, thus named after the television show *Arrow* (2012–2020), which was the first in what became a franchise of related shows, boasting many television crossover events. The other shows, all of which except *Supergirl* originated on the CW, include *The Flash* (2014–2023), *Supergirl* (2015–2021), *Legends of Tomorrow* (2016–2022), *Black Lightning* (2017–2021), *Batwoman* (2019–2022), and *Superman & Lois* (2021–present).

2. Lynda Carter was the star of the 1970s *Wonder Woman* television show. Her character's name in *Supergirl* is also an homage to Wonder Woman's creator, William Moulton Marston.

3. "Supergirl—Extended 'Wonder Woman' Promo," *YouTube*, 22 May 2017, https://www.youtube.com/watch?v=WLlwgBuKymo.

4. While the 2017 promo predates *WW84*, Diana will go on to share one of Kara's villains as well; the megalomaniacal businessman she faces in *WW84*, Maxwell Lord, is a recurring protagonist in season 1 of *Supergirl* (as well as in other parts of the DC universe, including the television show *Smallville* [2001–2011] and the comics).

5. This is not the first nor the last time Kara will be deemed Earth's hero. For example, in the five-episode Arrowverse crossover event "Crisis on Infinite Earths" (2019)—which encompassed five Arrowverse shows and their many characters—Supergirl is one of the seven Paragons (the Paragon of Hope) who survive the destruction of the multiverse and is tasked with bringing back a new universe.

6. Mon-El is, in fact, Kara's only sustained romantic interest throughout the series. Two other potential romances—with coworkers James Olsen (season 1) and William Dey (seasons 5 and 6)—fizzle out before they have begun, interrupted in both cases by Kara's Supergirl duties and her lack of interest significant enough to weather the challenge of dating alongside her two jobs.

7. Of course, these are only a few titles, and many episode titles are merely descriptive or function as referents to other aspects of popular/media culture or the events of the episode itself.

However, the season 2 finale episodes so explicitly reference feminist ideology—as discussed earlier—that these titles are instructive, especially when read alongside the show's broader progressive ethos.

8. On the origin of Clinton's slogan, see Tamara Keith, "How 'Stronger Together' Became Clinton's Response to 'Make America Great Again,'" NPR, 8 August 2016, https://www.npr.org/2016/08/08/489138602/trump-comment-gives-clinton-a-campaign-slogan-with-layered-meaning.

9. The DCEU and the Arrowverse have always had separate storylines and worlds, with character iterations who behave differently, sometimes have different origin stories, and are portrayed by different actors. Due to the scope of this chapter and the timing of its writing, there was no way to incorporate a discussion of Supergirl's 2023 entry into the DCEU. For a brief comparison of the Arrowverse and DCEU Karas, see Andy Behbakht, "DCU Theory: Flash Movie's Supergirl ISN'T Kara Danvers," *Screenrant*, 13 February 2023, https://screenrant.com/flash-movie-supergirl-dceu-not-kara-danvers-theory/.

10. Marcie Panutsos Rovan, "What to Do with Supergirl? Fairy Tale Tropes, Female Power and Conflicted Feminist Discourse," in *Girl of Steel: Essays on Television's* Supergirl *and Fourth-Wave Feminism*, ed. Melissa Wehler and Tim Rayborn (Jefferson, NC: McFarland, 2020), 18.

11. While my analysis does not extend to the comic versions of Supergirl, Alex Link's assessment of the character from the comics is relevant here: "Supergirl is typically obliged to maintain an impossibly low [standard] set for femininity by hiding her powers. Supergirl's shared secret with readers is not the specific identity of her mundane alter ego—as with readers who know Superman's secret identity—but that any mundane girl might be more powerful than she seems." Alex Link, "The Secret of Supergirl's Success," *Journal of Popular Culture* 46, no. 6 (2013): 1179.

12. There are many prominent male characters on *Supergirl*; however, given the scope of this chapter and the book, I focus on Kara's relationships with other women. Her relationships with male characters like J'onn, James, Winn, Mon-El, and Brainy are important to her growth in tangible but tangential ways (e.g., J'onn, as a defector father figure and mentor, frequently gives Kara and Alex advice), but it is Kara's relationships with women that fundamentally shift the nature of her character and the bulk of the show's season-long arcs.

13. One could invoke Jacques Lacan's mirror stage here, as it marks the moment a subject recognizes a split identity vis-à-vis their presumed wholeness in the mirror (and the wholeness they recognize in others). As Jane Gallop elaborates, "The mirror stage is a turning point. After it, the subject's relation to himself is always mediated through a totalizing image that has come from outside. For example, the mirror image becomes a totalizing ideal that organizes and orients the self. But since the 'self' is necessarily a totalized, unified concept—a division between an inside and an outside—there is no 'self' before the mirror stage." Jane Gallop, *Reading Lacan* (Ithaca, NY: Cornell University Press, 1985), 79.

14. Episode 2.12, "Luthors."

15. Mon-El returns for a significant portion of season 3. When he returns, he reveals that he was thrown into the thirty-first century; for him, seven years have passed, whereas for Kara, it has only been seven months. Mon-El has changed significantly during his absence, including joining the League of Superheroes and marrying fellow legionnaire Imra/Saturn Girl (Amy Jackson). Mon-El's return demonstrates how much Kara's guidance and principles affected his growth as a character; the Mon-El we meet in season 3 (and during a very brief return in season 6) is the model of a hero in the mold of Supergirl: thoughtful, altruistic, and noble.

16. See Caryn Murphy, "The CW: Media Conglomerates in Partnership," in *From Networks to Netflix: A Guide to Changing Channels*, ed. Derek Johnson (New York: Routledge, 2018), 37.

17. See Anaïs Fèvre-Berthelot, "*Gossip Girl* and the CW: Defining a New Network," *International Journal of TV Serial Narratives* 4, no. 2 (Winter 2018): 9–18.

18. For a host of essays on CW shows, coming-of-age, and the network's branding, see Ashley Lynn Carlson and Lisa K. Perdigao, eds., *The CW Comes of Age: Essays on Programming, Branding and Evolution* (Jefferson, NC: McFarland, 2022).

19. Murphy, "The CW," 40.

20. For example, the 2021 show *Kung Fu* is a reboot of a 1970s series that cast a white actor as a half-Chinese protagonist; this time around, the cast is majority Chinese American, including its young woman star (Olivia Liang). With *Batwoman* (2019–2022), already notable for being the first queer superhero to have her own TV show, the actor playing the role in the first season, Ruby Rose, an openly lesbian white actress, quit unexpectedly and was replaced with a Black bisexual actress, Javicia Leslie, for seasons 2 and 3. The *Charmed* reboot (2018–2022) pointedly diversified its cast with three main Latinx actresses, addressed the rampant heterosexism of the original by making one of the characters a lesbian, and revamped the entire series to explicitly reference contemporary social justice movements like #MeToo.

21. This transcription is from @cw_charmed (Charmed), "The CW's new initiative, We Defy, reinforces the network's commitment to inclusion and representation. #CWDareToDefy" [tweet with video], Twitter, 9 March 2019, https://mobile.twitter.com/cw_charmed/status/1104 539920243265537. A collection of these posts can be found here: "CW Stars 'Dare to Defy' with New Inclusion & Representation Initiative," *Just Jared Jr.*, 9 March 2019, https://www.justjaredjr.com/2019/03/09/cw-stars-dare-to-defy-with-new-inclusion-representation-initiative/.

22. Murphy, "The CW."

23. Fèvre-Berthelot, "*Gossip Girl* and the CW."

24. Fèvre-Berthelot, 15.

25. Anna Aupperle, "Teen Queens and Adrenaline Dreams: A History of the CW Television Network" (PhD diss., Pennsylvania State University, 2018), 6.

26. Josef Adelian, "The CW Is One of the Bigger TV Success Stories of the Decade," *Vulture*, 19 May 2016, www.vulture.com/2016/05/cw-is-a-tv-success-story.html.

27. See the Nexstar press release "Nexstar Media Group to Acquire the CW Network," 15 August 2022, https://www.nexstar.tv/nexstar-media-group-to-acquire-the-cw-network/.

28. In 2022, the CW canceled the most shows at one time ever in its history, half of which had women protagonists (most of the others were ensemble shows): *Batwoman* (2019–2022), *Charmed* (2018–2022), *Naomi* (2022), *Legacies* (2018–2022), and *In the Dark* (2019–2022). See Lesley Goldberg, "Mad about the CW Cancellations? Blame Streaming, but Also Its Unusual Corporate Structure," *Hollywood Reporter*, 13 May 2022, https://www.hollywoodreporter.com/tv/tv-news/the-cw-cancellations-blame-streaming-but-also-its-unusual-corporate-structure-1235146038/.

29. Maureen Ryan, "From 'Supergirl' to 'Crazy Ex-Girlfriend,' Women Are the Real Heroes of the CW," *Variety*, 16 October 2016, https://variety.com/2016/voices/columns/cw-gilmore-girls-crazy-ex-girlfriend-1201885544/.

30. For more, see Elizabeth Wagmeister, "CBS President Explains 'Supergirl' Moving to the CW," *Variety*, 18 May 2016, https://variety.com/2016/tv/news/supergirl-cbs-president-reaction-cw-1201777795/.

31. Murphy, "The CW," 40.

32. Jennifer Baumgardner and Amy Richards, *Manifesta: Young Women, Feminism, and the Future*, 2nd ed. (New York: Farrar, Straus and Giroux, 2010), 134–135.

33. Stéphanie Genz and Benjamin A. Brabon, *Postfeminism: Cultural Texts and Theories* (Edinburgh: Edinburgh University Press, 2009), 76.

34. Shauna Pomerantz, Rebecca Raby, and Andrea Stefanik, "Girls Run the World: Caught between Sexism and Postfeminism in School," *Gender and Society* 27, no. 2 (April 2013): 189.

35. Karen Boyle, "Feminism without Men: Feminist Media Studies in a Post-feminist Age," in *Feminist Television Criticism: A Reader*, 2nd ed., ed. Charlotte Brunsdon and Lynn Spigel (Berkshire, UK: Open University Press, 2008), 180.

36. See Angela McRobbie, "Post-feminism and Popular Culture," *Feminist Media Studies* 4, no. 3 (2004): 255–264, https://doi.org/10.1080/1468077042000309937.

37. Susan J. Douglas, *The Rise of Enlightened Sexism: How Pop Culture Took Us from Girl Power to Girls Gone Wild* (New York: St. Martin's Griffin, 2010), 9.

38. Sarah Banet-Weiser, *Empowered: Popular Feminism and Popular Misogyny* (Durham, NC: Duke University Press, 2018), 3.

39. Sara Ahmed, *Living a Feminist Life* (Durham, NC: Duke University Press, 2017), 26.

40. A few notable examples of recent gender nonconforming protagonists are found in the Canadian CBC sitcom *Sort Of* (2021–), which has a nonbinary lead; the Showtime dramedy series *Work in Progress* (2019–2021), with its butch lesbian protagonist who does not conform to feminine gender roles but also is not trans; and even a film such as *The Old Guard* (Netflix, 2020), which features two action heroines for whom gender roles seem antithetical to their being in the world—but these are all very much exceptions that prove the rule.

41. Kathryn Miller and Joshua Plencer, "*Supergirl* and the Corporate Articulation of Neoliberal Feminism," *New Political Science* 40, no. 1 (2018): 61.

42. Miller and Plencer, 62.

43. See, for example, Dara Goldberg, *Awaken Your Inner Goddess: Practical Tools for Self-Care, Emotional Healing, and Self-Realization* (Emeryville, CA: Rockridge Press, 2020) and Rachael Jayne Groover, *Powerful and Feminine: How to Increase Your Magnetic Presence and Attract the Attention You Want* (Loveland, CO: Groover Seminars, 2019). For a scholarly discussion of gender and self-help books, see Sarah Riley, Adrienne Evans, Emma Anderson, and Martine Robson, "The Gendered Nature of Self-Help," *Feminism and Psychology* 29, no. 1 (2019): 3–18.

44. Amy Stanton and Catherine Connors, *The Feminine Revolution: 21 Ways to Ignite the Power of Your Femininity for a Brighter Life and a Better World* (Berkeley, CA: Seal Press, 2018), 69.

45. Sheryl Sandberg, *Lean In: Women, Work and the Will to Lead* (New York: Alfred A. Knopf, 2013).

46. Ruth Whippman, "Enough Leaning In. Let's Tell Men to Lean Out," *New York Times*, 10 October 2019, https://www.nytimes.com/2019/10/10/opinion/sunday/feminism-lean-in.html.

47. Michelle Rodino-Colocino, "Me Too, #MeToo: Countering Cruelty with Empathy," *Communication and Critical/Cultural Studies* 15, no. 1 (2018): 98.

48. Banet-Weiser, *Empowered*, 46.

49. An actual term used on the show, the Superfriends encompass Kara and the other heroes who join her along the way. By the end of season 6, nearly all of Kara's close friends have superhero alter egos with costumes, with the notable exception of Lena, who is a technical genius and can perform magic (having discovered she inherited an affinity for witchcraft from her birth mother) but does most of her "hero work" in the lab.

50. Midway through season 5, the Arrowverse crossover event "Crisis on Infinite Earths," effectively *resets* the Earth Kara and others inhabit, eliminating the multiverse and combining all the Earths into one "Earth Prime." This also results in a reframing of certain relationships and histories, although Kara and her friends retain their memories from the prior Earth, so the plots adjust to the new timeline in relative stride even if the franchise's reasoning for reframing the Arrowverse in this way remains obtuse.

51. Lauren Berlant, *The Female Complaint: The Unfinished Business of Sentimentality in American Culture* (Durham, NC: Duke University Press, 2008), 5.

52. These include bosses Cat Grant (season 1, primarily) and Andrea Rojas (seasons 4 through 6); sister Alex (all seasons); and friends Lena (seasons 2 through 6), Sam (season 3), Nia (seasons 4 through 6), and Kelly (seasons 4 through 6). As part of Supergirl's team, male characters offer significant support as well, including father figure J'onn (all seasons); James (seasons 1 through 5); Winn (seasons 1 through 3, primarily); Mon-El (seasons 2 and 3); and Brainy (seasons 3 through 6).

53. The flashback episode 3.6, "Midvale," and time-travel episodes 6.5, "Prom Night!," and 6.6, "Prom Again," provide some insight into Kara's and Alex's relationships as teenagers. For more on the show's use of symbolic motherhood and sisterhood, see Courtney Lee Weida, "'Women

of Power and the Mothers Who Molded Them': Matriarchal Mentorship and Symbols of Sister-hood in *Supergirl*," in *Girl of Steel: Essays on Television's* Supergirl *and Fourth-Wave Feminism*, ed. Melissa Wehler and Tim Rayborn (Jefferson, NC: McFarland, 2020), 180–198.

54. Astra dies in episode 1.13, "For the Girl Who Has Everything," and Alex admits to killing Astra in episode 1.15, "Solitude."

55. The plot arc that has Kara reuniting with her mother and traveling to Argo City occurs over the last four episodes of season 3, beginning with 3.20, "The Dark Side of the Moon."

56. A robust fan campaign for Kara and Lena to become a romantic couple grew throughout the show's tenure, described by the portmanteau "Supercorp." The show's frequent use of romantic tropes to define the relationship between Kara and Lena—Supergirl literally swoop-ing in to rescue Lena from harm, carrying her in her arms like the quintessential damsel in distress, or Lena articulating in season 5 how Kara "broke [her] heart" by lying about her identity—caused some fans to accuse the show's writers of queerbaiting. These concerns, while compelling, are too tangential and speculative to tackle here, although they bear acknowledging. For more on queerbaiting in *Supergirl* and other shows, see Annemarie Navar-Gill and Mel Stanfill, "'We Shouldn't Have to Trend to Make You Listen': Queer Fan Hashtag Campaigns as Production Interventions," *Journal of Film and Video* 70, no. 3–4 (Fall/Winter 2018): 85–100.

57. While it is difficult to pinpoint this with absolute certainty (without exhaustively review-ing costuming in each episode), Kara's work clothes in the early seasons tend to favor more androgynous belted slacks and button-up shirts; her Supergirl suit during this period is skirted, with high boots. At the beginning of season 5, the Supergirl suit changes to one with pants, but Kara's work wardrobe accordingly shifts almost entirely to form-fitting dresses. This observa-tion suggests that efforts were made to maintain some overtly feminine aspect of Kara's costum-ing once Supergirl's suit no longer has its signature skirt.

58. For that matter, Lena is also an adopted stepchild of Lillian Luthor (a product of her dead husband's infidelity), and while Lena is not an alien, she discovers in season 6 that her birth mother was a witch and she is as well.

59. Episode 2.2, "The Last Children of Krypton."

60. Allen names the "three basic sense[s] of *power* that our conception will have to illuminate: power-over, power-to, and power-with." Amy Allen, *The Power of Feminist Theory: Domination, Resistance, Solidarity* (Boulder, CO: Westview Press, 1999), 123.

61. Bernadette Barton and Lisa Huebner, "Feminine Power: A New Articulation," *Psychology and Sexuality* 13, no. 1 (2022), 2–3, https://doi.org/10.1080/19419899.2020.1771408.

62. bell hooks, *Feminism Is for Everybody* (Boston: South End Press, 2000), 15.

63. Bonnie Thornton Dill, "Race, Class, and Gender: Prospects for an All-Inclusive Sister-hood," *Feminist Studies* 9, no. 1 (Spring 1983): 131.

64. bell hooks, "Sisterhood: Political Solidarity between Women," *Feminist Review* 23 (1986): 127.

65. Berlant, *Female Complaint*, 6.

66. See, for example, a related essay about the WB show *Smallville* (2001–2011), which chroni-cles the coming-of-age of Clark Kent/Superman: the chapter "Teen Programming: Isolation, Alienation and Emerging Manhood," in Rebecca Feasey, *Masculinity and Popular Television* (Edinburgh: Edinburgh University Press, 2008), 45–55.

67. From the appropriately titled episode 3.1, "Girl of Steel."

68. In episode 3.18, "Shelter from the Storm," J'onn tells Kara that her secret weapon is "her heart," as opposed to Reign, who seems soulless.

69. Nxly is a complicated case, as she is somewhat sympathetic due to her backstory and refusal to harm an innocent child, Alex and Kelly's adopted daughter Esme. She is ultimately punished by the show because of her (unsolicited) connection to Lex and the presumption that she is uncontrollable and too powerful.

70. Supergirl is worshipped as a god by the fringe group Cult of Rao in season 3; however, she strenuously resists the cult's assignation of her divinity. See, for example, episode 3.4, "The Faithful."

71. Episode 5.8, "The Wrath of Rama Khan."

72. Episode 5.1, "Event Horizon."

73. Episode 5.7, "Tremors."

74. Villains like Lex and Ben Lockwood, aka Agent Liberty, leader of the anti-alien terrorist group Children of Liberty (season 4) try to figure out Supergirl's identity to nefarious ends. However, women in power over Kara, like bosses Cat and Andrea, also investigate Supergirl's identity in the interest of journalistic truth and clickbait fodder, respectively.

75. Episode 5.8, "The Wrath of Rama Khan"

76. Episode 5.13, "It's a Super Life." In an amusing conceit that offers a metareferential perspective on the show and television viewing, Mxy offers Kara the chance to see what happens when she "controls the narrative" and then proceeds to let these realities play out for her on variety of screens: a 16mm film projector, a laptop using the streaming service "Myxflx," and via "Betamyx" tapes.

77. Episode 2.6, "Changing."

78. Episode 3.3, "Far from the Tree." This episode also features a parallel storyline in which J'onn reunites with his father, presumed dead after the genocide that obliterated almost all of J'onn's race of Green Martians; his father initially rejects J'onn, thinking him an imposter.

79. This storyline emerges in an episode codirected by Tesfai that aired on 21 September 2021— and so was likely written with the summer 2020 Black Lives Matter protests in mind. The use of a gentrifying councilwoman with supernatural powers as a villain further cements the show's intersection of the political with the fantastical. Episode 6.12, "Blindspots."

80. For example, in episode 3.14, "Schott through the Heart," J'onn, a shapeshifter, tells Alex that he has chosen to stay in the body of a Black man, despite being a shapeshifter, in solidarity with African Americans who were and are persecuted the way his race of Green Martians have been. In episode 3.19, "Fight or Flight," James debates the merits of coming out as the hero Guardian since the police do not believe he could be a hero due to his Blackness; however, he also considers the difference he could make by showing the public the face behind the mask for the same reasons.

81. Episode 4.11, "Blood Memory." In episode 6.16, "A Nightmare in National City," Nia is forced to work with Maeve, and the two begin a process of reconciliation.

82. Episode 4.19, "American Dreamer."

83. The DREAM Act, also known as DACA (Deferred Action for Childhood Arrivals), was put into place to protect immigrant children from deportation by President Obama in 2012. It was then terminated by President Trump in 2017. Its status has since been reinstated and contested a number of times. See, for example, Miriam Jordan, "Judge Rules DACA Is Unlawful and Suspends Applications," *New York Times*, 15 July 2021, https://www.nytimes.com/2021/07/16/us/court-daca-dreamers.html.

84. Episode 4.21, "Red Dawn."

85. In episode 5.15, "Reality Bytes," Nia's trans roommate is catfished and attacked in an attempt to punish Dreamer for being an openly trans hero. While Supergirl eventually convinces Dreamer that she cannot enact revenge against the attacker, she is also forced to acknowledge that she does not fully understand Nia's experiences and needs to be a better ally by listening.

86. Episode 4.2, "Fallout."

87. In episode 1.20, "Better Angels," Supergirl's speech allows citizens globally to resist the forces of her aunt Astra's mind-control weapon, Myriad. In episode 5.19, "Immortal Kombat," Supergirl convinces billions of users of the virtual reality Obsidian Platinum server to disconnect from their VR simulations in order to prevent a mass-casualty event orchestrated by Lex

and a vengeful goddess of technology, Gamemnae (Cara Buono). In the series finale, episode 6.20, "Kara," discussed further at the end of this chapter, Supergirl again uses her powers of persuasive speech to rally the world's population to believe in their own power.

88. In a later episode, a character even asserts this outright. When Kara speaks with erudite convict Steve Lomeli (Willie Garson) about the "power of the press in pursuit of justice," Steve rejoins, "The pen is mightier than the sword," and Kara adds, "Maybe even mightier than a cape." Episode 4.18, "Crime and Punishment."

89. Kaznia is a small, fictional Eastern European country used in DC Comics media as a stand-in for a Balkan nation with a history of civil wars. The Kaznian language is Russian or Russian-adjacent.

90. Season 4 of *Supergirl* aired during 2018–2019, with Kara receiving her Pulitzer at the beginning of the fifth season, in fall 2019. In the spring of 2018, when it is likely the fourth season of *Supergirl* was being plotted out, journalists from the *New York Times* and the *Washington Post* received Pulitzers for "deeply sourced, relentlessly reported coverage in the public interest that dramatically furthered the nation's understanding of Russian interference in the 2016 presidential election and its connections to the Trump campaign, the president-elect's transition team and his eventual administration." See "2018 Pulitzer Prizes: Journalism," *The Pulitzer Prizes,* accessed 20 July 2022, https://www.pulitzer.org/prize-winners-by-year/2018.

91. The Red Daughter storyline dominates the latter half of season 4; during the season finale, episode 4.22, "The Quest for Peace," Red Daughter dies in Kara's arms after having defended her from Lex's Kryptonite attack.

92. These examples occur throughout the series, but comparisons with Superman and The Flash occur primarily during Arrowverse crossover events.

93. The Overgirl storyline occurs as part of an Arrowverse crossover event, "Crisis on Earth-X." Overgirl expresses her disdain for Kara in *Arrow*, episode 6.8; wonders why Kara does not use her "blond, white, Aryan perfection" to her advantage in *Flash*, episode 4.8; and dies in the conclusion of *Legends of Tomorrow*, episode 3.8.

94. For a compelling article on Overgirl, see Doyle Greene, "Supergirl vs. Overgirl," *Film Criticism* 42, no. 4 (2018), http://dx.doi.org/10.3998/fc.13761232.0042.409.

95. Episode 6.13, "The Gauntlet."

96. Episode 6.20, "Kara."

97. Episode 1.2, "Stronger Together."

98. The lyrics "Well, I've been afraid of changin' / 'Cause I've built my life around you / But time makes you bolder / Even children get older" punctuate the last minute of the show.

99. Interestingly, Superman's motto has now also changed to "Truth, Justice and a Better Tomorrow," signifying, perhaps, DC's attempts to move away from the overt patriotism of the past. "Superman Changes Motto to 'Truth, Justice and a Better Tomorrow,' Says DC Chief," NBC News, 17 October 2021, https://www.nbcnews.com/pop-culture/pop-culture-news/superman-changes-motto-truth-justice-better-tomorrow-says-dc-chief-n1281716.

100. I am, of course, referring to President Barack Obama's best-selling memoir, *The Audacity of Hope: Thoughts on Reclaiming the American Dream* (New York: Crown, 2006), the thesis of which also significantly undergirded his presidential campaigns in 2008 and 2012.

101. Amy Brandzel, *Against Citizenship: The Violence of the Normative* (Champaign: University of Illinois Press, 2016), 5.

CHAPTER 4   MOTHERHOOD AND MYTH

1. Episode 6.1, "Rebirth."

2. Alex even worries that her desire for motherhood and her work are incompatible, admitting to her mentor and former boss, J'onn, "One day, I will be [a mother]. . . . I know that's what I want and I know that that is who I am. Just as I know that I'm the person who's going to jump the building to stop the bad guy. And I keep wondering, can those two people coexist? And is that fair? Is it fair to the person that I'm coming home to?" Episode 3.20, "The Dark Side of the Moon."

3. *Dark Fate* was considered a box office disappointment (despite relatively good critical reviews), which some, including Hamilton herself, attributed to viewers' fatigue with the franchise and its continuous reboots, which often overwrote the prior films' timelines. Many reviews and box office analyses note this reason. Based on an imperfect but compelling metric such as Rotten Tomatoes aggregated critic and audience scores, *Dark Fate* ranks third in the franchise (behind the first two blockbusters) in terms of number of viewers who liked the film. The films have the following scores, respectively, with the first number listed the critics' score and the second the audience score: *Terminator*, 100 percent/89 percent; *Terminator: Judgment Day*, 93 percent/95 percent; *Terminator: Rise of the Machines*, 69 percent/46 percent; *Terminator: Salvation*, 33 percent/53 percent; *Terminator: Genisys*, 26 percent/52 percent; *Terminator: Dark Fate*, 70 percent/82 percent. These numbers show how overall satisfaction with the sequels dwindles after the second film and then reemerges with the final installment. "*Terminator*—Franchise," *Rotten Tomatoes*, accessed 1 October 2022, https://www.rottentomatoes.com/franchise/terminator. For box office information on the franchise, see "Franchise: Terminator," Box Office Mojo by IMDbPro, accessed 1 October 2022, https://www.boxofficemojo.com/franchise/fr3175583493/. For Hamilton's comments on the box office, see Mike Reyes, "Linda Hamilton Thinks Box Office May Have Finally Killed the Terminator Franchise," *Cinema Blend*, 30 January 2020, https://www.cinemablend.com/news/2489354/linda-hamilton-thinks-box-office-may-have-finally-killed-the-terminator-franchise.

4. Jane Gallop, *The Daughter's Seduction: Feminism and Psychoanalysis* (Ithaca, NY: Cornell University Press, 1982), 115.

5. Jennifer Baumgardner and Amy Richards, *Manifesta: Young Women, Feminism, and the Future*, 2nd ed. (New York: Farrar, Straus and Giroux, 2010), 211.

6. Andrea O'Reilly, "Outlaw(ing) Motherhood: A Theory and Politic of Maternal Empowerment for the Twenty-First Century," in *21st Century Motherhood: Experience, Identity, Policy, Agency*, ed. Andrea O'Reilly (New York: Columbia University Press, 2010), 369–370.

7. Jacqueline Rose, *Mothers: An Essay on Love and Cruelty* (New York: Farrar, Straus and Giroux, 2018), 134.

8. Simone de Beauvoir, *The Second Sex* [1949], trans. H. M. Parshley (New York: Vintage Books, 1989), 512.

9. Andrea O'Reilly and Marie Porter, "Introduction," in *Motherhood: Power and Oppression*, ed. Marie Porter, Patricia Short, and Andrea O'Reilly (Toronto: Women's Press, 2005), 6.

10. Adrienne Rich, *Of Woman Born: Motherhood as Experience and Institution* (New York: W. W. Norton, 1995), 13.

11. Sigmund Freud, *Civilization and Its Discontents*, trans. James Strachey (New York: W. W. Norton, 2010), 84.

12. Linda Ahall, "Motherhood, Myth and Gendered Agency in Political Violence," *International Feminist Journal of Politics* 14, no. 1 (2012): 107.

13. Ahall, 109.

14. For two of many such critical discussions of motherhood and myth, see Mary Beard, *Women and Power: A Manifesto* (New York: W. W. Norton, 2017), and Rose, *Mothers*.

15. Maria Tatar, *The Heroine with 1,001 Faces* (New York: Liveright, 2021), 2.

16. Rose, *Mothers*, 27.

17. Jessica Benjamin, "The Omnipotent Mother: A Psychoanalytic Study of Fantasy and Reality," in *Representations of Motherhood*, ed. Donna Bassin, Margaret Honey, and Meryle Mahrer Kaplan (New Haven, CT: Yale University Press, 1994), 142.

18. See Ahall, "Motherhood, Myth and Gendered Agency," and Laura Sjoberg and Caron Gentry, *Mothers, Monsters, Whores: Women's Violence in Global Politics* (London: Zed Books, 2007), for more on the tensions between ideals of motherhood and violent action.

19. Joe McGovern, "'The Terminator' at 30: An Oral History," *Entertainment Weekly*, 17 July 2014, https://ew.com/article/2014/07/17/the-terminator-oral-history/.

20. Karen B. Mann, "Narrative Entanglements: 'The Terminator,'" *Film Quarterly* 43, no. 2 (1989): 25.

21. Judith Butler, *Gender Trouble* (New York: Routledge, 1990), 125.

22. Donald Palumbo, "The Monomyth in James Cameron's *The Terminator*: Sarah as Monomythic Heroine," *Journal of Popular Culture* 41, no. 3 (2008): 416.

23. Julia Baumgold, "Killer Women: Here Come the Hardbodies," *New York*, 29 July 1991, 26.

24. The film's status as "most successful" is generally agreed upon (see box office numbers in note 3). It is also discussed in this oral history: Alan Siegel, "The Tin Man Gets His Heart: An Oral History of 'Terminator 2: Judgment Day,'" *The Ringer*, 30 June 2021, https://www.theringer.com/movies/2021/6/30/22555687/terminator-2-judgement-day-t2-oral-history.

25. Jeffrey A. Brown, *Dangerous Curves: Action Heroines, Gender, Fetishism, and Popular Culture* (Jackson: University Press of Mississippi, 2011).

26. Jeffrey A. Brown, "Gender and the Action Heroine: Hardbodies and the 'Point of No Return,'" *Cinema Journal* 35, no. 3 (Spring 1996): 56.

27. Yvonne Tasker, *Spectacular Bodies: Gender, Genre and the Action Cinema* (New York: Routledge, 1993), 149.

28. Marc O'Day, "Beauty in Motion: Gender, Spectacle and Action Babe Cinema," in *Action and Adventure Cinema*, ed. Yvonne Tasker (New York: Routledge, 2004), 203.

29. Sherrie Inness, *Tough Girls: Women Warriors and Wonder Women in Popular Culture* (Philadelphia: University of Pennsylvania Press, 1999), 126.

30. George Faithful, "Survivor, Warrior, Mother, Savior: The Evolution of the Female Hero in Apocalyptic Science Fiction Film of the Late Cold War," *Implicit Religion* 19, no. 3 (2016): 349.

31. Barbara Creed, *The Monstrous Feminine* (London: Routledge, 1993), 27.

32. Mark Jancovich, "Modernity and Subjectivity in *The Terminator*: The Machine as Monster in Contemporary American Culture," *Velvet Light Trap* 30 (1992): 11.

33. Lisa Purse, *Contemporary Action Cinema* (Edinburgh: Edinburgh University Press, 2011), 81.

34. Sharon Willis, *High Contrast: Race and Gender in Contemporary Hollywood Film*, 2nd ed. (Durham, NC: Duke University Press, 2002), 119.

35. Siegel, "Tin Man Gets His Heart."

36. The other films in the franchise do not all belong to the same timelines, especially in relation to the television show, which puts the latter installments in the franchise in a murky category somewhere between reboots, sequels, and remakes.

37. Beauvoir, *Second Sex*, 516.

38. Beauvoir, 516.

39. Episode 1.2 "Gnothi Seauton."

40. For a discussion of the "castrating mother" in the *Alien* trilogy, see Creed, *Monstrous Feminine*. Freud's and Lacan's ideas about castration anxiety and women are also discussed by Juliet Mitchell and Jacqueline Rose in their respective introductions to Jacques Lacan, *Feminine Sexuality: Jacques Lacan and the école freudienne* (New York: W. W. Norton, 1985) and by Gayle Rubin in "The Traffic in Women: Notes on the 'Political Economy' of Sex," in *Women, Class, and the Feminist Imagination*, ed. Karen Hansen and Ilene Philipson (Philadelphia: Temple University Press, 1990), 74–113, among other texts.

41. See Gallop's chapter on the phallic mother, "The Phallic Mother: Fraudian Analysis," in *Daughter's Seduction*.

42. Sjoberg and Gentry, *Mothers, Monsters, Whores*, 33.

43. Jean Bethke Elshtain, *Women and War* (New York: Basic Books, 1995), 4.

44. Sara Ruddick, *Maternal Thinking: Towards a Politics of Peace* [1989] (Boston: Beacon Press, 2002), 137.

45. Sara Ruddick, "On 'Maternal Thinking,'" *Women's Studies Quarterly* 37, no. 3/4 (2009): 308.

46. Ranjana Khanna, "Reflections on Sara Ruddick's 'Maternal Thinking,'" *Women's Studies Quarterly* 37, no. 3/4 (2009): 303.

47. Rose, *Mothers.*

48. Stephanie Hartzell, "An (In)visible Universe of Grief: Performative Disidentifications with White Motherhood in the We Are Not Trayvon Martin Blog," *Journal of International and Intercultural Communication* 10, no. 1 (2017): 65.

49. Rose, *Mothers,* 29.

50. Elshtain, *Women and War,* 9.

51. Susan Faludi, *The Terror Dream: Myth and Misogyny in an Insecure America* (London: Picador, 2007), 15.

52. Shepard writes, "Ordinary Decent Citizens were exhorted in the aftermath of 9/11: 'live your lives, and hug your children . . . be calm and resolute' . . . A positive link was made between 'every American family and the family of America' . . . connoting 'family values' and therefore a valorization of the (assumed nuclear) family unit." In Laura Shepard, "Veiled References: Constructions of Gender in the Bush Administration Discourse on the Attacks on Afghanistan Post-9/11," *International Feminist Journal of Politics* 8, no. 1 (2006): 22. See Faludi, *Terror Dream.*

53. It is of little consequence to my particular analysis, but worth noting for clarity, that Kyle Reese's brother, Derek (hence, John's uncle) is also sent back in time during the run of *The Chronicles* and John is able to interact with this other family member.

54. Marianne Kac-Vergne, "From Sarah Connor 2.0 to Sarah Connor 3.0: Women Who Kill in the *Terminator* Franchise," in *Women Who Kill: Gender and Sexuality in Film and Series of the Post-feminist Era,* ed. David Roche and Cristelle Maury (London: Bloomsbury, 2020), 122.

55. Kac-Vergne, 123.

56. Episode 2.22, "Born to Run."

57. Since the show was canceled after the second season, it is difficult to know if Cameron would have eventually been revived after her seeming self-sacrifice. The cancellation of the series left many other loose ends as well, including what happened to John and Sarah after the former traveled into the future.

58. *Terminator* and *Judgment Day* are part of the same timeline, and *The Sarah Connor Chronicles* takes off from the timeline of the second film. The subsequent three films were not written and directed by James Cameron, and each film reimagines the timeline in slightly different ways. The final film, *Dark Fate,* returns to the original timelines of the first two films (but not the events of *The Chronicles*).

59. For more on the *Genisys* timeline and its premise, see Phillip E. Wegner, "Relics from a Deleted Timeline: The Economics of *Terminator Genisys,*" *Science Fiction Film and Television* 10, no. 1 (2017): 115–124.

60. Ruby C. Tapia, *American Pietàs: Visions of Race, Death, and the Maternal* (Minneapolis: University of Minnesota Press, 2011), 27.

61. I am basing his age on the age of the character in *Judgment Day*. John's age shifts depending on the film and which timeline it uses. For example, in the third film and *The Chronicles,* John's experiences running from the terminators with his mother in *Judgment Day* are discussed as if they happened when he was a teenager, despite the second film being set in 1995 and the first film (his conception date) being set in 1984.

62. Unlike in the earlier films, Skynet has been averted; a new sentient AI, Legion, comes into power. However, since the differences between Skynet and Legion seem to be fairly minimal and result in more or less the same dystopian future, it is not worth belaboring their differences here.

63. It is not made clear who would be the "mommy" and who the "daddy" in this situation. Both Grace and Sarah tip toward the masculine side of the scale in terms of dress—although their sartorial choices may more accurately be read as "combat-ready"—and they both have a gruff, hardheaded demeanor.

64. As part of her cybernetic implants, Grace has a boosted metabolism that runs on an implanted power core. It allows her to have superhuman speed, strength, and endurance, as well as the ability to self-heal to an extent; however, Grace is only capable of these feats in short, intense bursts, after which she needs to recharge via an injection (of a concoction of drugs she steals from a pharmacy early in the film with Dani's help). At the end of the film, she has run out of her "medicine" and has been expending too much energy too rapidly; her power core is failing.

65. For example, Iris Marion Young writes, "The logic of masculinist protection positions leaders, along with some other officials such as soldiers and firefighters, as protectors and the rest of us in the subordinate position of dependent protected people. Justifications for the suspension of due process or partial abrogation of privacy rights and civil liberties, as well as condemnation of dissent, rest on an implicit deal: that these are necessary trade-offs for effective protection." Iris Marion Young, "The Logic of Masculinist Protection: Reflections on the Current Security State," *Signs: Journal of Women in Culture and Society* 29, no. 1 (2003): 16.

66. Sjoberg and Gentry, *Mothers, Monsters, Whores*, 2.

67. Grace is also of above average height for a woman, but the film's explicit rendering of her preference for men's clothing even when women's clothing is available suggests that height is not the only factor.

68. By the same token, the terminator sent back to assassinate Dani is in a body portrayed by a Mexican American actor (Gabriel Luna). During the fight and escape scene that takes place at the U.S. border detention center, it seems that only border patrol agents are killed by the terminator as they try to stop him, whereas Sarah, Dani, and Grace set most of the detainees free as they themselves flee.

69. Yvonne Tasker, *Working Girls: Gender and Sexuality in Popular Cinema* (New York: Routledge, 1998), 69.

70. Barbara Gurr, "Introduction," in *Race, Gender, and Sexuality in Post-apocalyptic TV and Film*, ed. Barbara Gurr and Brayton Polka (London: Palgrave Macmillan, 2015), 1.

CHAPTER 5   AT THE END OF THE WORLD

1. Alice interacts closely with several children in the films, although these children rarely reappear in subsequent sequels, suggesting that despite Alice's intervention they are eventually killed or captured. In *Apocalypse*, Alice rescues a girl, Angie (Sophie Vavasseur), who also has blood that bonds with the T-virus, although her storyline is dropped in later films. In *Extinction*, a teen in Claire's convoy, who goes by the nickname K-Mart (Spencer Locke), plays a prominent role and seems to have a strong connection with both Alice and Claire. Finally, in *Retribution*, Alice rescues a cloned deaf girl, Becky (Aryana Engineer), who believes she is Alice's daughter because an Alice clone was used in her simulation to play her mother; Becky disappears after the end of the film.

2. By "motherless child," I am referring here to the well-known antebellum spiritual.

3. Alice is not in the games, and she is not referenced in the newest film or streaming show.

4. See Scott Mendelson, "How 'Resident Evil' Became the Most Successful Video Game–Based Franchise Ever," *Forbes*, 23 January 2017, https://www.forbes.com/sites/scottmendelson/2017/01/23/why-resident-evil-became-the-most-successful-video-game-based-franchise-ever. Box office numbers for the franchise can be found here: "Franchise: Resident Evil," Box Office Mojo by IMDbPro, accessed 1 October 2022, https://www.boxofficemojo.com/franchise/fr3578236677/.

5. *The Last of Us* has a similar premise to *Resident Evil* in that Ellie's immunity to the apocalyptic virus is constructed as central to humanity's salvation and, hence, part of her value as a character. Unlike Alice, Ellie is fourteen and thus is still a child requiring protection.

6. See, for example, Dominic Arsenault, "Video Game Genre, Evolution and Innovation," *Eludamos: Journal for Computer Game Culture* 3 (October 2009): 149–176.

7. See Stephen Cadwell, "Opening Doors: Art-Horror and Agency," in *Unraveling Resident Evil: Essays on the Complex Universe of the Games and Films*, ed. Nadine Farghaly (Jefferson, NC: McFarland, 2014), 45–61.

8. Nick Jones, "This Is My World: Spatial Representation in the *Resident Evil* Films," *Continuum: Journal of Media and Cultural Studies* 30, no. 4 (2016): 479.

9. Thomas M. Sipos, *Horror Film Aesthetics: Creating the Visual Language of Fear* (Jefferson, NC: McFarland, 2010), 25–26.

10. Daniel Müller, "Survival and System in *Resident Evil* (2002): Remembering, Repeating and Working-Through," in *Unraveling Resident Evil: Essays on the Complex Universe of the Games and Films*, ed. Nadine Farghaly (Jefferson, NC: McFarland, 2014), 19–20.

11. Unlike Alice, Claire is a recurring character in the games, as well. In the films, many characters die; some are then cloned and die again or are captured by Umbrella and corrupted, only to be defeated (these include characters such as Rain Ocampo, Jill Valentine, Carlos Olivera, and Luther West). There are other characters who we do not see die, but their disappearance from the subsequent films implies their death (e.g., children like Angie and Becky who seem to survive at the end of their respective films but then do not return in sequels).

12. The phrase *Et in Arcadia Ego*, used in the heading for this section, is the title of two famous baroque paintings: one by the Italian Giovanni Francesco Barbieri (commonly known as Guercino; the painting is from ca. 1618–1622) and the other by the French Nicolas Poussin (ca. 1637–1638). These paintings both depict shepherds; in Guercino's version, the two shepherds peer at a skull placed on a pedestal in which the title's words have been carved; in Poussin's version, the words are engraved on a tombstone. One of the prevailing interpretations of both paintings and the use of the phrase in this manner is that they serve the function of a memento mori, reminding viewers that even in Arcadia, there is death. However, other interpretations suggest that Poussin's version may actually illustrate nostalgia for our dreams of the past, rather than death, which adds yet another layer to the concept of Arcadia as an impossible site. See Erwin Panofsky, "*Et in Arcadia Ego*: Poussin and the Elegiac Tradition" [1936], in *Meaning in the Visual Arts* (Chicago: University of Chicago Press, 1967), 295–320.

13. Jacques Lacan, *The Seminar of Jacques Lacan, Book XI: The Four Fundamental Concepts of Psychoanalysis* [1973], ed. Jacques-Alain Miller, trans. Alan Sheridan (New York: W. W. Norton, 1998), 67.

14. Kirsten Moana Thompson, *Apocalyptic Dread: American Film at the Turn of the Millennium* (Albany: State University of New York Press, 2007), 23.

15. Thompson, 22.

16. Thompson, 1.

17. Stephen Harper, "'I Could Kiss You, You Bitch': Race, Gender, and Sexuality in *Resident Evil* and *Resident Evil 2: Apocalypse*," *Jump Cut: A Review of Contemporary Media* 49 (Spring 2007), https://www.ejumpcut.org/archive/jc49.2007/HarperResEvil/.

18. Andrea Harris, "Woman as Evolution: The Feminist Promise of the Resident Evil Film Series," in *Race, Gender, and Sexuality in Post-apocalyptic TV and Film*, ed. Barbara Gurr and Brayton Polka (New York: Palgrave Macmillan, 2015), 99.

19. The six films that are the main subject of my analysis were released post-9/11 and pre-COVID-19. However, the Netflix streaming series, which aired in July 2022, explicitly references COVID-19 as a corollary to the T-virus.

20. Todd A. Comer and Lloyd Isaac Vayo, "Introduction," in *Terror and the Cinematic Sublime: Essays on Violence and the Unpresentable in Post-9/11 Films*, ed. Todd A. Comer and Lloyd Isaac Vayo (Jefferson, NC: McFarland, 2013), 6.

21. W.J.T. Mitchell, "The Unspeakable and the Unimaginable: Word and Image in a Time of Terror," *ELH* 72 (2005): 295.

22. Mitchell, 300.

23. See also Jean Baudrillard, *Simulations* (New York: Semiotext[e], 1983).

24. Slavoj Žižek, *The Metastases of Enjoyment: Six Essays on Woman and Causality* (New York: Verso, 1994), 31.

25. Sigmund Freud, *Beyond the Pleasure Principle*, ed. and trans. James Strachey (New York: W. W. Norton, 1961), 15.

26. Jones, "This Is My World," 485.

27. Lewis Carroll, *Alice's Adventures in Wonderland* (Project Gutenberg e-book, 1991).

28. Margo Collins, "'I Barely Feel Human Anymore': Project Alice and the Posthuman in the Films," in *Unraveling Resident Evil: Essays on the Complex Universe of the Games and Films*, ed. Nadine Farghaly (Jefferson, NC: McFarland, 2014), 202.

29. Slavoj Žižek, *The Sublime Object of Ideology* (New York: Verso, 1989), 149.

30. I am referring here to the Marquis de Sade's novel *The 120 Days of Sodom* (1785) and Pier Paolo Pasolini's film adaptation *Salò, or the 120 Days of Sodom* (1975).

31. Jeff May, "Zombie Geographies and the Undead City," *Social and Cultural Geography* 11, no. 3 (May 2010): 290.

32. Jones, "This Is My World," 485.

33. Jenn Webb and Sam Byrnand, "Some Kind of Virus: The Zombie as Body and as Trope," *Body and Society* 14, no. 2 (June 2008): 88.

34. Webb and Byrnand, 96.

35. Miriam Ross, "The 3-D Aesthetic: *Avatar* and Hyperhaptic Visuality," *Screen* 53, no. 4 (2012): 386.

36. Julia Kristeva, *Powers of Horror: An Essay on Abjection*, trans. Leon S. Roudiez (New York: Columbia University Press, 1982), 4.

37. Barbara Creed, *The Monstrous Feminine* (London: Routledge, 1993), 11.

38. Isabel Cristina Pinedo, *Recreational Terror: Women and the Pleasures of Horror Film Viewing* (Albany: State University of New York Press, 1997), 23.

39. See Immanuel Kant, *Critique of Judgement*, trans. J. H. Bernard (New York: Macmillan, 1914).

40. Cornelia Klinger, "The Concepts of the Sublime and the Beautiful in Kant and Lyotard," in *Feminist Interpretations of Immanuel Kant*, ed. Robin May Schott (Philadelphia: Pennsylvania State University Press, 1997), 197.

41. Jean-François Lyotard, *The Postmodern Explained: Correspondence 1982–1985*, trans. Morgan Thomas (Minneapolis: University of Minnesota Press, 1992), 10.

42. Kant, *Critique of Judgment*, 104.

43. Klinger, "Concepts of the Sublime and the Beautiful," 196.

44. Helga Geyer-Ryan, "Effects of Abjection in the Texts of Walter Benjamin," *MLN* 107, no. 3 (1992): 513.

45. Kristeva, *Powers of Horror*, 11.

46. Kristeva, 4.

47. Roland Barthes, *The Pleasure of the Text*, trans. Richard Miller (New York: Hill and Wang, 1975), 6–7.

48. In between the first *Resident Evil* and its sequel, *Apocalypse*, Alice is captured by Umbrella and forcibly injected with the T-virus. Instead of turning her undead, the virus bonds with her DNA, making her stronger and seemingly giving her superhuman powers.

49. Jones further describes Anderson's conception of the film "with as many tight, claustrophobic environments or wide landscapes as possible in order to exploit the 3D format, which is for him a 'holistic' experience." Nick Jones, "Variation within Stability: Digital 3D and Film Style," *Cinema Journal* 55, no. 1 (2015): 61.

50. Jones, 64.

51. It is worth noting that other characters' deaths barely seem to register for Alice except in the case of a select few. When Rain (Michelle Rodriguez) dies at the end of the first film, Alice briefly mourns her loss, as she does when her marginal love interest—they share one kiss—Carlos Olivera sacrifices himself in *Extinction* to provide a path to safety for the others. Alice also refuses to fight Project Nemesis in *Apocalypse* once she realizes the enormous patchwork monster is a mutated version of a fellow survivor, Matt (Eric Mabius). Later deaths, like that of Abigail (Ruby Rose) in *The Final Chapter*, are drawn-out, pathos-filled scenes that feel closer to torture porn than the majority of scenes from the franchise. Alice is affected by Abigail's death, and the many others who die in the film, but has no choice but to carry on with her mission. By contrast, in *Afterlife*, when survivor Crystal is attacked and viciously dragged away by a zombie after volunteering to help Alice and Chris gather weapons from the prison's armory, Alice barely reacts; in fact, moments later she is gleeful on finding an array of weapons in the armory, seeming to have forgotten entirely about Crystal's sudden demise.

52. Jones, "Variation within Stability," 65.

53. James Stone, "'My Name Is Alice and I Remember Everything!' Surviving Sexual Abuse in the *Resident Evil* Films," in *Unraveling Resident Evil: Essays on the Complex Universe of the Games and Films*, ed. Nadine Farghaly (Jefferson, NC: McFarland, 2014), 100. Notably, a marauder threatens Alice with rape in *Extinction*, but it is clear she is never in any danger, and she defeats him and his accomplices with relative ease.

54. Laura Wilson, "Race, the Other and *Resident Evil*," *Ethnicity and Race in a Changing World: A Review Journal* 3, no. 2 (2012): 31. Suzan Aiken writes, "The silences often present an opposition to expectations, an extension of masculine-feminine power dynamics, and a complication of scenes that might typically presume an action hero to use other tactics." Suzan Aiken, "The Strong, Silent Type: Alice's Use of Rhetorical Silence as Feminist Strategy," in *Unraveling Resident Evil: Essays on the Complex Universe of the Games and Films*, ed. Nadine Farghaly (Jefferson, NC: McFarland, 2014), 81.

55. Wilson, 31.

56. Harper, "'I Could Kiss You, You Bitch,'" n.p.

57. Harper, n.p.

58. See Jenny Platz, "The Woman in the Red Dress: Sexuality, Femmes Fatales, the Gaze and Ada Wong," in *Unraveling Resident Evil: Essays on the Complex Universe of the Games and Films*, ed. Nadine Farghaly (Jefferson, NC: McFarland, 2014).

59. Harris, "Woman as Evolution," 107.

60. Creed, *Monstrous Feminine*, 1.

61. Creed, 11.

62. Roland Barthes, *The Pleasure of the Text*, 7.

63. Notably, in *The Final Chapter*, Dr. Isaacs is killed by his own clone, as they argue over who is real. Wesker returns as an antagonist in the 2021 prequel, *Welcome to Racoon City*, and, as a more nuanced character, a cloned version of the first Wesker, in the 2022 streaming series.

64. Mary Ann Doane, *Femmes Fatales: Feminism, Film Theory, Psychoanalysis* (New York: Routledge, 1991), 1.

65. Doane, 2.

66. Slavoj Žižek, *Looking Awry: An Introduction to Jacques Lacan through Popular Culture* (Cambridge, MA: MIT Press, 1991), 65.

67. Žižek, *Metastases of Enjoyment*, 70.

68. Julie Grossman, *The Femme Fatale* (New Brunswick, NJ: Rutgers University Press, 2020), 15.

69. Carol Clover, *Men, Women, and Chain Saws: Gender in the Modern Horror Film* (Princeton, NJ: Princeton University Press, 1992), 35.

70. Janet Staiger, "The Slasher, the Final Girl and the Anti-denouement," in *Style and Form in the Hollywood Slasher Film*, ed. Wickham Clayton (London: Palgrave Macmillan, 2016), 225.

71. Jacques Derrida, *The Gift of Death* (Chicago: University of Chicago Press, 1995), 41.

72. Michel Foucault, *History of Sexuality: An Introduction, Volume 1* [1978] (New York: Vintage Books, 1990), 138.

73. Foucault, 144.

74. Sigmund Freud, *Civilization and Its Discontents*, trans. James Strachey (New York: W. W. Norton, 2010), 71.

75. Freud, 142.

76. Harris, "Woman as Evolution," 102.

77. E. Ann Kaplan, *Motherhood and Representation: The Mother in Popular Culture and Melodrama* (New York: Routledge, 1992), 43.

78. Jacques Lacan, "God and the *Jouissance* of the Woman: A Love Letter," in *Feminine Sexuality: Jacques Lacan and the* école freudienne, ed. Juliet Mitchell and Jacqueline Rose, trans. Jacqueline Rose (New York: W. W. Norton, 1985), 153.

CONCLUSION

1. Robin Givhan, "Kamala Harris Made History with Quiet, Exquisite Power," *Washington Post*, 7 November 2020, https://www.washingtonpost.com/nation/2020/11/07/kamala-harris-made-history-with-quiet-exquisite-power/.

2. "Watch Kamala Harris' Full Victory Speech," CNN, 7 November 2020, *YouTube*, https://www.youtube.com/watch?v=ExPm_hJQYpQ.

3. Hillary Clinton, "Power Shortage," *The Atlantic*, October 2020, https://www.theatlantic.com/magazine/archive/2020/10/hillary-clinton-womens-rights/615463.

4. Clinton.

5. Political power is, of course, not the only way in which women's professional lives can have agentic meaning. However, it is perhaps the clearest stand-in for the fictional role of the action hero because of the degree of publicity, control, and ostensible real-world utility political power holds.

6. Michelle Ruiz, "AOC's Next Four Years," *Vanity Fair*, 28 October 2020, https://www.vanityfair.com/news/2020/10/becoming-aoc-cover-story-2020.

7. See the introduction to Simone de Beauvoir, *The Second Sex* [1949], trans. H. M. Parshley (New York: Vintage Books, 1989). The observations of the dual or even triple othering of women of color can be found, not necessarily always using this exact language, in the works of Anna Julia Cooper, discussed in the introduction, but also in Patricia Hill Collins's work on "controlling images" and Kimberlé Crenshaw's work on "intersectionality"—to name only a few.

8. Wonder Woman is deliberately excluded from this list, as neither the 2017 film nor its sequel convey much in the way of significant attempts at intersectional representation.

BIBLIOGRAPHY

Adelian, Josef. "The CW Is One of the Bigger TV Success Stories of the Decade." *Vulture*, 19 May 2016. www.vulture.com/2016/05/cw-is-a-tv-success-story.html.

Adler, Ali, Greg Berlanti, and Andrew Kreisberg, creators. *Supergirl*. Television show. CBS, aired 2015–2016. CW, aired 2016–2021. Accessed on Netflix.

Ahall, Linda. "Motherhood, Myth and Gendered Agency in Political Violence." *International Feminist Journal of Politics* 14, no. 1 (2012): 103–120.

Ahmed, Sara. *Living a Feminist Life*. Durham, NC: Duke University Press, 2017.

Aiken, Suzan. "The Strong, Silent Type: Alice's Use of Rhetorical Silence as Feminist Strategy." In *Unraveling Resident Evil: Essays on the Complex Universe of the Games and Films*, edited by Nadine Farghaly, 80–98. Jefferson: McFarland, 2014.

Akil, Salim, creator. *Black Lightning*. Television show. CW, aired 2017–2021.

Albertson, Cory. "The New Wonder Woman." *Contexts* 15, no. 3 (2016): 66–69.

Allen, Amy. *The Power of Feminist Theory: Domination, Resistance, Solidarity*. Boulder, CO: Westview Press, 1999.

———. "Rethinking Power." *Hypatia* 13, no. 13 (Winter 1998): 21–40.

Allen, Prudence. *The Concept of Woman*. Vol. 1, *The Aristotelian Revolution, 750 B.C.–A.D. 1250*. Grand Rapids, MI: William B. Eerdmans, 1997.

Al-Mahadin, Salam. "Wonder Woman: Goddess of Fictional and Actual Wars." *Journal of Middle East Women's Studies* 14, no. 2 (2018): 246–249.

Anderson, Paul W. S., dir. *Resident* Evil. Film, 2002. DVD, Sony Pictures Home Entertainment, 2018.

———, dir. *Resident Evil: Afterlife 3D*. Film, 2010. 3D Blu-ray, Screen Gems, 2010.

———, dir. *Resident Evil: Retribution*. Film, 2012. DVD, Sony Pictures Home Entertainment, 2018.

———, dir. *Resident Evil: The Final Chapter*. Film, 2016. DVD, Sony Pictures Home Entertainment, 2018.

Arsenault, Dominic. "Video Game Genre, Evolution and Innovation." *Eludamos*: *Journal for Computer Game Culture* 3 (October 2009): 149–176.

Asimov, Isaac. "Feminine Intuition." In *Robot Visions*, 218–244. New York: Penguin, 1990.

Aupperle, Anna. "Teen Queens and Adrenaline Dreams: A History of the CW Television Network." PhD diss., Pennsylvania State University, 2018.

Azzopardi, Chris. "Elizabeth Banks Talks Queering 'Charlie's Angels' & How Kristen Stewart Is 'Definitely Gay' in the Movie." *Pride Source*, 12 November 2019. https://pridesource.com/article/elizabeth-banks-talks-queering-charlies-angels-how-kristen-stewart-is-definitely-gay-in-the-movie/.

Banet-Weiser, Sarah. *Empowered: Popular Feminism and Popular Misogyny*. Durham, NC: Duke University Press, 2018.

Banet-Weiser, Sarah, Rosalind Gill, and Catherine Rottenberg. "Postfeminism, Popular Feminism and Neoliberal Feminism? Sarah Banet-Weiser, Rosalind Gill and Catherine Rottenberg in Conversation." *Feminist Theory* 21, no. 1 (2020), https://doi.org/10.1177/1464700119842555.

Banks, Elizabeth, dir. *Charlie's Angels*. Film, 2019. DVD, Sony Pictures, 2019.

Barthes, Roland. *The Pleasure of the Text*. Translated by Richard Miller. New York: Hill and Wang, 1975.

Barton, Bernadette, and Lisa Huebner. "Feminine Power: A New Articulation." *Psychology and Sexuality* 13, no. 1 (2022): 23–32. https://doi.org/10.1080/19419899.2020.1771408.

Bastién, Angelica Jade. "The Strange, Complicated, Feminist History of Wonder Woman's Origin Story." *Vulture*, 8 June 2017. https://www.vulture.com/2017/06/wonder-woman-origin-story-the-strange-feminist-history.html.

Baudrillard, Jean. *Simulations*. New York: Semiotext[e], 1983.

Baumgardner, Jennifer, and Amy Richards. *Manifesta: Young Women, Feminism, and the Future.* 2nd ed. New York: Farrar, Straus and Giroux, 2010.

Baumgold, Julie. "Killer Women: Here Come the Hardbodies." *New York*, 29 July 1991, 23–29.

Beard, Mary. *Women and Power: A Manifesto.* New York: W. W. Norton, 2017.

———. "Women in Power." *London Review of Books* 39, no. 6 (16 March 2017): https://www.lrb.co.uk/the-paper/v39/n06/mary-beard/women-in-power.

Beauvoir, Simone de. *The Second Sex* [1949]. Translated by H. M. Parshley. New York: Vintage Books, 1989.

Beck, Koa. *White Feminism: From the Suffragettes to Influencers and Who They Leave Behind.* New York: Atria Books, 2021.

Behbakht, Andy. "DCU Theory: Flash Movie's Supergirl ISN'T Kara Danvers." *Screenrant*, 13 February 2023. https://screenrant.com/flash-movie-supergirl-dceu-not-kara-danvers-theory/.

Bendix, William, and Gyung-Ho Jeong. "Gender and Foreign Policy: Are Female Members of Congress More Dovish Than Their Male Colleagues?" *Political Research Quarterly* 73, no. 1 (March 2020): 126–140.

Benioff, David, and D. B. Weiss, creators. *Game of Thrones.* Television show. HBO, aired 2011–2019.

Benjamin, Jessica. "The Omnipotent Mother: A Psychoanalytic Study of Fantasy and Reality." In *Representations of Motherhood*, edited by Donna Bassin, Margaret Honey, and Meryle Mahrer Kaplan, 129–146. New Haven, CT: Yale University Press, 1994.

Berlant, Lauren. *The Female Complaint: The Unfinished Business of Sentimentality in American Culture.* Durham, NC: Duke University Press, 2008.

Berlanti, Greg, Marc Guggenheim, and Phil Klemmer, creators. *DC's Legends of Tomorrow.* Television show. CW, aired 2016–2022.

Berlanti, Greg, Geoff Johns, and Andrew Kreisberg, creators. *The Flash.* Television show. CW, aired 2014–2023.

Berlatsky, Noah. *Wonder Woman: Bondage and Feminism in the Marston/Peter Comics.* New Brunswick, NJ: Rutgers University Press, 2015.

Blondell, Ruby, Mary-Kay Gamel, Nancy Sorkin Rabinowitz, and Bella Zweig, trans. and eds. *Women on the Edge: Four Plays by Euripides.* New York: Routledge, 1999.

Boyle, Karen. "Feminism without Men: Feminist Media Studies in a Post-feminist Age." In *Feminist Television Criticism: A Reader*, 2nd ed., edited by Charlotte Brunsdon and Lynn Spigel, 174–190. Berkshire, UK: Open University Press, 2008.

Brandzel, Amy. *Against Citizenship: The Violence of the Normative.* Champaign: University of Illinois Press, 2016.

Brown, Jeffrey A. *Dangerous Curves: Action Heroines, Gender, Fetishism, and Popular Culture.* Jackson: University Press of Mississippi, 2011.

———. "Gender and the Action Heroine: Hardbodies and the 'Point of No Return.'" *Cinema Journal* 35, no. 3 (Spring 1996): 52–71.

———. *The Modern Superhero in Film and Television: Popular Genre and American Culture.* New York: Routledge, 2017.

Burge, Constance M., Jessica O'Toole, and Amy Rardin, creators. *Charmed.* Television show. CW, aired 2018–2022.

Butler, Judith. *Gender Trouble.* New York: Routledge, 1990.

———. "Performative Acts and Gender Constitution: An Essay in Phenomenology and Feminist Theory." *Theatre Journal* 40, no. 4 (December 1988): 519–531.

Cadwell, Stephen. "Opening Doors: Art-Horror and Agency." In *Unraveling Resident Evil: Essays on the Complex Universe of the Games and Films*, edited by Nadine Farghaly, 45–61. Jefferson, NC: McFarland, 2014.

Cameron, James, dir. *The Terminator*. Film, 1984. Terminator: Six Film Collection. Blu-ray, Warner Brothers Home Entertainment, 2020.

———, dir. *Terminator 2: Judgment Day*. Film, 1991. Terminator: Six Film Collection. Blu-ray, Warner Brothers Home Entertainment, 2020.

Carlson, Ashley Lynn, and Lisa K. Perdigao, eds. *The CW Comes of Age: Essays on Programming, Branding and Evolution*. Jefferson, NC: McFarland, 2022.

Carroll, Lewis. *Alice's Adventures in Wonderland*. Project Gutenberg e-book, 1991.

Chocano, Carina. "Tough, Cold, Terse, Taciturn and Prone to Not Saying Goodbye When They Hang Up the Phone." *New York Times Magazine*, 1 July 2011. https://www.nytimes.com/2011/07/03/magazine/a-plague-of-strong-female-characters.html.

Christie, Agatha. *The Murder of Roger Ackroyd* [1926]. New York: HarperCollins, 2009.

Clinton, Hillary. "Power Shortage." *The Atlantic*, October 2020. https://www.theatlantic.com/magazine/archive/2020/10/hillary-clinton-womens-rights/615463.

Clover, Carol. *Men, Women, and Chain Saws: Gender in the Modern Horror Film*. Princeton, NJ: Princeton University Press, 1992.

Cocca, Carolyn. "Negotiating the Third Wave of Feminism in Wonder Woman." *Political Science and Politics* 47, no. 1 (January 2014): 98–103.

———. *Superwomen: Gender, Power, and Representation*. London: Bloomsbury, 2016.

Cohn, Carol, ed. *Women and Wars: Contested Histories, Uncertain Futures*. Cambridge, UK: Polity, 2012.

Collins, Margo. "'I Barely Feel Human Anymore': Project Alice and the Posthuman in the Films." In *Unraveling Resident Evil: Essays on the Complex Universe of the Games and Films*, edited by Nadine Farghaly, 201–215, NC: McFarland, 2014.

Collins, Patricia Hill. *Black Feminist Thought: Knowledge, Consciousness and the Politics of Empowerment*. 2nd ed. New York: Routledge, 2000.

Comer, Todd A., and Lloyd Isaac Vayo, eds. *Terror and the Cinematic Sublime: Essays on Violence and the Unpresentable in Post-9/11 Films*. Jefferson, NC: McFarland, 2013.

Cooper, Anna Julia. *A Voice from the South* [1892]. Electronic edition. Published online in *Documenting the American South*. Chapel Hill, NC: University of North Carolina at Chapel Hill, 2000. https://docsouth.unc.edu/church/cooper/cooper.html.

Cooper, Mark Garrett. "Pearl White and Grace Cunard: The Serial Queen's Volatile Present." In *Flickers of Desire: Movie Stars of the 1910s*, edited by Jennifer M. Bean, 174–195. New Brunswick, NJ: Rutgers University Press, 2011.

Creed, Barbara. *The Monstrous Feminine*. London: Routledge, 1993.

@cw_charmed (Charmed). "The CW's new initiative, We Defy, reinforces the network's commitment to inclusion and representation. #CWDareToDefy" [Tweet with video], Twitter, 9 March 2019. https://mobile.twitter.com/cw_charmed/status/1104539920243265537.

"CW Stars 'Dare to Defy' with New Inclusion & Representation Initiative." *Just Jared Jr.*, 9 March 2019. https://www.justjaredjr.com/2019/03/09/cw-stars-dare-to-defy-with-new-inclusion-representation-initiative/.

Dabb, Andrew, creator. *Resident Evil*. Television show. Netflix, 2022.

Daniels, Les. *The Life and Times of the Amazon Princess Wonder Woman: The Complete History*. San Francisco: Chronicle Books, 2000.

de Lauretis, Teresa. *Technologies of Gender: Essays on Theories, Film, and Fiction*. Bloomington: Indiana University Press, 1987.

Derrida, Jacques. *The Gift of Death*. Chicago: University of Chicago Press, 1995.

Dill, Bonnie Thornton. "Race, Class, and Gender: Prospects for an All-Inclusive Sisterhood." *Feminist Studies* 9, no. 1 (Spring 1983): 131–150.

DiPaolo, Marc. *War, Politics, and Superheroes: Ethics and Propaganda in Comics and Film*. Jefferson, NC: McFarland, 2011.

Doane, Mary Ann. *Femmes Fatales: Feminism, Film Theory, Psychoanalysis*. New York: Routledge, 1991.

———. "Film and the Masquerade: Theorizing the Female Spectator." *Screen* 23, no. 3–4 (September/October 1982): 74–88.

Douglas, Susan J. *The Rise of Enlightened Sexism: How Pop Culture Took Us from Girl Power to Girls Gone Wild*. New York: St. Martin's Griffin, 2010.

Dove-Viebahn, Aviva. "Despite a Promising Beginning, 'Wonder Woman 1984' Falls into the Same Old Traps." *Ms.*, 28 December 2020. https://msmagazine.com/2020/12/28/wonder-woman-1984-ww84/.

———. "How Much Longer Will Straight White Women Be Our Queer Superhero Stand-Ins?" *Xtra*, 18 June 2021. https://xtramagazine.com/culture/tv-film/straight-white-women-queer-superhero-203171.

———. "Peace Strength Wisdom Wonder." *Ms.*, Fall 2017, 31–32.

Dries, Caroline, creator. *Batwoman*. Television show. CW, aired 2019–2022.

Druckmann, Neil, and Craig Mazin, creators. *The Last of Us*. Television show. HBO Max, aired 2023–present.

Edgar, Joanne. "Wonder Woman Revisited." *Ms.*, July 1972, 54–55.

Elshtain, Jean Bethke. *Women and War*. New York: Basic Books, 1995.

Emad, Mitra. "Reading Wonder Woman's Body: Mythologies of Gender and Nation." *Journal of Popular Culture* 39, no. 6 (2006): 954–984.

Euripides. *The Trojan Women*. Translated by Alan Shapiro. Oxford: Oxford University Press, 2009.

Faircloth, Kelly. "'Strong Female Characters' Aren't Enough, Goddammit." *Jezebel*, 17 June 2014. https://jezebel.com/strong-female-characters-arent-enough-goddammit-1592135553.

Faithful, George. "Survivor, Warrior, Mother, Savior: The Evolution of the Female Hero in Apocalyptic Science Fiction Film of the Late Cold War." *Implicit Religion* 19, no. 3 (2016): 347–370.

Faludi, Susan. *The Terror Dream: Myth and Misogyny in an Insecure America*. London: Picador, 2007.

Feasey, Rebecca. *Masculinity and Popular Television*. Edinburgh: Edinburgh University Press, 2008.

Fèvre-Berthelot, Anaïs. "*Gossip Girl* and the CW: Defining a New Network." *International Journal of TV Serial Narratives* 4, no. 2 (Winter 2018): 9–18.

Finn, Michelle R. "William Marston's Feminist Agenda." In *The Ages of Wonder Woman: Essays on the Amazon Princess in Changing Times*, edited by Joseph J. Darowski, 8–21. Jefferson, NC: McFarland, 2014.

Foucault, Michel. *History of Sexuality: An Introduction, Volume 1* [1978]. New York: Vintage Books, 1990.

———. *Power*. Vol. 3 of *The Essential Works of Michel Foucault, 1954–1984*. New York: New Press, 2001.

"Franchise: Resident Evil." Box Office Mojo by IMDbPro. Accessed 1 October 2022. https://www.boxofficemojo.com/franchise/fr3578236677/.

"Franchise: Terminator." Box Office Mojo by IMDbPro. Accessed 1 October 2022. https://www.boxofficemojo.com/franchise/fr3175583493/.

Friedan, Betty. *The Feminine Mystique*. 4th ed. [1963]. New York: W. W. Norton, 1997.

Friedman, Josh, creator. *Terminator: The Sarah Connor Chronicles*. Television show. Fox, aired 2008–2009. DVD, Warner Brothers Home Entertainment, 2009.

Freud, Sigmund. *Beyond the Pleasure Principle*. Edited and translated by James Strachey. New York: W. W. Norton, 1961.

———. *Civilization and Its Discontents*. Translated by James Strachey. New York: W. W. Norton, 2010.

Gallagher, Mark. *Action Figures: Men, Action Films, and Contemporary Adventure Narratives*. London: Palgrave Macmillan, 2006.

Gallop, Jane. *The Daughter's Seduction: Feminism and Psychoanalysis*. Ithaca, NY: Cornell University Press, 1982.

———. *Reading Lacan*. Ithaca, NY: Cornell University Press, 1985.

Gay, Penny. *As She Likes It: Shakespeare's Unruly Women*. New York: Routledge, 2002.

Genz, Stéphanie, and Benjamin A. Brabon. *Postfeminism: Cultural Texts and Theories*. Edinburgh: Edinburgh University Press, 2009.

Geyer-Ryan, Helga. "Effects of Abjection in the Texts of Walter Benjamin." *MLN* 107, no. 3 (1992): 499–520.

Gill, Rosalind. *Gender and the Media*. Cambridge, UK: Polity, 2007.

Givhan, Robin. "Kamala Harris Made History with Quiet, Exquisite Power." *Washington Post*, 7 November 2020. https://www.washingtonpost.com/nation/2020/11/07/kamala-harris-made-history-with-quiet-exquisite-power/.

Goldberg, Dara. *Awaken Your Inner Goddess: Practical Tools for Self-Care, Emotional Healing, and Self-Realization*. Emeryville, CA: Rockridge Press, 2020.

Goldberg, Lesley. "Mad about the CW Cancellations? Blame Streaming, but Also Its Unusual Corporate Structure." *Hollywood Reporter*, 13 May 2022. https://www.hollywoodreporter.com/tv/tv-news/the-cw-cancellations-blame-streaming-but-also-its-unusual-corporate-structure-1235146038/.

Gordon, Lyndall. *Vindication: A Life of Mary Wollstonecraft*. London: Virago, 2005.

Gough-Yates, Anna. "Angels in Chains? Feminism, Femininity and Consumer Culture in *Charlie's Angels*." In *Action TV: Tough-Guys, Smooth Operators and Foxy Chicks*, edited by Bill Osgerby and Anna Gough-Yates, 83–99. New York: Routledge, 2001.

Greene, Doyle. "Supergirl vs. Overgirl." *Film Criticism* 42, no. 4 (2018). http://dx.doi.org/10.3998/fc.13761232.0042.409.

Groover, Rachael Jayne. *Powerful and Feminine: How to Increase Your Magnetic Presence and Attract the Attention You Want*. Loveland, CO: Groover Seminars, 2019.

Gross, Rita M. *Buddhism after Patriarchy: A Feminist History, Analysis, and Reconstruction of Buddhism*. Albany: State University of New York Press, 1992.

Grossman, Julie. *The Femme Fatale*. New Brunswick, NJ: Rutgers University Press, 2020.

Gurr, Barbara, and Brayton Polka, eds. *Race, Gender, and Sexuality in Post-apocalyptic TV and Film*. London: Palgrave Macmillan, 2015.

Gutowitz, Jill. "Dear Men: You Should Absolutely Feel Excluded from 'Wonder Woman.'" *DAME*, 6 June 2017. https://www.damemagazine.com/2017/06/06/dear-men-you-should-absolutely-feel-excluded-wonder-woman/.

Hall, Stuart. "Encoding/Decoding." In *Culture, Media, Language*, edited by Stuart Hall, Dorothy Hobson, Andrew Lowe, and Paul Willis, 117–127. New York: Routledge, 1980.

Hanley, Tim, and Jonathan Hahn. *Wonder Woman Unbound: The Curious History of the World's Most Famous Heroine*. Chicago: Chicago Review Press, 2014.

Harper, Stephen. "'I Could Kiss You, You Bitch': Race, Gender, and Sexuality in *Resident Evil* and *Resident Evil 2: Apocalypse*." *Jump Cut: A Review of Contemporary Media* 49 (Spring 2007), https://www.ejumpcut.org/archive/jc49.2007/HarperResEvil/.

Harris, Aisha. "*Black Panther*'s Dialect Coach on Wakanda's Regional Accents and Prepping Actors." *Slate*, 21 February 2018. https://slate.com/culture/2018/02/an-interview-with-black-panthers-dialect-coach.html.

Harris, Andrea. "Woman as Evolution: The Feminist Promise of the Resident Evil Film Series." In *Race, Gender, and Sexuality in Post-apocalyptic TV and Film*, edited by Barbara Gurr and Brayton Polka, 99–112. New York: Palgrave Macmillan, 2015.

Hartzell, Stephanie. "An (In)visible Universe of Grief: Performative Disidentifications with White Motherhood in the We Are Not Trayvon Martin Blog." *Journal of International and Intercultural Communication* 10, no. 1 (2017): 62–79.

Helbing, Todd, and Greg Berlanti, creators. *Superman & Lois*. Television show. CW, aired 2021–present.

Higashi, Sumiko. "Hold It! Women in Television Adventure Series." *Journal of Popular Film and Television* 8, no. 3 (1980): 26–37.

Holmes, Linda. "The New 'Charlie's Angels': The Depressing Spectacle of a Project No One Loves." NPR, 22 September 2011. https://www.npr.org/2011/09/22/140700388/the-new -charlies-angels-the-depressing-spectacle-of-a-project-no-one-loves.

———. "The Only One: A Talk with Shonda Rhimes." NPR, 22 September 2014. https://www .npr.org/2014/09/22/350563549/the-only-one-a-talk-with-shonda-rhimes.

Holmlund, Chris. *Impossible Bodies: Femininity and Masculinity at the Movies*. New York: Routledge, 2002.

hooks, bell. *Ain't I a Woman: Black Women and Feminism*. New York: Routledge, 1981.

———. *Feminism Is for Everybody*. Boston: South End Press, 2000.

———. *Reel to Real: Race, Class, and Sex at the Movies*. New York: Routledge, 1996.

———. "Sisterhood: Political Solidarity between Women." *Feminist Review* 23 (1986): 125–138.

Hoskin, Rhea A. "Femme Theory: Refocusing the Intersectional Lens." *Atlantis* 38, no. 1 (2017): 95–109.

Inness, Sherrie. *Tough Girls: Women Warriors and Wonder Women in Popular Culture*. Philadelphia: University of Pennsylvania Press, 1999.

Irigaray, Luce. *The Sex Which Is Not One*. Translated by Catherine Porter. Ithaca, NY: Cornell University Press, 1985.

———. *Speculum of the Other Woman* [1974]. Translated by Gillian Gill. Ithaca, NY: Cornell University Press, 1985.

Jancovich, Mark. "Modernity and Subjectivity in *The Terminator*: The Machine as Monster in Contemporary American Culture." *Velvet Light Trap* 30 (1992): 3–17.

Jenkins, Patty, dir. *Wonder Woman*. Film, 2017. DVD, Warner Brothers Home Entertainment, 2017.

———, dir. *Wonder Woman 1984*. Film. HBO Max, 2020.

Johnson, Jessica. "TV Review: Charlie's Angels." *Time Out Chicago*, 22 September 2011. https:// www.timeout.com/chicago/tv/tv-review-charlies-angels.

Jones, Nick. "This Is My World: Spatial Representation in the *Resident Evil* Films." *Continuum: Journal of Media and Cultural Studies* 30, no. 4 (2016): 477–488.

———. "Variation within Stability: Digital 3D and Film Style." *Cinema Journal* 55, no. 1 (2015): 52–73.

Jordan, Miriam. "Judge Rules DACA Is Unlawful and Suspends Applications." *New York Times*, 15 July 2021. https://www.nytimes.com/2021/07/16/us/court-daca-dreamers.html.

Kac-Vergne, Marianne. "From Sarah Connor 2.0 to Sarah Connor 3.0: Women Who Kill in the *Terminator* Franchise." In *Women Who Kill: Gender and Sexuality in Film and Series of the Post-feminist Era*, edited by David Roche and Cristelle Maury, 117–133. London: Bloomsbury, 2020.

Kang, Inkoo. "The Dutiful Feminism of the New *Charlie's Angels* Made Me Miss the Sleazy Camp of the Old Ones." *Slate*, 14 November 2019. https://slate.com/culture/2019/11 /charlies-angels-2019-movie-reboot-kristen-stewart.html.

Kant, Immanuel. *Critique of Judgement*. Translated by J. H. Bernard. New York: Macmillan, 1914.

———. *Observations of the Beautiful and the Sublime* [1764]. Translated by J. T. Goldthwait. Berkeley: University of California Press, 1960.

Kaplan, E. Ann. *Motherhood and Representation: The Mother in Popular Culture and Melodrama*. New York: Routledge, 1992.

Keith, Tamara. "How 'Stronger Together' Became Clinton's Response to 'Make America Great Again.'" NPR, 8 August 2016. https://www.npr.org/2016/08/08/489138602/trump-comment -gives-clinton-a-campaign-slogan-with-layered-meaning.

Kent, Miriam. *Women in Marvel Films*. Edinburgh: Edinburgh University Press, 2021.

Khanna, Ranjana. "Reflections on Sara Ruddick's 'Maternal Thinking.'" *Women's Studies Quarterly* 37, no. 3/4 (2009): 302–304.

Kilkenny, Katie. "How a Magazine Cover from the 1970s Helped Wonder Woman Win Over Feminists." *Pacific Standard*, 22 June 2017. https://psmag.com/social-justice/ms-magazine -helped-make-wonder-woman-a-feminist-icon.

Kim, Christina M., creator. *Kung Fu*. Television show. CW, aired 2021–present.

Klinger, Cornelia. "The Concepts of the Sublime and the Beautiful in Kant and Lyotard." In *Feminist Interpretations of Immanuel Kant*, edited by Robin May Schott, 191–212. Philadelphia: Pennsylvania State University Press, 1997.

Krishna, Rachael, and Rose Troup Buchanan. "Here's Why a Muslim Editor Called Out a Company for Working with Gal Gadot." *BuzzFeed News*, 22 January 2018. https://www.buzzfeed-news.com/article/krishrach/heres-why-a-muslim-editor-criticized-a-company-for-working.

Kristeva, Julia. *Powers of Horror: An Essay on Abjection*. Translated by Leon S. Roudiez. New York: Columbia University Press, 1982.

Lacan, Jacques. *Feminine Sexuality: Jacques Lacan and the école freudienne*. Edited by Juliet Mitchell and Jacqueline Rose. Translated by Jacqueline Rose. New York: W. W. Norton, 1985.

———. *The Seminar of Jacques Lacan, Book XI: The Four Fundamental Concepts of Psychoanalysis* [1973]. Edited by Jacques-Alain Miller. Translated by Alan Sheridan. New York: W. W. Norton, 1998.

Lamb, Christina. *Our Bodies, Their Battlefields: War through the Lives of Women*. New York: Scribner Books, 2020.

Landler, Mark. "How Hillary Clinton Became a Hawk." *New York Times*, 21 April 2016. https://www.nytimes.com/2016/04/24/magazine/how-hillary-clinton-became-a-hawk.html.

Lane, Lydia. "Frills Delight This 'Angel.'" *Los Angeles Times*, 24 October 1976, F22.

Lauzen, Martha M. "Boxed In: Women on Screen and behind the Scenes on Broadcast and Streaming Television in 2021–22." Center for the Study of Women in Television and Film, 2022.

———. "Boxed In 2019–20: Women on Screen and behind the Scenes in Television." Center for the Study of Women in Television and Film, 2020.

———. "It's a Man's (Celluloid) World: On-Screen Representations of Female Characters in the Top 100 Films of 2011." Center for the Study of Women in Television and Film, 2012.

Lenz, Carolyn Ruth Swift, Gayle Greene, and Carol Thomas Neely, eds. *The Woman's Part: Feminist Criticism of Shakespeare*. Champaign: University of Illinois Press, 1983.

Lepore, Jill. *The Secret History of Wonder Woman*. New York: Alfred A. Knopf, 2014.

LeVine, Deborah Joy, Joe Shuster, and Jerry Siegel, creators. *Lois & Clark: The New Adventures of Superman*. Television show. ABC, aired 1993-1997.

Levine, Elana. "Sex as a Weapon: Programming Sexuality in the 1970s." In *NBC: America's Network*, edited by Michele Hilmes, 224–239. Berkeley: University of California Press, 2007.

Lewis, Rachel Charlene. "In 2019, 'Charlie's Angels' Isn't Just about Girl Power—It's a Critique of Male Leadership." *Bitch Media*, 27 November 2019. https://www.bitchmedia.org/article /charlies-angels-reboot-feminist-review.

Link, Alex. "The Secret of Supergirl's Success." *Journal of Popular Culture* 46, no. 6 (2013): 1177–1197.

Loughrey, Clarisse. "Charlie's Angels Review: A more Daring Film Lurks beneath the Surface of This Toothless Sequel." *The Independent*, 28 November 2019. https://www.independent.co .uk/arts-entertainment/films/reviews/charlies-angels-review-film-sequel-cast-kristen -stewart-elizabeth-banks-a9221116.html.

Luscombe, Belinda. "12 Questions with Patty Jenkins, Director of Wonder Woman." *Time*, 15 June 2017. https://time.com/4819569/patty-jenkins-wonder-woman-director-interview/.

Lyons, Deborah. *Gender and Immortality: Heroines in Ancient Greek Myth and Cult*. Princeton, NJ: Princeton University Press, 1997.

Lyotard, Jean-François. *The Postmodern Explained: Correspondence 1982–1985*. Translated by Morgan Thomas. Minneapolis: University of Minnesota Press, 1992.

Mann, Karen B. "Narrative Entanglements: 'The Terminator.'" *Film Quarterly* 43, no. 2 (1989): 17–27.

Manzano, Angie. "Charlie's Angels: Free-Market Feminism." *Off Our Backs* 30, no. 11 (December 2000): 10.

Marston, William Moulton. "Why 100,000,000 Americans Read Comics." *American Scholar*, Winter 1943–1944, 42–43. https://theamericanscholar.org/wonder-woman/.

——. *Wonder Woman (Archives, volume 1)*. Burbank, CA: DC Comics, 1998.

Matsuuchi, Ann. "Wonder Woman Wears Pants: Wonder Woman, Feminism and the 1972 'Women's Lib' Issue." *Colloquy* 24 (2012): 118–142.

May, Jeff. "Zombie Geographies and the Undead City." *Social and Cultural Geography* 11, no. 3 (May 2010): 285–298.

McCann, Hannah. "Is There Anything 'Toxic' about Femininity? The Rigid Femininities That Keep Us Locked In." *Psychology and Sexuality* 13, no. 1 (2022): 9–22 https://doi.org/10.1080 /19419899.2020.1785534.

McDougall, Sophia. "I Hate Strong Female Characters." *New Statesman*, 15 August 2013. https:// www.newstatesman.com/culture/2013/08/i-hate-strong-female-characters.

McG, dir. *Charlie's Angels*. Film, 2000. DVD, Sony Pictures Home Entertainment, 2002.

——, dir. *Charlie's Angels: Full Throttle*. Film, 2003. DVD, Sony Pictures Home Entertainment, 2003.

——, dir. *Terminator: Salvation*. Film, 2009. Terminator: Six Film Collection. Blu-ray, Warner Brothers Home Entertainment, 2020.

McGovern, Joe. "'The Terminator' at 30: An Oral History." *Entertainment Weekly*, 17 July 2014. https://ew.com/article/2014/07/17/the-terminator-oral-history/.

McNulty, Rose. "The Badass Real Women Playing Amazons in 'Wonder Woman.'" *Muscle and Fitness*. Accessed 1 October 2020. https://www.muscleandfitness.com/muscle-fitness-hers /hers-athletes-celebrities/badass-real-women-playing-amazons-wonder-woman/.

McRobbie, Angela. "Post-feminism and Popular Culture." *Feminist Media Studies* 4, no. 3 (2004): 255–264. https://doi.org/10.1080/1468077042000309937

Mead, Margaret. "Why Do We Speak of Feminine Intuition?" *Anima* 8 (1981): 50–55.

Mendelson, Scott. "How 'Resident Evil' Became the Most Successful Video Game–Based Franchise Ever." *Forbes*, 23 January 2017. https://www.forbes.com/sites/scottmendelson /2017/01/23/why-resident-evil-became-the-most-successful-video-game-based-franchise -ever.

Miller, Catriona. *Cult TV Heroines: Angels, Aliens and Amazons*. London: Bloomsbury, 2020.

Miller, Kathryn, and Joshua Plencer. "*Supergirl* and the Corporate Articulation of Neoliberal Feminism." *New Political Science* 40, no. 1 (2018): 51–69.

Miller, Tim, dir. *Terminator: Dark Fate*. Film, 2019. Terminator: Six Film Collection. Blu-ray, Warner Brothers Home Entertainment, 2020.

Millett, Kate. *Sexual Politics* [1970]. New York: Columbia University Press, 2016.

Mitchell, W.J.T. "The Unspeakable and the Unimaginable: Word and Image in a Time of Terror." *ELH* 72 (2005): 291–308.

Mizejewski, Linda. *Hardboiled and High Heeled: The Woman Detective in Popular Culture.* New York: Routledge, 2004.

Mogilevich, Mariana. "Charlie's Pussycats." *Film Quarterly* 55, no. 3 (2002): 38–51.

Mostow, Jonathan, dir. *Terminator: Rise of the Machines.* Film, 2003. Terminator: Six Film Collection. Blu-ray, Warner Brothers Home Entertainment, 2020.

Mulcahy, Russell, dir. *Resident Evil: Extinction.* Film, 2007. DVD, Sony Pictures Home Entertainment, 2018.

Müller, Daniel. "Survival and System in *Resident Evil* (2002): Remembering, Repeating and Working-Through." In *Unraveling Resident Evil: Essays on the Complex Universe of the Games and Films,* edited by Nadine Farghaly, 19–33. Jefferson, NC: McFarland, 2014.

Murcott, Susan. *The First Buddhist Women: Translations and Commentary on the Therigatha.* Berkeley, CA: Parallax Press, 1991.

Murphy, Caryn, "The CW: Media Conglomerates in Partnership." In *From Networks to Netflix: A Guide to Changing Channels,* edited by Derek Johnson, 35–43. New York: Routledge, 2018.

Muschietti, Andy, dir. *The Flash.* Film. Warner Brothers Picutres, 2023.

Navar-Gill, Annemarie, and Mel Stanfill. "'We Shouldn't Have to Trend to Make You Listen': Queer Fan Hashtag Campaigns as Production Interventions." *Journal of Film and Video* 70, no. 3–4 (Fall/Winter 2018): 85–100.

Neff, Katherine L., Stacy L. Smith, and Katherine Pieper. "Inequality across 1,500 Popular Films: Examining Gender and Race/Ethnicity of Leads/Co Leads from 2007 to 2021." Annenberg Inclusion Initiative. University of Southern California, 2020.

Negra, Diane. *What a Girl Wants: Fantasizing the Reclamation of Self in Postfeminism.* New York: Routledge, 2009.

Newman, Louise Michele. *White Women's Rights: The Racial Origins of Feminism in the United States.* Oxford: Oxford University Press, 1999.

"Nexstar Media Group to Acquire the CW Network." *Nexstar,* 15 August 2022. https://www.nexstar.tv/nexstar-media-group-to-acquire-the-cw-network/.

"1977–78 Ratings History." *The TV Ratings Guide.* Accessed 1 February 2023. http://www.thetvratingsguide.com/2020/02/1977-78-ratings-history.html.

Obama, Barack. *The Audacity of Hope: Thoughts on Reclaiming the American Dream.* New York: Crown, 2006.

O'Day, Marc. "Beauty in Motion: Gender, Spectacle and Action Babe Cinema." In *Action and Adventure Cinema,* edited by Yvonne Tasker, 201–218. New York: Routledge, 2004.

O'Reilly, Andrea. "Outlaw(ing) Motherhood: A Theory and Politic of Maternal Empowerment for the Twenty-First Century." In *21st Century Motherhood: Experience, Identity, Policy, Agency,* edited by Andrea O'Reilly, 366–380. New York: Columbia University Press, 2010.

Orenstein, Peggy. *Cinderella Ate My Daughter: Dispatches from the Front Lines of the New Girlie-Girl Culture.* New York: Harper, 2012.

Palumbo, Donald. "The Monomyth in James Cameron's *The Terminator*: Sarah as Monomythic Heroine." *Journal of Popular Culture* 41, no. 3 (2008): 413–427.

Panofsky, Erwin. "*Et in Arcadia Ego*: Poussin and the Elegiac Tradition" [1936]. In *Meaning in the Visual Arts,* 295–320. Chicago: University of Chicago Press, 1967.

Pinedo, Isabel Cristina. *Recreational Terror: Women and the Pleasures of Horror Film Viewing.* Albany: State University of New York Press, 1997.

Platz, Jenny. "The Woman in the Red Dress: Sexuality, Femmes Fatales, the Gaze and Ada Wong." In *Unraveling Resident Evil: Essays on the Complex Universe of the Games and Films,* edited by Nadine Farghaly, 117–134. Jefferson, NC: McFarland, 2014.

Pomerantz, Shauna, Rebecca Raby, and Andrea Stefanik. "Girls Run the World: Caught between Sexism and Postfeminism in School." *Gender and Society* 27, no. 2 (April 2013): 185–207.

Pomeroy, Sarah. *Goddesses, Whores, Wives, and Slaves: Women in Classical Antiquity*. New York: Schocken Books, 1975.

Porter, Marie, Patricia Short, and Andrea O'Reilly, eds. *Motherhood: Power and Oppression*. Toronto: Women's Press, 2005.

Purse, Lisa. *Contemporary Action Cinema*. Edinburgh: Edinburgh University Press, 2011.

Rackin, Phyllis. *Shakespeare and Women*. Oxford: Oxford University Press, 2005.

Radner, Hilary. *Neo-feminist Cinema: Girly Films, Chick Flicks, and Consumer Culture*. New York: Routledge, 2011.

Reyes, Mike. "Linda Hamilton Thinks Box Office May Have Finally Killed the Terminator Franchise." *Cinema Blend*, 30 January 2020. https://www.cinemablend.com/news/2489354/linda-hamilton-thinks-box-office-may-have-finally-killed-the-terminator-franchise.

Rich, Adrienne. *Of Woman Born: Motherhood as Experience and Institution*. New York: W. W. Norton, 1995.

Riley, Sarah, Adrienne Evans, Emma Anderson, and Martine Robson. "The Gendered Nature of Self-Help." *Feminism and Psychology* 29, no. 1 (2019): 3–18.

Riviere, Joan. "Womanliness as a Masquerade." *International Journal of Psychoanalysis* 9 (1929): 303–313.

Roberts, Johannes, dir. *Resident Evil: Welcome to Racoon City*. Film, 2021. DVD, Sony Pictures Home Entertainment, 2022.

Robinson, Tasha. "We're Losing All Our Strong Female Characters to Trinity Syndrome." *The Dissolve*, 16 June 2014. http://thedissolve.com/features/exposition/618-were-losing-all-our-strong-female-characters-to-tr/.

Rodino-Colocino, Michelle. "Me Too, #MeToo: Countering Cruelty with Empathy." *Communication and Critical/Cultural Studies* 15, no. 1 (2018): 96–100.

Rosa, Christopher. "This Unfinished 'Wonder Woman' Script by Joss Whedon Is Getting Crucified on Twitter." *Glamour*, 19 June 2017. https://www.glamour.com/story/unfinished-wonder-woman-script-joss-whedon-twitter.

Rose, Jacqueline. *Mothers: An Essay on Love and Cruelty*. New York: Farrar, Straus and Giroux, 2018.

———. *Sexuality in the Field of Vision*. East Peoria, IL: Verso, 1986.

Rosenberg, Alyssa. "'Wonder Woman' Is a Beautiful Reminder of What Feminism Has to Offer Women—and Men." *Washington Post*, 5 June 2017. https://www.washingtonpost.com/news/act-four/wp/2017/06/05/wonder-woman-is-a-beautiful-reminder-of-what-feminism-has-to-offer-women-and-men/.

Ross, Miriam. "The 3-D Aesthetic: *Avatar* and Hyperhaptic Visuality." *Screen* 53, no. 4 (2012): 381–397.

Ross, Stanley Ralph, creator. *Wonder Woman*. Television show. ABC, aired 1975–1977. CBS, aired 1977–1979.

Rottenberg, Catherine. *The Rise of Neoliberal Feminism*. Oxford: Oxford University Press, 2018.

Rousseau, Jean-Jacques. *Emile, Or Treatise on Education* [1762]. Translated by William H. Payne. New York: D. Appleton and Company, 1909.

Rovan, Marcie Panutsos. "What to Do with Supergirl? Fairy Tale Tropes, Female Power and Conflicted Feminist Discourse." In *Girl of Steel: Essays on Television's Supergirl and Fourth-Wave Feminism*, edited by Melissa Wehler and Tim Rayborn, 11–26. Jefferson, NC: McFarland, 2020.

Rubin, Gayle. "The Traffic in Women: Notes on the 'Political Economy' of Sex." In *Women, Class, and the Feminist Imagination*, edited by Karen Hansen and Ilene Philipson, 74–113. Philadelphia: Temple University Press, 1990.

Ruddick, Sara. *Maternal Thinking: Towards a Politics of Peace* [1989]. Boston: Beacon Press, 2002.

———. "On 'Maternal Thinking.'" *Women's Studies Quarterly* 37, no. 3/4 (2009): 305–308.

Ruiz, Michelle. "AOC's Next Four Years." *Vanity Fair*, 28 October 2020. https://www.vanityfair.com/news/2020/10/becoming-aoc-cover-story-2020.

Ryan, Maureen. "From 'Supergirl' to 'Crazy Ex-Girlfriend,' Women Are the Real Heroes of the CW." *Variety*, 16 October 2016. https://variety.com/2016/voices/columns/cw-gilmore-girls-crazy-ex-girlfriend-1201885544/.

Sandberg, Sheryl. *Lean In: Women, Work and the Will to Lead*. New York: Alfred A. Knopf, 2013.

Sapiro, Virginia. *A Vindication of Political Virtue: The Political Theory of Mary Wollstonecraft*. Chicago: University of Chicago Press, 1992.

Scott, Joan W. "Gender: A Useful Category of Historical Analysis." *American Historical Review* 91, no. 5 (December 1986): 1053–1075.

Serano, Julie. *Whipping Girl: A Transsexual Woman on Sexism and the Scapegoating of Femininity*. 2nd ed. Berkeley, CA: Seal Press, 2016.

Shepard, Laura. "Veiled References: Constructions of Gender in the Bush Administration Discourse on the Attacks on Afghanistan Post-9/11." *International Feminist Journal of Politics* 8, no. 1 (2006): 19–41.

Siegel, Alan. "The Tin Man Gets His Heart: An Oral History of 'Terminator 2: Judgment Day.'" *The Ringer*, 30 June 2021. https://www.theringer.com/movies/2021/6/30/22555687/terminator-2-judgement-day-t2-oral-history.

Sipos, Thomas M. *Horror Film Aesthetics: Creating the Visual Language of Fear*. Jefferson, NC: McFarland, 2010.

Sjoberg, Laura. *Gender, War, and Conflict*. Cambridge, UK: Polity, 2014.

Sjoberg, Laura, and Caron Gentry. *Mothers, Monsters, Whores: Women's Violence in Global Politics*. London: Zed Books, 2007.

Smith, Cecil. "ABC's High-Flying Hit Charlie's Angels." *Los Angeles Times*, 2 January 1977, R4.

Snyder, Zack, dir. *Batman v Superman: Dawn of Justice*. Film. HBO Max, 2016.

Spelling, Aaron, creator. *Charlie's Angels*. Television show. ABC, aired 1976–1981. DVD, Sony Pictures Home Entertainment, 2016.

———, creator. *Charlie's Angels*. Television show. ABC, aired 2011. Amazon Prime Video, 2011.

Staiger, Janet. "The Slasher, the Final Girl and the Anti-denouement." In *Style and Form in the Hollywood Slasher Film*, edited by Wickham Clayton, 213–228. London: Palgrave Macmillan, 2016.

Stanley, Alessandra. "Female Detectives Revived: One Tough, Others Stylish." *New York Times*, 21 September 2011. https://www.nytimes.com/2011/09/22/arts/television/prime-suspect-and-charlies-angels-tv-review.html.

Stanley, Kelli E. "'Suffering Sappho': Wonder Woman and the (Re)Invention of the Feminine Ideal." *Helios* 32, no. 2 (2005): 143–171.

Stanton, Amy, and Catherine Connors. *The Feminine Revolution: 21 Ways to Ignite the Power of Your Femininity for a Brighter Life and a Better World*. Berkeley, CA: Seal Press, 2018.

Stone, James. "'My Name Is Alice and I Remember Everything!' Surviving Sexual Abuse in the *Resident Evil* Films." In *Unraveling Resident Evil: Essays on the Complex Universe of the Games and Films*, edited by Nadine Farghaly, 99–116. Jefferson, NC: McFarland, 2014.

"Supergirl—Extended 'Wonder Woman' Promo." *YouTube*, 22 May 2017. https://www.youtube.com/watch?v=WLlwgBuKymo.

"Superman Changes Motto to 'Truth, Justice and a Better Tomorrow,' Says DC Chief." NBC News, 17 October 2021. https://www.nbcnews.com/pop-culture/pop-culture-news/superman-changes-motto-truth-justice-better-tomorrow-says-dc-chief-n1281716.

Tapia, Ruby C. *American Pietàs: Visions of Race, Death, and the Maternal*. Minneapolis: University of Minnesota Press, 2011.

Tasker, Yvonne, ed. *Action and Adventure Cinema.* New York: Routledge, 2004.

———. *Spectacular Bodies: Gender, Genre, and the Action Cinema.* New York: Routledge, 1993.

———. *Working Girls: Gender and Sexuality in Popular Cinema.* New York: Routledge, 1998.

Tasker, Yvonne, and Diane Negra, eds. *Interrogating Post-feminism.* Durham, NC: Duke University Press, 2007.

Tatar, Maria. *The Heroine with 1,001 Faces.* New York: Liveright, 2021.

Taylor, Alan, dir. *Terminator: Genisys.* Film, 2015. Terminator: Six Film Collection. Blu-ray, Warner Brothers Home Entertainment, 2020.

"*Terminator*—Franchise." *Rotten Tomatoes.* Accessed 1 October 2022. https://www.rottento matoes.com/franchise/terminator.

Thompson, Ayanna. "Shakespeare's Female Icons: Doing and Embodying." *Upstart Crow: A Shakespeare Journal* 31 (2012): 115–120.

Thompson, Kirsten Moana. *Apocalyptic Dread: American Film at the Turn of the Millennium.* Albany: State University of New York Press, 2007.

Towns, Ann E. "'Diplomacy Is a Feminine Art': Feminised Figurations of the Diplomat." *Review of International Studies* 46, no. 5 (2020): 573–593.

Travers, Peter. "Elizabeth Banks' Crew of Woke Angels Rescue Latest 'Charlie's Angels' Reboot." *Rolling Stone,* 14 November 2019. https://www.rollingstone.com/movies/movie -reviews/charlies-angels-review-elizabeth-banks-910689/.

Tucker, Ken. "'Charlie's Angels': Minka Kelly, Rachel Taylor and Annie Ilonzeh Fought Crime in a Silly Hour." *Entertainment Weekly,* 22 September 2011. https://ew.com/article/2011/09 /22/charlies-angels-minka-kelly-rachel-taylor/.

"2018 Pulitzer Prizes: Journalism." *The Pulitzer Prizes.* Accessed 20 July 2022. https://www .pulitzer.org/prize-winners-by-year/2018.

Wagmeister, Elizabeth. "CBS President Explains 'Supergirl' Moving to the CW." *Variety,* 18 May 2016. https://variety.com/2016/tv/news/supergirl-cbs-president-reaction-cw-1201777795/.

Warner, Kristen. "Blue Skies Again: Streamers and the Impossible Promise of Diversity." *Los Angeles Review of Books,* 24 June 2021. https://lareviewofbooks.org/article/blue-skies-again -streamers-and-the-impossible-promise-of-diversity/.

"Watch Kamala Harris' Full Victory Speech." CNN, 7 November 2020. *YouTube,* https://www .youtube.com/watch?v=ExPm_hJQYpQ.

Wayne, Rachel. "Fierce Femmes: The Problem with Strong Female Characters." *Medium,* 9 August 2018. https://medium.com/@rachelwayne/fierce-femmes-the-problem-with-strong -female-characters-6c4e23847b8f.

Webb, Jenn, and Sam Byrnand. "Some Kind of Virus: The Zombie as Body and as Trope." *Body and Society* 14, no. 2 (June 2008): 83–98.

Wegner, Phillip E. "Relics from a Deleted Timeline: The Economics of *Terminator Genisys.*" *Science Fiction Film and Television* 10, no. 1 (2017): 115–124.

Weida, Courtney Lee. "'Women of Power and the Mothers Who Molded Them': Matriarchal Mentorship and Symbols of Sisterhood in *Supergirl.*" In *Girl of Steel: Essays on Television's Supergirl and Fourth-Wave Feminism,* edited by Melissa Wehler and Tim Rayborn, 180–198. Jefferson, NC: McFarland, 2020.

Whedon, Joss. *Wonder Woman* [unproduced screenplay], 7 August 2006. Accessed 1 October 2020, https://indiegroundfilms.files.wordpress.com/2014/01/wonder-woman-aug7-07 -joss-whedon.pdf.

Whedon, Joss, and Zack Snyder, dirs. *Justice League.* Film. HBO Max, 2017.

Whippman, Ruth. "Enough Leaning In. Let's Tell Men to Lean Out." *New York Times,* 10 October 2019. https://www.nytimes.com/2019/10/10/opinion/sunday/feminism-lean-in.html.

Willis, Sharon. *High Contrast: Race and Gender in Contemporary Hollywood Film.* 2nd ed. Durham, NC: Duke University Press, 2002.

Wilson, Laura. "Race, the Other and *Resident Evil*." *Ethnicity and Race in a Changing World: A Review Journal* 3, no. 2 (2012): 30–34.

Winfrey, Lee. "'Charlie's Angels' as Bad as Its Stars Are Beautiful." *Chicago Tribune*, 26 November 1976, A14.

Witt, Alexander, dir. *Resident Evil: Apocalypse*. Film, 2004. DVD, Sony Pictures Home Entertainment, 2018.

Wollstonecraft, Mary. *A Vindication of the Rights of Woman: With Strictures on Political and Moral Subjects* [1792]. London: T. Fisher Unwin, 1891.

"Wonder Woman Director Interview—Patty Jenkins." *YouTube*, uploaded by Flicks and The City Clips, 23 May 2017. https://www.youtube.com/watch?v=uTT-v8TvuQg.

Young, Iris Marion. "The Logic of Masculinist Protection: Reflections on the Current Security State." *Signs: Journal of Women in Culture and Society* 29, no. 1 (2003): 1–25.

Žižek, Slavoj. *Looking Awry: An Introduction to Jacques Lacan through Popular Culture*. Cambridge, MA: MIT Press, 1991.

———. *The Metastases of Enjoyment: Six Essays on Woman and Causality*. New York: Verso, 1994.

———. *The Sublime Object of Ideology*. New York: Verso, 1989.

INDEX

abortion, 3, 92, 95

Abrams, Stacey, 145

action-adventure (genre), 85, 97, 117–119

action heroines, 5, 22–23, 39, 41, 63, 96, 115, 163n40

activism, 3, 14, 68, 80, 83

Alex (*Charlie's Angels*), 34–38, 40

Alice (*Resident Evil*), 7, 18, 117–127, 129, 131–143, 170n1, 170n3, 171n5, 172n48, 173n51, 173n53

Alice's Adventures in Wonderland, or *Alice in Wonderland*, 126

altruism: as feminine virtue, 2, 6–7, 27, 47, 50, 53, 62, 79, 87; as heroic quality, 17, 56, 63, 70, 84, 91, 119, 139, 161n15

Amazons (*Wonder Woman*), 26, 29, 33, 45–47, 49–56

American Dream, 79

Anderson, Paul W. S., 132, 172n49

androgyny, 22, 113–114, 136, 146, 164n57

Andromache, 16–17

antifeminism, 29, 44

Antiope (*Wonder Woman*), 51, 53–55

apocalypse: in the future, 90, 93, 96, 98, 104, 107, 110, 113–114; imagery of the, 123–124; as masculinist, 6; post-, 7, 115, 117, 124–125, 135, 171n5; and the sublime, 126; and trauma, 140; zombie, 117–118, 120

Ares, 26, 49–50, 52–53

Arias, Sam (*Supergirl*), 70, 73, 76, 164n68

Arrowverse, 16, 57–58, 61, 63–66, 160n1, 160n5, 161n9, 163n50, 166n92

Balinska, Ella, 39–40, 143

Banet-Weiser, Sarah, 15, 67, 70, 151n8

Banks, Elizabeth, 26, 39–43

Barthes, Roland, 116, 131, 135

Batman v. Superman: Dawn of Justice, 48

Batwoman, 162n20, 162n28

beauty: as aesthetics, 122; as feminine virtue, 17, 38, 49; and horror, 119, 128, 134–135; as physical attribute, 30, 35, 36, 38, 42, 48–50, 119; and the sublime, 7, 10, 119, 126, 130

Beauvoir, Simone de, 12–13, 19, 89, 92, 99–100, 145

belonging (to community), 7, 57–58, 63–64, 66, 68–87, 141, 146

Berlant, Lauren, 57, 71, 75

Bible, The (allusions to), 105, 107, 109

biopower (Foucault), 141

bisexuality. *See* LGBTQ representation

Black Lives Matter, 3, 70, 80, 165n79

blackness, 11–15, 33, 75, 80, 143, 145, 159n58, 162n20, 165n80

Bosley (*Charlie's Angels*), 26, 32–34, 39–43, 157n28

business (field), 1–2, 69, 147

Calisto (fictional technology), 39, 41

Callisto (Greek myth), 157n30

Cameron (*Sarah Connor Chronicles*), 99–100, 102, 104–106, 113

Cameron, James, 94, 98

camp (as aesthetic), 18, 34, 47, 64

Carter, Lynda, 47, 57–58, 160n2

Cassandra, 16–17, 96, 154n37

castration anxiety, 100, 124, 141, 168n40

Charlie's Angels (1970s TV show), 29–32, 155n3, 156n11, 156n21, 157n23

Charlie's Angels (2000 film), 34–36, 67

Charlie's Angels (2011 TV show), 32–34, 156n16

Charlie's Angels (2019 film), 25–26, 28–43, 143, 146, 157n29, 157n32

Charlie's Angels (franchise), 5–7, 18, 26–28, 38–39, 43–44, 47, 56, 62–63, 113

Charlie's Angels: Full Throttle, 34–38, 67, 157n22

Charmed, 162n20, 162n21, 162n28

Cheetah (*Wonder Woman*). *See* Minerva, Barbara (*Wonder Woman*)

children: and agency, 20, 92, 94, 101, 109; as allegory, 7, 93, 115, 117; as characters, 170n1, 171n5, 171n11; and education, 11–12, 46; forced birth of, 18, 95; harm to, 17, 73, 108, 136, 142–143, 154n39; protection of, 98–99, 101, 104, 113, 164n69, 165n83; in psychoanalysis, 100–101; raising, 7, 11, 91, 92, 93. *See also* motherhood

Children of Liberty (*Supergirl*), 70, 76, 79, 81–83, 165n74 citizenship, 15, 87–88, 108

Clinton, Hillary, 8, 23–24, 60–61, 144–145

cloning, 7, 70, 84, 117–126, 131–135, 138–141, 143

Clover, Carol, 140–141

Collins, Patricia Hill, 15, 174n7

comedy (genre), 34, 156n21

coming of age, 6, 45, 61, 64–65, 71, 75, 79, 85–88

Connor, John (*Terminator*): as an adult, 107–108; as a child, 93, 96; conception of, 95; death of, 108, 110–112; as imagined hero, 90, 95–96, 99–100, 109; relationship with Cameron, 99–100, 105–106; relationship with Sarah, 94, 97–106, 108–109, 111, 114

Connor, Sarah (*Terminator*): in *Dark Fate*, 110–115; death, 107; evolution of, 90, 95–96; as hero, 95–98, 106–109; relationship with John, 94, 97–106, 108–109, 111, 114; and trauma, 17–18. *See also* Hamilton, Linda; maternal instinct; motherhood

consumerism, 14–15, 33, 65

Cooper, Anna Julia, 11–12, 174n7

costuming, 35, 51, 72, 80, 84, 136, 157n22, 163n49, 164n57

COVID-19 pandemic, 85, 124, 171n19

Creed, Barbara, 97, 129, 137

CW (television network), 6, 62–66, 70, 74, 160n1, 162n20, 162n28

DACA (Deferred Action for Childhood Arrivals). *See* DREAM Act

Danvers, Alex (*Supergirl*): as mother, 164n69, 166n2; relationship with Kara, 57–58, 60–61, 71–73, 75, 78–80, 84, 86, 89

Danvers, Kara (*Supergirl*): anxiety, 59, 62–63, 72–73, 76, 87; costuming, 57–58, 72, 164n57; friendship with Lena, 58–59, 61–62, 70, 72–73, 84–86, 164n56; as journalist, 61, 72, 75–76, 78, 87; relationship with Alex, 57–58, 60–61, 71–73, 75, 78–80, 84, 86, 89; relationship with Mon El, 58–60, 63, 70, 75, 160n6, 161n15; rift with Lena, 70, 75–79; secret identity, 58, 70–73, 76–79, 84–85, 87. *See also* Supergirl (character)

Davids, Sharice, 145

DC Comics, 6, 47, 61, 64–65

DC Extended Universe (DCEU), 48, 61, 161n9

democracy, 7–8, 12, 45, 49, 87, 90

Dill, Bonnie Thornton, 13–14, 74

diplomacy, 2–3, 7–8, 24

diversity, equity, and inclusion (DEI), 1, 3, 15, 33, 63–64, 87, 115, 151n5

divinity, 14, 22, 46, 48–49, 56, 165n70

domination (as power), 13, 15, 42, 56, 74, 76, 121, 164n60

double entanglement (McRobbie), 67

DREAM Act, 81, 165n83

Dreamer (*Supergirl*). *See* Nal, Nia (*Supergirl*)

Dylan (*Charlie's Angels*), 34–38, 40, 157n23

Elena (*Charlie's Angels*), 39–42, 157n32

empathy, 2, 7, 23, 47, 51–53, 70, 76, 82, 112, 137

empowerment: and consumerism, 15, 33, 67; and femininity, 41–44, 69; and feminism, 28, 60, 67, 70; individual v. collective, 14, 67–68, 83, 87; narratives, 3, 67–68; tenuous, 29, 38–39, 146; women's, 7, 15, 18, 23, 30, 32, 47, 56, 146–147

Enlightenment, The, 10–11, 13

environmental sustainability, 24, 71, 86, 124

Et in Arcadia Ego, 171n12

fantasy (genre), 81, 98, 117

Fawcett, Farrah, 30

feminine intuition, 2–10, 14, 18, 23, 27–29, 32, 39, 43, 47, 63, 67–68, 87, 147

feminine virtues, 10–11, 22, 49. *See also* altruism; beauty; diplomacy; empathy; hope; love; sacrifice; sisterhood

feminism: first wave (suffrage), 11; as ideology, 7, 33, 79, 91, 160–161n7; as a movement, 13–14, 67; as performative, 1, 26, 28, 39; second wave, 12, 30, 105–106; third wave, 66, 91. *See also* antifeminism; girl power; intersectionality; neoliberal feminism; popular feminism; postfeminism

femme fatale, 136, 139–140

final girl (Clover), 139–141

Flash, The (DC universe), 48, 61, 65, 84, 161n9

fort-da game (Freud), 20–21, 126

Fortress of Solitude, 77

Foucault, Michel, 4, 15, 141

Freud, Sigmund, 19–21, 93, 100, 123, 125, 141

Friedan, Betty, 13

Gadot, Gal, 48–49, 159n57

Game of Thrones, 159n62

gender binary, 10, 13, 22, 113, 156

gendered exceptionalism, 2–7, 13, 16, 18, 21–22, 26–28, 32, 38, 49, 56, 65, 75, 79, 144–147

gender performance, 12, 16, 43, 67
gender roles, 2, 6–7, 10–12, 15–19, 45, 66–67, 99, 115, 140, 146, 152n10, 153n5, 163n40
girl power, 3, 14, 65–69
global conflict, 3, 93, 124. *See also* war
Grant, Cat (*Supergirl*), 59–60, 68–69, 72, 86, 164n74
Greek mythology, 16–17, 49, 93, 122, 152n4, 157n30

Haaland, Deb, 145
Hamilton, Linda, 96, 105, 108, 110, 167n3
Harris, Kamala, 144–145
Hatcher, Teri, 58
Hecuba, 16–17
Helen of Troy, 17, 154n38
hero (archetype), 4, 8, 16–17, 22, 44–46, 53–54, 72, 85, 89, 99. *See also* heroine (archetype); hero's journey
heroine (archetype), 4–5, 17, 22–24, 29, 46, 56, 71, 94. *See also* hero (archetype)
hero's journey, 59, 93–94
heterosexuality, 31, 37–40, 53, 55, 66, 160n67
Hippolyta (*Wonder Woman*), 45–47, 49–50
homophobia, 64, 80
hooks, bell, 13–14, 74–75
hope, 6, 62, 76, 79–82, 87, 90, 103, 112, 141
horror (genre), 95, 97–98, 115–121, 124–125, 128–131, 134–137, 140–143

identity politics, 3, 14–15, 81, 146
immigration, 62, 79, 80, 82, 112–114. *See also* DREAM Act
intersectionality, 2, 13, 15, 18, 33, 39, 63–68, 79–81, 87, 113, 146, 174n7
intimate public (Berlant), 71, 75

Jackson, Kate, 30
Jade (*Resident Evil*), 143
Jane (*Charlie's Angels*), 39–42, 157n28
Jenkins, Patty, 8, 24–26, 44–45, 49, 53, 56
Jesus Christ, 25, 105, 111
Jill (*Charlie's Angels*), 29–31
jouissance (Lacan), 142
Jovovich, Milla, 142
Justice League, 48–49, 61

Kant, Immanuel, 10–11, 129–130
Kelly (*Charlie's Angels*), 29–31, 37, 42, 56
Kent, Clark (DC universe). *See* Superman

Kristeva, Julia, 129–131
Kryptonite, 59, 62, 76–77, 166n91
Kung Fu, 162n20

Lacan, Jacques, 4, 19–21, 28, 43, 100, 123, 127, 142
Last of Us, The, 120, 171n5
lesbianism. *See* LGBTQ representation
LGBTQ representation, 13, 40, 62, 86, 145–146, 162n20; bisexual, 40; lesbian, 31, 72, 80, 163n40; nonbinary, 68, 146, 163n40; transgender, 3, 42, 62, 68, 81, 146, 165n85. *See also* intersectionality; queerbaiting; queer coding
Lois and Clark: The New Adventures of Superman, 58
Lord, Maxwell (DC universe), 54–55, 160n4
love: as feminine virtue, 2, 6–8, 23–24, 26, 47; maternal, 13, 46, 92, 101, 103; patriotic, 82; platonic, 73, 77–78, 84; in psychoanalysis, 19, 28; romantic, 17, 38–40, 44, 53, 55–56, 63–64, 70, 108–109, 160n6; as source of power, 29, 49–53, 56, 69, 74, 84, 129
Luthor, Lena (*Supergirl*): animosity with Supergirl, 72–73; friendship with Kara, 58–59, 61–62, 70, 72–73, 84–86, 164n56; potential villain, 62, 70, 76, 82; relationship with family, 62, 72, 76, 78, 89, 164n58; rift with Kara, 70, 75–79. *See also* Supercorp
Luthor, Lex (DC universe), 48, 59, 62, 70–71, 76–77, 83–86

male gaze, 41, 56, 128, 134
male privilege, 48, 101
marriage, 11, 13, 17, 23, 154n39, 157n23
Marston, William Moulton, 44–47, 53, 160n2
Marvel Cinematic Universe (MCU), 151n6
masculinity, 12–13, 16–17, 46, 67, 97
mastery: aesthetic, 128, 134; assumed, 20–22, 28, 31–32, 43, 56, 62, 87, 94, 146; intuitive, 4, 36, 119; through repetition, 5, 27, 119, 121–123, 125, 131
maternal instinct, 90, 94–98, 103
maternal thinking (Ruddick), 103–104, 113
matrix of domination (Collins), 15
Me Too, 3, 68, 70, 162n20
microaggressions, 18, 40, 68
Minerva, Barbara (*Wonder Woman*), 54–55, 160n67

misogyny, 3, 38, 44, 64, 67, 69, 151n8
Mizejewski, Linda, 29
Mon-El (*Supergirl*), 58–60, 63, 70, 75, 78, 85, 87, 160n6, 161n12, 161n15
monstrous feminine (Creed), 97, 137
motherhood: and femininity, 6, 115; forced, 95, 99; as form of power, 23, 73, 90, 97; as justification for violence; and psychoanalysis, 100–101; as role, 90–94, 101–103; and work-life balance, 89, 166–167n2
mother privilege, 99–102, 113
musculinity (Tasker), 97, 114

Nal, Nia (*Supergirl*), 81, 86, 165n81, 165n85
Natalie (*Charlie's Angels*), 34–38, 36, 40, 157n22
nature v. culture, 118, 130, 137
neoliberal feminism, 6, 28, 38, 64, 68–70
9/11. *See* September 11
nonbinary. *See* LGBTQ representation
normative femininity, 14–18, 23, 27, 39, 154n32

Obama, Barack, 87, 165n83, 166n100
Ocampo, Rain (*Resident Evil*), 135, 171n11, 173n51
Ocasio-Cortez, Alexandria, 145
Oedipus complex, 100
Olsen, James (*Supergirl*), 78, 80, 83, 86, 160n6, 161n12, 165n80
Olsen, Kelly (*Supergirl*), 80
Omar, Ilhan, 145
Other, the (psychoanalytic), 28, 142, 153n18
Overgirl (*Supergirl*), 84, 166n93

patriarchy, 34, 69, 74, 106
patriotism, 45, 47, 49, 108, 166n99
peace, 3, 11, 46, 53, 59, 82, 87, 102–104, 113
Perils of Pauline, The, 23
phallic mother, 100–101
politics, women in, 1–2, 24, 84, 102–103, 113, 144–147, 174n5
popular feminism, 3, 14–16, 34, 38, 67, 70, 151n8
postfeminism, 6, 14–16, 38, 66
Presley, Ayanna, 145
Prince, Diana (*Wonder Woman*): and the Amazons, 49–50, 52–56; childhood, 50, 53–54, 56; relationship with Steve, 26, 45–47, 49–56, 160n64. *See also* Wonder Woman (character)

queerbaiting, 160n67, 164n56
queer coding, 40, 160n67. *See also* queerbaiting

racial justice, 3, 62, 68, 70, 79–80, 165n79. *See also* Black Lives Matter
rape, 17, 33, 154n39, 156n21, 157n30, 173n53
Red Daughter (*Supergirl*), 70, 84, 166n91
Redfield, Claire (*Resident Evil*), 122, 132–139, 142–143, 170n1, 171n11
Reese, Kyle (*Terminator*), 95–96, 107–109, 112
Reign (*Supergirl*). *See* Arias, Sam (*Supergirl*)
repetition, 2–5, 18–23, 28, 39, 67, 117–121, 123–126, 146. *See also* seriality
repetition compulsion, 20, 123
reproductive rights, 3, 92, 95
Resident Evil (franchise), 7, 18, 90, 117–126, 142
Resident Evil (2002 film), 118–119, 126–127, 135–136
Resident Evil (2022 TV show), 143
Resident Evil (video games), 118, 120–123
Resident Evil: Afterlife, 122, 127, 128–136
Resident Evil: Apocalypse, 126–127, 136
Resident Evil: Extinction, 122, 125, 127, 136–137
Resident Evil: Retribution, 122, 127, 136
Resident Evil: The Final Chapter, 127, 137–139
Roe v. Wade, 3
Rose, Jacqueline, 4, 19, 89, 92, 94, 103, 168n40
Rosseau, Jean-Jacques, 10–11
Ruddick, Sara, 103

Sabina (*Charlie's Angels*), 25–26, 39–42
Sabrina (*Charlie's Angels*), 29–31, 157n23
sacrifice: of children, 17, 108, 113; of happiness, 55, 60; of power, 55; of self, 26, 84, 108, 110, 123, 173n51; as self-effacement, 92, 94; virgin, 17
Sawyer, Maggie (*Supergirl*), 80
Schwarzenegger, Arnold. *See* Terminator (character)
science fiction (genre), 81, 98, 137
Scott, Naomi, 40
Second Sex, The (Beauvoir), 12, 89, 99, 153n18, 174n7
self-help (genre), 69–70
September 11th, 104, 124, 169n52, 171n19
seriality, 5, 18–23, 27–28, 63, 68. *See also* repetition
sexism, 45, 67–68, 74, 144

sisterhood: adoptive, 58–60, 78–79, 81, 163n53; friendship as, 73, 78; metaphorical, 6–7, 55, 63, 69, 71–75, 79, 84; political, 14, 66, 74, 87

Smallville, 160n4, 164n66

Smith, Jaclyn, 30, 37, 42, 157n29

social justice, 14, 61–64, 71, 79–81, 85–86, 146–147, 162n20

solidarity politics, 14, 70–71, 74, 77, 165n80

Spelling, Aaron, 26, 29, 32–33

split subjectivity (Lacan), 20–21, 126–127, 161n13

STEM fields, 1, 69

Stewart, Kristen, 40

stronger together: Kryptonian motto, 60–61, 71, 73, 82, 86; political slogan, 60–61

strong female characters, 27–28, 38, 56, 146

subject-supposed-to-know (Lacan), 4, 19–21, 28, 43, 62, 94, 100, 123, 142

sublime, 7, 10, 119, 124–131, 136–137, 142

Supercorp, 78, 164n56. *See also* queerbaiting

Supergirl (character): and American patriotism, 57, 63, 75, 79, 82–84, 87; animosity with Lena, 72–73; inspiring hope, 62, 76, 81–82, 87, 160n5; loss of power, 71, 85–87; relationship to Wonder Woman, 57–58, 61; as Superman's cousin, 57, 59–62, 70–71, 84; vulnerability to Kryptonite, 62, 76–77. *See also* Danvers, Kara (*Supergirl*)

Supergirl (TV show): season one, 60, 65, 69–72; season two, 59–60, 62–63, 65, 69–72, 74, 79–80; season three, 70, 73–75; season four, 70, 76, 79–83; season five, 70, 72, 76–79; season six, 71, 76, 80, 85–87. *See also* Supergirl (character)

Superman (DC universe), 45–46, 48, 57–59, 61–62, 72, 84, 87, 160n1, 164n66, 166n92, 166n99

Tasker, Yvonne, 14, 22, 97, 114–115

Terminator (character): as played by Schwarzenegger, 95–98, 107–108, 110–115; various other, 96, 99–102, 107–112

Terminator (franchise), 6–7, 90–94, 167n3

Terminator, The, 94–96

Terminator: Dark Fate, 90, 98–99, 103, 106–107, 109–113, 117, 167n3, 169n58

Terminator: The Sarah Connor Chronicles, 90, 99–102, 104–107, 109, 113, 117, 169n53, 169n58, 169n61

Terminator 2: Judgment Day, 92–93, 96–99, 101, 104, 107–109, 114, 117, 169n58, 169n61

Terminator 3: Rise of the Machines, 107, 109

Terminator Genisys, 90, 107–109, 111–112

Terminator Salvation, 107, 109

terrorism, 70, 76, 83–84, 124–125, 165n74

3D technology, 119, 128–136, 172n49

Times Up, 3

Tlaib, Rashida, 145

tokenism, 3, 144–145

toxic masculinity, 16

transference, 19–20

transgender. *See* LGBTQ representation

transphobia, 62, 68, 81

trauma, 17–18, 21, 71, 116–121, 127, 140–142; as abyss, 116, 123–125, 130; bodily, 127, 154n39; familial, 89–90; of loss, 18, 85; of racial injustice, 62, 80; and repetition, 123, 126

Trevor, Steve (*Wonder Woman*), 26, 45–47, 49–56, 160n64

Trojan Women, The, 16–17, 93

Trump, Donald, 54, 60–61, 68, 80, 84, 165n83, 166n90

Valentine, Jill (*Resident Evil*), 134, 136, 142, 171n11

violence, 47, 49, 116, 128–129, 131; against women, 17–18, 81, 140; masculine, 44, 76, 113; perpetrated by women, 40, 52, 59, 76, 93–99, 102–104, 113–114, 125; repeated, 123, 126; sexual, 17, 33, 135, 154n39, 156n21, 157n30, 173n53; structural, 33, 67, 79, 99

vulnerability: emotional, 22–23, 40, 59, 76, 79, 84–85, 112; physical, 29, 62, 125, 135; as risk, 4, 16–17, 27, 71, 73, 90, 118–119, 121, 147

war (concept), 6, 90, 95, 102–103. *See also* global conflict

Welcome to Racoon City, 142–143

whiteness, 1, 11, 30, 33, 48–49, 80, 108, 113–114, 166n93

white privilege, 13–14, 60, 74–75, 80, 104, 135, 144–145

white supremacy, 33, 69, 79, 166n93

Wollstonecraft, Mary, 10–12, 153n11

women of color, 3, 13, 33–34, 64, 80, 114, 135, 145, 162n20, 174n7. *See also* intersectionality

Wonder Woman (1970s TV show), 47, 155n3, 160n2

Wonder Woman (2017 film), 6, 17, 26, 28, 44–45, 49–53, 57

Wonder Woman (character): fighting style, 48, 52–53; as icon, 28, 43–47, 54, 56; and love as power, 26, 29, 43–47, 49–50, 52–53, 55–56; and truth, 29, 46–47, 54. *See also* Prince, Diana (*Wonder Woman*)

Wonder Woman (comics), 44–47, 55

Wonder Woman 1984, 26–28, 53–56, 160n67, 160n4

Wong, Ada (*Resident Evil*), 134, 136

World War I, 26, 49

World War II, 45, 49

xenophobia, 68, 103

Zeus, 46, 50, 53, 157n30

Žižek, Slavoj, 125–126, 140

zombies, 117–121, 124, 127, 131–132, 137, 143

ABOUT THE AUTHOR

AVIVA DOVE-VIEBAHN is an assistant professor of film and media studies in the Department of English at Arizona State University, where she also previously taught as part of Barrett, The Honors College. She has a PhD in visual and cultural studies from the University of Rochester, an MA in art history from the University of Virginia, and a BA from Mary Baldwin University (formerly Mary Baldwin College). She is coeditor (with Carrie N. Baker) of *Public Feminisms: From Academy to Community* and has published many peer-reviewed essays and book chapters, including recent articles on femme resistance in *Fleabag* and white feminist "othering" in *Captain Marvel*. In addition to her scholarship, she is a screenwriter, editor of the Professional Notes section for the *Journal of Cinema and Media Studies*, and director of the Scholars' Writing Program at *Ms.* magazine, where she also frequently publishes articles and reviews in print and online.

Printed and bound by CPI Group (UK) Ltd, Croydon, CR0 4YY

09/06/2025

14685742-0001